人文社科
高校学术研究论著丛刊

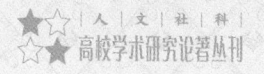

英汉外宣修辞与翻译研究

麦红宇 著

中国书籍出版社
China Book Press

图书在版编目(CIP)数据

英汉外宣修辞与翻译研究 / 麦红宇著. -- 北京：中国书籍出版社, 2022.3

ISBN 978-7-5068-8959-9

Ⅰ.①英… Ⅱ.①麦… Ⅲ.①中国对外政策–宣传工作–语言翻译–研究 Ⅳ.①H059

中国版本图书馆CIP数据核字（2022）第042835号

英汉外宣修辞与翻译研究

麦红宇 著

丛书策划	谭　鹏　武　斌
责任编辑	李　新
责任印制	孙马飞　马　芝
封面设计	东方美迪
出版发行	中国书籍出版社
地　　址	北京市丰台区三路居路97号(邮编：100073)
电　　话	（010）52257143（总编室）　（010）52257140（发行部）
电子邮箱	eo@chinabp.com.cn
经　　销	全国新华书店
印　　厂	三河市德贤弘印务有限公司
开　　本	710毫米×1000毫米　1/16
字　　数	230千字
印　　张	13.25
版　　次	2023年1月第1版
印　　次	2023年1月第1次印刷
书　　号	ISBN 978-7-5068-8959-9
定　　价	72.00元

版权所有　翻印必究

目 录

第一章 绪论   1

    第一节 英汉宣传平行文本对比的研究背景   1
    第二节 中西方修辞对比理论研究   3
    第三节 外宣翻译研究   6

第二章 英汉外宣修辞对比研究方法   11

    第一节 研究问题   11
    第二节 研究对象   12
    第三节 研究方法和框架   13
    第四节 研究过程   14
    第五节 创新之处   14

第三章 英汉外宣修辞对比研究范畴   17

    第一节 语音修辞对比   17
    第二节 修辞格对比   20
    第三节 文化修辞对比   25

第四章 英汉外宣修辞对比与翻译案例   **29**

    第一节 中英文企业简介修辞对比与翻译   29
    第二节 中英产品手册修辞对比与翻译   49
    第三节 中英网站修辞对比与翻译   55
    第四节 会展致辞的修辞对比与翻译   79
    第五节 中英城市形象宣传片的修辞对比和翻译   84
    第六节 中国—东盟商务致辞的修辞比较及翻译   89
    第七节 中英演讲中元话语标记劝说功能的跨文化比较   93

第五章 英汉外宣修辞对比与翻译启示   **111**

    第一节 广西外宣翻译中存在的问题   112
    第二节 平行文本语料库的建设与应用   119
    第三节 平行文本的修辞对比对外宣翻译的启示   121
    第四节 外宣翻译策略的使用   123
    第五节 提高广西外宣翻译质量的对策   129

参考文献   **135**

附录1：英汉宣传语篇平行文本   **141**

附录2：英汉翻译语篇平行文本   **163**

后　记   **203**

第一章　绪论

第一节　英汉宣传平行文本对比的研究背景

自2004年以来，中国—东盟博览会每年在南宁举行，博览会既是一次经贸盛会，又是一次多边国际活动，推动着中国与东盟区域经济合作的深入发展。在国际性展会上，翻译是完成语言沟通与表达的重要工具，翻译的质量直接对会展业相关企业产生正面或者负面的效应。但现实中许多英译文本质量参差不齐，不能达到最佳的沟通效果。因此，本书拟收集英汉宣传平行文本进行修辞对比，研究中英文的差异，为广西外宣翻译添砖加瓦。

20世纪80年代初期，我国学者开始进行英汉修辞对比的研究。经过几十年的发展，研究范围从辞格比较和对比修辞学学科建设的讨论发展到语音、词汇、句法、语篇等各个方面。在此期间涌现出一批影响力较大的英汉修辞对比专著，包括李国南的《英汉修辞格对比研究》、侯广旭的《汉英谚语结构与修辞比较》、胡曙中的《英汉修辞比较研究》、蔡建基的《英汉写作修辞对比》和温科学的《中西比较修辞论》等。

胡曙中（1993）对英汉修辞学的历史发展进行了宏观上的比较，梳理了英汉修辞学的发展历史、研究方法和修辞传统，同时，进行了英汉的修辞格、语言结构、段落发展等方面微观上的比较。李国南（1992）从语言与文化两个方面比较和分析英、汉修辞格。蔡基刚（2001）从语篇、句法和修辞等几个方面比较了中国学生的英文作文中存在的问题以及这些存在问题的语言、文化和思维方式的根源。温科学（2009）以高度的哲学视野对中西修辞学理论加以对接融合，比较了中西修辞学的结构体系和基础结构等。总的来说，我国修辞学研究更多地从宏观上对中英两种语言对比，也更多偏向中英文写作的研究。

也有一些学者通过英汉的修辞对比来研究翻译中的问题。例如，李定坤（1994）对英汉修辞进行了全面的比较分析，提出了直译、替代和自由翻译等建议。袁昌明从五个方面比较了英汉表达的差异：形合与形合、动与静态、人与物、主动与被动、复合与简单，并阐述了修辞比较对翻译的指导作用。陈小慰（2014）从当代修辞理论角度对比分析汉英商务画册语言在话语内容、诉求策略、建构方式和美学手段上的差异，提出商务画册的文字翻译应以受众为转移，关注话语的修辞性。越来越多的学者肯定对比修辞研究对翻译的指导作用，但从微观上进行具体修辞研究的论文数量不多，研究的文体也较少。

综上所述，我们发现，由于中西方文化的差异，英语和汉语语篇的修辞手段存在较大差异，对英汉语篇进行修辞对比研究是提高翻译质量的重要步骤。但现有的英汉修辞对比研究更多着眼于宏观的语言修辞对比和写作教学，较少服务于应用翻译的教学。因此，对英汉宣传平行文本进行收集、整理和研究工作显得尤为紧迫和重要。

平行文本在翻译中具有极大的参考价值，要达到译文对译者、读者产生的效果与原文对原文读者产生的效果一致，我们必须使译文符合目的语的文本规范和文化规范。本研究对英汉宣传平行文本的修辞研究，可以很好地应用到广西外宣翻译实践活动和翻译课堂教学中，提高外宣译文的可读性和可接受程度，提高译文翻译的质量。

第二节　中西方修辞对比理论研究

　　西方古典修辞是说服力和论据的结合。在古希腊和罗马时期（大约从公元前五世纪到中世纪早期），修辞学的最初宗旨在于培养演讲和辩论能力，这个时代的修辞学更适合称为"诡辩术"，代表学者是亚里士多德。亚里士多德认为"修辞术是论辩术的对应物"，辩证是寻找真理的要素，而修辞的功能是用于真理的交流。他还提出了三种说服策略：第一种是道德诉求，强调讯息来源的可信度；第二种是理性诉求，强调传播内容的逻辑性，即通过讲道理来达到说服功能；第三种是情感诉求，强调用感情去说服。亚里士多德的修辞理论对后世的修辞研究产生了巨大而深远的影响。20世纪以来，英语修辞学不仅仅继承了西方古典修辞学，更从哲学、语言学、美学、心理学、生理学等其他人文学科中不断吸收养分，发展成为一门庞大的学科，包括语体学、风格学、辞格理论、实践修辞学、论辩修辞学、小说修辞学等多个分支。

　　古代汉语修辞学把"修辞"理解为对语言进行修饰和调整，从而使语言表达得准确、鲜明、生动、有力。《易经》中有记载："修辞立其诚。"这就是修饰文辞的意思。修辞中的"辞"既可指"文辞"（书面语），也可指"言辞"（口头语），但最初的修辞研究的重心在"言辞"方面，后来重心才向文辞发展。《修辞鉴衡》列举了各种不同的文体，并分析了不同文体中的风格和技巧。作者认为，"修辞"是风格和技巧的结合。五四运动以后，修辞学脱离文学批评成为一门独立的学科。发展到了现在，现代汉语修辞学已经完全脱离了以修辞格为中心的学科格局，在修辞格的语用学范畴、修辞语境、修辞风格等方面的研究都不断地得以加强。

　　汉语修辞学和英语修辞学的不断发展，为英汉对比修辞研究打下了良好的基础。20世纪80年代初期，我国英汉对比修辞开始起步，经过几十年的发展，研究范围不断扩大，英汉修辞对比研究涵盖了英汉语音对比、英汉词汇对比、英汉语句对比、英汉语篇修辞对比和英汉辞格对比等领域。

　　在语音比较方面，刘英凯的《英汉语音修辞学》具有较大的影响力。这是一本专门研究英语和汉语语音修辞的专著。作者使用大量语料作为支撑，从头韵、双声、同音异形、同音同形异义词、同形异音异义词、异义词、拟声词、押韵词、语音双关、语音仿拟、回环等方面来进行中英文的语音对比。

词汇对比包括词义的选择、词的搭配、词的辨析与应用等。例如，对颜色词语的英汉比较。侯广旭的《汉英谚语结构与修辞比较》从音韵、节奏、辞格和字词句的选择等方面对汉英谚语进行了系统的对比，揭示了汉英谚语在修辞方面的共同之处、为达到良好的表达效果所遵循的共同原则。习语的表达离不开修辞，对习语的修辞比较研究促进了修辞学的发展。

句子研究包括句型的选择、句型的变化和句型衔接等方面。语篇结构的比较包括英汉段落的修辞结构和衔接手段。一般而言，英语段落的修辞结构是线性的，而汉语段落的修辞结构是螺旋的。

在我国英汉对比修辞研究中，英汉修辞格对比占有十分重要的地位。李国南（1992）从语言与文化两个方面，对比较常见的英汉修辞格进行了比较详尽的对比研究，包括明喻、拟人、反复、仿拟、通感、借代、夸张、拟声、隐喻、委婉、双关以及对顶、对偶和排比。

1966年，美国南加州大学教授罗伯特·卡普兰在《跨文化教育中的文化思维模式》一文中首先提出了语篇对比修辞学的概念（Kaplan，1966）。卡普兰认为，每种语言和文化都有独特的修辞传统，逻辑和修辞是相互依存的，不同的文化和语言现象会产生不同的文本模式。由于在美国学习的中国学生人数众多，因此英语和汉语的比较修辞已经成为该领域学者关注的焦点之一。在卡普兰的研究基础上，许多国内外学者对英汉语篇修辞进行了对比研究。蔡冠军提出，中国学生的写作深受八股文影响，习惯以间接的方式提出论题（Cai，1993）。胡曙中的研究结论表明，英汉写作结构之间存在着较大差异，而中国学生所写作的英文语篇既不像纯粹的英文语篇，也不像纯粹的中文语篇。英文的段落往往以主题句开头，呈直线型；中文的段落既有螺旋形的也有归纳型的。中国学生的英文语篇中，这几种语篇模式都存在。

汉兹是另一个对英汉语篇修辞研究产生重大影响的学者。他提出了读者—作者责任的分类方式，认为英语语篇是作者责任型，而汉语语篇是读者责任型（Hinds & Kaplan,1987）。英文语篇中，作者需对语篇的连贯负责，必须表明各个部分之间的联系和衔接；而在汉语语篇中，读者来担负这一责任，读者需要通过自己的努力来猜测作者写作意图，明确语篇中各部分的关联。现代汉语正从读者责任型语篇向作者责任型语篇过渡。同时，汉兹还把语篇分成"归纳式"和"演绎式"，汉语语篇偏归纳式，论点出现在段落的最后，而英语语篇偏"演绎式"，论点出现在文章的开头部分。汉兹进一步提出，汉语议论文结构遵循"起—承—转—合"的固定顺序。这一点得到了许多学者的支持，他们发现汉语的议论文篇章通常采用间接的组织结构，论述迂回起伏，而标准的英语议论文往往直接得多，观点在段落开头就被明确提出。

开普伦认为思维与语篇结构相关，而篇章的结构是作者思维模式的体现。研究者认为，在中文文本中，中文的主题陈述句法结构会影响中国人的思维方式，进而影响中文口头和书面的语篇结构，导致中国人倾向于将写作的论点放在文章末尾。而其他研究者认为影响语言修辞的是文化。麦塔琳（Metalen）认为中国的宗教哲学都否认个人的重要性而更强调集体，这种特点决定了汉语的修辞特征。申凡（Fan Shen）与司考伦（Scollen）则用中国文化对"自我"的认知来解析汉语修辞的间接性。他们指出，中国文化中的"自我"不是孤立的，而是受到各种关系限制和制约的"自我"。因此，中国人在写作中因为需要考虑到与他人的关系建构，很难直接表达个人的观点。

研究者们的结论大多只是建立在对中国人的英语作文的分析上，假设中国人在使用英文进行写作的时候，汉语修辞习惯会影响英文的表达。但这类研究并没考虑到学习者语言水平对语言表达的影响。也就是说，中国学生的英文写作所表现出的修辞模式，很可能是因为他们英文水平不够而犯的错误，而不一定是母语对第二语言学习的影响。其次，对比修辞研究中还普遍存在一个分析样本过小的问题，分析样本过小，研究结果中所呈现的特征很难说是因作者个人写作风格所导致的，还是因中英文化差异所造成的。

第三节　外宣翻译研究

外宣翻译实践历史悠久。20世纪七八十年代以来，中国确立了改革开放的政策，伴随着中国的开放，大量的外宣文本需要翻译，提供了外宣翻译的实践良机。而随着中国经济实力的增强与国际地位的提高，中国文化的输出成为国家战略需要。中国对外宣传翻译的需求不断增长，大量的宣传文本需要翻译成不同的语言。然而，相对于日益增长的市场需求，我国的外宣翻译研究也必须跟上市场的需求。外宣翻译质量的高低，直接影响着对外宣传效果的好坏，也同时关系到中国在国际舞台上的形象。我们有必要对外宣翻译的研究进行系统梳理和总结，以构建具有中国特色的外宣翻译研究理论体系。

相对于文学翻译而言，外宣翻译研究的历史并不长。改革开放后，我国对外宣翻译的需求大大增加，一群翻译工作者为了中国的对外宣传工作默默耕耘，并对翻译实践中的经验进行了总结。此阶段的外宣翻译研究多以"中译英""汉英翻译""对外传播与翻译"和"商务文本汉译英"等名称出现，以译者经验总结为主，例如对翻译中常见错误的归纳和总结。

2004年和2005年，黄友义提出了"贴近中国发展的实际，贴近外国受众对中国信息的需求，贴近国外受众的思维习惯"的外宣三贴近原则（黄友义，2004；2005），促进了外宣翻译研究的发展。自此，外宣翻译受到越来越多研究者的关注。

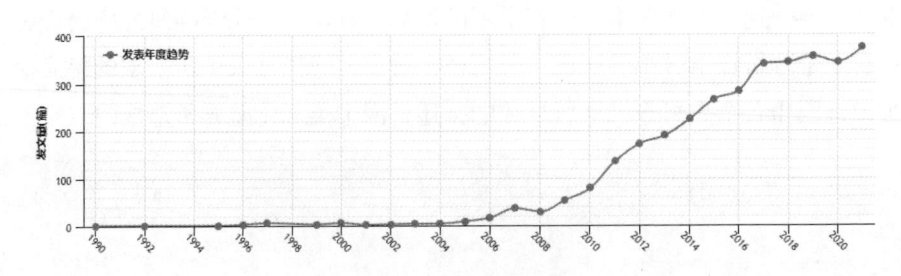

图1-1　以"外宣翻译"为主题的论文发表年度趋势

笔者以"外宣翻译"为主题关键词，在中国知网上搜索，共得到文献总数2942篇，文献数量在2004年后逐步上扬，在2010年后发展迅速。2010年发表的"外宣翻译"相关论文有78篇，而2020年则达到了343篇，研究在近10年内呈现爆发式增长（如图1-1），外宣翻译成为翻译研究的一个热点。与此同时，外宣翻译的专著和图书也陆续出版。以"外宣翻译"为关键词在网上书店当当网进行搜索，发现关于外宣翻译的专著和图书已有600多本。比较有影响力的图书包括衡孝军（2011）的《对外宣传翻译理论与实践：北京市外宣用语现状调查与规范》、卢小军（2016）的《国家形象与外宣翻译策略研究》、卢彩虹（2016）的《传播视角下的外宣翻译研究》和张健（2014）的《外宣翻译导论》等。综上所述，外宣翻译已经成为我国翻译研究中一个重要的领域。

什么是"外宣翻译"？张健（2013）认为，外宣翻译"包括各种媒体报道、政府文件公告、政府及企事业单位的介绍、公示语、信息资料等实用文体的翻译"。方梦之（2003）则认为外宣翻译"包括人们日常接触和实际应用的各类文字，涉及对外宣传、社会生活、生产领域、经营活动等方方面面，但不包括文学及纯理论文本"。杨惠莹（2011）则把外宣翻译定义为"以外国读者受众为中心，以交际翻译为主要手段，将源信息翻译成目的语的一种翻译实践"。虽然至今为止，并没有一个对"外宣翻译"的统一定义，但专家学者们的论述中都对外宣翻译的范畴达成了一定的共识：（1）外宣翻译的主体主要为实用文体，涉及人们日常接触的各类宣传文体；（2）外宣翻译的目标读者为外国读者，因此必须考虑译者的阅读习惯及对译文的接受度；（3）外宣翻译主要是中文信息翻译成外语，进行对外宣传。由于外宣翻译的单向性，外宣翻译的研究者主要以国内学者为主，他们从多个理论角度对外宣翻译展开了多视角的研究。

一、功能学派翻译理论视角下的外宣翻译

1971年，翻译目的论的创始人凯瑟琳娜·赖斯（Katharina Reiss）提出

了功能主义翻译批评理论,首次将功能类别引入翻译批评,将语言功能、文本类型和翻译策略联系在一起。赖斯的学生汉斯·维米尔（Hans Vermeer）继续发展了这一理论,提出了目的论。他认为"任何形式的翻译,包括翻译本身,都可以视为一种行为。任何行为都有目的"。目的论包含三个原则:"目的原则（Skopos Rule）、连贯原则（Coherence Rule）和忠实原则（Fidelity Rule）。"在这三个原则中,最重要的是目的原则（Nord,2001:27-33）。

功能学派翻译理论学认为翻译目的决定了所有翻译行为,包括翻译策略的选择。译文优劣的评估标准在于译文是否在跨文化语境中获得等值的交际功能。连贯性原则是译文要具有可读性和可接受性,符合文本语内连贯（intratextual coherence）的标准,符合目的语读者的文化语境和阅读习惯。忠实性原则指译文文本必须忠实于原文。

功能翻译理论被介绍到中国后,许多翻译研究者把它应用到外宣翻译的研究中,不少学者从功能翻译理论的角度对不同文体的翻译进行了研究。例如,徐敏和胡艳红（2010）以功能翻译理论为理论依据,提出在对企业外宣文本进行翻译时应关注译文的外宣效果,并从宣传效果中的"了解层次、认同层次和诱动层次"三个方面阐述了企业外宣文本的翻译原则和翻译策略。白蓝（2010）运用功能翻译的理论分析了张家界旅游资料英译,提出可使用解释、增补及改译等具体的翻译策略来达到旅游宣传文本的目的。王丽丽（2010）进行了翻译目的论视角下的旅游网站翻译研究,提出旅游文本的翻译应该坚持"内外有别"的原则,充分实现旅游文本"呼唤"功能,从而达到旅游网站应有的广告效应,吸引国外游客。

莱斯建议"不同类型的文本采用不同的翻译方法"（Reiss,1976:20）。也就是说,翻译行为和翻译策略应该根据翻译目的进行灵活调整。功能翻译理论视角下的外宣翻译研究以读者为中心,以达到良好的外宣效果为目的,对翻译实践具有重要的理论和现实指导意义。

二、传播学视角下的外宣翻译

传播学是研究人类一切传播行为和传播过程规律的学问，是研究人类如何运用符号进行社会信息交流的学科。在传播学领域，活动或行为的最基本要素是符号。传播学即是"研究人类如何运用符号进行社会信息交流的学科"（董璐，2008）。传播学所关注的问题与翻译学极其相似，都是如何能够正确地传达信息。所不同之处在于，传播学研究的对象是同一文化环境下的传播现象，而翻译学研究的则是跨文化的传播活动。不少学者把传播学理论和外宣翻译结合在一起，为外宣翻译的研究提供了新的研究视角。

吕俊教授是较早提出将传播学和翻译研究相结合的学者。他提出翻译的本质就是传播，呼吁使用传播学的理论框架对翻译进行研究（吕俊，1997）。张健教授基于斯韦尔（Harold Lassewell）所提出的"传播五要素"，提出对外报道翻译必须注重传播效果（张健，2001）。王银泉等（2007）探讨了外宣电视新闻导语的译写策略，强调以外宣为导向的汉英电视新闻翻译必须兼顾源语的新闻事实和译语的表达习惯，以实现最佳跨文化传播和外宣效果。

杨雪莲（2010）对比了《今日中国》中英文版本，提出需要合理平衡语篇层面上的归化和异化策略，以提高译文的可读性和可接受性。李茜和刘冰泉（2011）研究了温家宝总理答中外记者问的现场回答及其翻译案例，提出外宣翻译要将"文化差异、思维习惯、情感内涵融会贯通"，从而提高传播效果。

传播学视角下的外宣翻译研究为外宣翻译的研究提供了一个新的研究视角，能很好地解析外宣翻译中的翻译行为，丰富了外宣翻译研究的范畴和领域。传播学视角下的外宣翻译研究更注重传播受众，关注点在于如何使得译文信息为传播的受众所理解和接受，对外宣翻译的实践有着重要的指导意义。

三、国家形象视角下的外宣翻译

国家形象指的是在国际舞台上，公众对某一特定国家形成的综合印象与评价。改革开放以来，中国经济发展迅速，但西方国家对中国的国家制度和意识形态依然存在着不少偏见，在国际舆论中不断"妖魔化"中国，影响着普通外国民众对中国的印象。外宣翻译是我国对外宣传的主要手段，外宣翻译与国家形象的塑造密切关联，外宣翻译文本要求具备准确性和可读性，译文质量的高低，都会对我国的国际形象产生直接或间接的影响（余秋平，2016）。因此，许多学者都强调要从国家形象建构的角度来认识和研究外宣翻译。

胡洁（2010）从社会建构主义角度出发，探讨外宣中的国家形象建构，提出在外宣译文中应如何兼顾语篇的语言意义与社会意义。卢小军（2015）从"准确性与国家形象、可读性与国家形象、政治性与国家形象"三个方面探讨了外宣翻译与国家形象之间的关系，对我国外宣翻译中常见的误译类型进行了分类和原因剖析，进而提出了具体的外宣翻译策略。

在国家形象建构的视角下研究外宣翻译，是我国翻译研究的一个特色。随着国际交往的进一步发展，中国在世界政治舞台上软实力的进一步增强，中国大国形象的建构和提升势在必行。国家形象视角下的外宣翻译，将成为外宣翻译研究发展的主要方向之一。

经过二十多年的发展，我国外宣翻译研究成就显著。外宣翻译研究从无到有，从早期的经验总结到近期的多元学科体系建构，外宣翻译在现阶段已经发展成为翻译界的一个重要研究领域。同时，外宣翻译的范围涉及从政治外宣到文化外宣、企业外宣、旅游外宣等多个领域，研究角度包括译者主体性、外宣受众、外宣传播效果、文化和意识形态对翻译的影响等。研究的人群也从高校教师和学生拓展到了政府官员、媒体记者、译者和各类研究机构的研究人员。同时，外宣研究的发展呈现出多元化发展态势，外宣翻译研究不仅借鉴了传统翻译学领域的理论，还吸收了来自多个人文学科的思想，研究的视野得到了较大的扩展和延伸。

第二章　英汉外宣修辞对比研究方法

第一节　研究问题

　　自2004年以来,中国—东盟博览会每年在南宁举行,博览会既是一次经贸盛会,又是一次多边国际活动,务实地推动着中国与东盟国家区域经济合作的深入发展。在国际性展会上,翻译是完成语言沟通与表达的重要工具,翻译的质量直接对会展业相关企业产生正面或者负面的效应。但现实中许多英译文本质量参差不齐,不能达到最佳的沟通效果。因此,本书拟通过英汉宣传平行文本的修辞对比研究,提高本土英语人才的翻译水平,提高广西外宣翻译的质量,为每年在南宁举行的中国—东盟博览会提供助力。

　　本书的研究问题为英汉宣传平行文本的修辞比较,具体问题可分为:

　　(1)英汉宣传平行文本在修辞格的使用上有什么异同?

　　(2)英汉宣传平行文本在语篇修辞上有什么异同?

　　(3)对广西外宣翻译研究有何启示?

　　比较修辞研究一直是学术研究的热点和前沿,不同文化逻辑思维方式的不同，导致了中英两种语篇的修辞方式存在较大差异。译者如果不研究中英语言的修辞差别，不学习英文平行语篇的文本规范和文化规范，就很难提高翻译的质量。因此，我们需要对中英文平行语篇进行研究，以提高广西外宣翻译的质量。

第二节　研究对象

本书的研究对象为英汉宣传平行文本，在比较语篇学中，平行文本（parallel text）指的是不同文化中具有相似交际功能的语篇类型。德国学者（Hartmann，1994）把平行文本分为三种类型：A类为形式上高度一致的译文及原文；B类为同一信息在不同语言中的对应表达，即可逐句对照阅读的原文及其译文；C类为语域对应语料，具有相似内容或相近内容的多语言文本，可作为原文翻译的参考材料。本书的研究包括B类和C类。我们在语料的收集中，既收集原文和对应译文构成的语料，也收集在语言上彼此独立，但是在相同情境下产生的不同文本。广西中文和英文的对外宣传资料，包括网上企业介绍、产品介绍、旅游宣传文本等。

平行文本的作用有：

（1）帮助译员加深对原文的理解。语言是文化的载体，一句话有可能除了字面意思还含有深层含义，有时候译者会难以发现或者理解不了原文的深层含义。通过阅读平行文本，译者可以获取相关的文本信息，从而对原文难以解读的部分进行重新解读，理解是进行翻译的前提，深入的理解是进行正确翻译的前提，阅读平行文本可以帮助译员加深对原文的理解。

（2）帮助译员进行文体风格的构建。非文学翻译的文本种类繁多，每种文本都有特定的文体风格。平行文本可以帮助译员进行遣词造句，特定的句式和用词从而帮助译文向一定的文体风格靠拢，译员在进行非文学翻译时，阅读平行文本可以对译文的文体风格有一定的把握，所以，平行文本可以帮助译员进行文体风格的构建。

（3）帮助译员提高翻译效率和质量。平行文本可以提供专业的术语翻译参考，重叠的翻译文本，译员可以进行比较，进行模仿翻译，从而得到更地道、更针对目标人群的译文，并节省一定的时间，提高翻译效率和质量。

综上所述，在翻译过程中，平行文本是多个问题解决方法的集合，研究平行文本，合理利用平行文本，可以使译者的译文语言表达更准确，内容传达更清晰，文体风格更专业。

第三节　研究方法和框架

本书主要在语言学、文体学、修辞学的理论指导下对英汉平行语篇进行研究，从文化差异的角度阐述动态等值翻译所需要注意的问题。在具体研究方法上主要采取对比研究、语篇分析等研究方法对平行语篇进行定性分析。

本书的总体框架包括：

（1）中西方对比修辞理论与实证研究的梳理。

（2）英汉宣传平行文本的收集、整理和归类。

（3）从文本结构、推理方式、说服策略和修辞格的运用等方面比较平行文本的修辞。

（4）研究修辞理论在中国—东盟博览会上广西本土企业和产品的对外宣传和翻译中的应用。

（5）研究成果翻译在课堂教学中的应用，提高翻译课堂效率，促进本土翻译人才的培养。

本书的重点在于通过对比汉英平行语料的修辞区别，寻找汉英两种语言深层语言内在机制和文化思维差异。本书的难点在于寻找角度新颖的研究切入点。

第四节　研究过程

第一步：进行比较修辞研究的文献梳理工作。笔者所在学校图书馆藏书丰富，拥有CKNI、万方、人大复印资料、SAGE、SPRINGER、剑桥全文等多个中英文学术论文数据库，为研究文献的收集整理提供了极大方便。

第二步：完成宣传平行语料的收集和整理工作。研究语料通过两个途径解决：(1)网络途径。通过网络可很方便地收集到一部分资料，如企业介绍、产品介绍和公众演讲的文本等；(2)现场收集。中国—东盟博览会每年都在南宁举行，而申请人所在学院每年都为博览会派出大量教师和学生参与会展工作，因此，会比较方便通过博览会收集到一些对外宣传的文本资料。

第三步：论文写作修改、中期成果发表等。本研究对汉英宣传平行文本进行修辞对比，揭示中英两种语言背后的语言内核与文化差异，本研究将促进宣传文本翻译研究，提升广西对外宣传的质量，为中国—东盟博览会提供更好的翻译人力资源培养。

第四步：研究成果整理，专著撰写和出版。本书将把话语分析理论、修辞学理论和传播学理论等引入进来，多视角的运用使得该研究可多方面运用至英语本科、研究生教学中，丰富翻译教学的内容，为区域翻译人才的培养添砖加瓦。

第五节　创新之处

我国修辞学研究更多地从宏观上对中英两种语言对比，也更多偏向中英文写作的研究。虽然也有部分学者通过英汉的修辞对比来研究翻译中的问题（朱丽田，1993；李定坤，1994；邵志洪，2009；陈小慰，2012；陈小慰，

2014等），但从微观上进行具体修辞研究的论文数量并不多，研究的文体也较少，其中针对广西宣传文本的研究就更少。广西是国家"一带一路"倡仪中与东盟国家建立联系的重要枢纽，中国—东盟博览会是我国对东盟各国展示经济、政治和外交实力的多领域多层次交流合作的新平台。因此，对英汉宣传平行文本进行收集、整理，研究广西对外宣传翻译的工作显得尤为紧迫和重要。

第三章　英汉外宣修辞对比研究范畴

第一节　语音修辞对比

　　以韵律作为修辞手段的广告标题、金句，因其节奏感和顺口，只要多次接触，很容易在读者脑海中留下深刻印象。由于英文中的押韵句都比较短小精悍（太长就会使韵味淡化），而中文中最推崇的广告句式却是四字一句、八字一句的对偶句，故最佳的方法就是将英文的韵句译成这一类形式中的中文对偶句。如果达不到既对仗又押韵就退而求其次，用朴素一点的意译。

　　谐音。谐音指的是利用语言一音多义的特征来转换概念。如一个电熨斗的广告，"百衣百顺"，巧妙改"依"为"衣"，风趣新奇，暗示了电熨斗的出色和完美的性能令人印象深刻。

　　自行车广告"骑乐无穷"表明，骑这种自行车不仅可以满足人们对自行车功能的需求，而且可以使人们享受"骑行"的乐趣。英文广告也有谐音和同音替代，例如希尔顿的广告：The "in" idea in business travel—Hilton Inns. 但它们却不如中文广告突出和丰富多彩，因为中文与英语具有不同的语音系统特征。

  叠音。叠音形指的是把两个相同的音节叠合在一起，用以加强表达情感。叠音是中文独特的文化现象。例如，晶晶亮，透心凉（雪碧），以及上上下下的享受（三菱电梯）。雪碧广告为单纯叠音，而三菱电梯为合成叠音。

  押韵。韵律是中国诗歌文化中运用最广泛、历史最悠久的修辞手段。在现代中国广告创作和翻译中，押韵尤其是押尾韵，几乎是所有对偶式的附加要求。中国传统对偶句绝大部分由七字句构成，除了音韵上平仄讲究外，在词性上通常也比较严格：名词对名词，动词对动词，数词对数词，虚词对虚词。英语广告语言在语音上有头韵和尾韵等修辞手法，但最突出的特点是押头韵，如英国《星期六晚报》的广告，"Health, humor and happiness? It's a gift we'd love to give."其中前三个词health、humor、happiness押的是[h]的这个音，而后面的gift 和give押的就是[g]的头韵。再如"全球通信，就近付款"这句广告词的英文翻译就是"Talk global, pay local"其中global和local 通过押尾韵来增强节奏感，突出了音乐美妙，荡气回肠。

  第一类，由重复词构成的尾韵句。在以下例句中，尾韵词ahead、time、hand被加以重复，使得广告词朗朗上口。例如：

Every time a good time.

秒秒钟欢聚欢笑（McDonald'——麦当劳餐厅）

Plan Ahead. Get Ahead.

专业策划　安享退休（信安强积金）

UPS. On time, every time.

——准时的典范（UPS）

Hand in Hand, Future in Your Hand.

伴你同行　齐握未来（太平人寿）

  第二类，标准尾韵句。例如：

Shining and Caring

关怀周详　一生照亮（加拿大永明人寿保险公司）

Always listening. Always understanding.

用心聆听　更知你心（英国保诚保险）

  第三类，头韵句。例如：

Real food, Real people, Real place.

真滋味　真心意　真我天地（KFC）

Extra Value Extra Fun.

增值　增精彩（Compass VISA）

第四类，头尾韵。例如：

在广告的翻译中，往往寻求译句的韵律，一般把两个意思连贯或语气递进的成语、短句，经过改良的四字词堆放在一起，便成一则金句。例如：

Prepare to want one.

众望所归，翘首以待（Hyundai——现代汽车）

Your world of financial service.

金融荟萃　服务全球（HSBC——香港上海汇丰银行）

The future of the automobile.

领导时代　驾驭未来（Mercedes-Benz——汽车）

Be good to yourself. Fly emirates.

纵爱自己　纵横万里（Emirates——阿联酋）

Striving today for all your tomorrows.

为你未来，做好现在（中银集团）。

传统的七字句逐渐走向消失的主要原因与广告创作的宗旨有关。好的广告要易读易记，四字成语式广告既短又朗朗上口，自然人们对四字句情有独钟。中国人对双数的偏好以及对八字带有吉利寓意的观念，也进一步促使四字一句、八字一对的对偶句在广告中广泛流行。为了使这类广告金句念起来节奏感强，更加顺口，以便成为"口头禅"，从而深入人心，达到家喻户晓，绝大部分这类对偶式广告都是基本押韵的。

第二节　修辞格对比

所谓宣传文本，指的是用于介绍本公司、本地区或宣传产品的文本，包括官网宣传和纸质宣传册子等，其目的是为了吸引目标客户对本公司或相关产品的兴趣。在中英文的宣传文本中，都大量使用了修辞格。

一、比喻

比喻，就是用相似的事物来打比方，是最基本、最重要、最古老的一种修辞手法。正如《文心雕龙》所说："或喻于声，或方于貌，或拟于心，或譬于事。"比喻就是把抽象的、深奥的、晦涩难懂的事物用具体的、浅显的、形象鲜明的事物来描述或说明，使得事物、景观愈加鲜明，便于人们接受。

（1）南宁的绿肺，景区内山峦起伏，群峰叠翠，泉清石奇，素以山不高而秀，水不深而清著称。（南宁青秀山）

（2）A White Sail in the Sea, and a Best Palace of Culture and Art. Sydney Opera House looks like a white sail in the sea, side by side with the surrounding scenery. It spreads out like petals floating in the air. People have been amazed for years.（悉尼歌剧院）

例（1）是广西壮族自治区首府南宁一处著名景点——青秀山的介绍。运用比喻的修辞，把青秀山比作南宁的"绿肺"，表现了青秀山位于南宁这座绿城，即其地理位置。除此之外，"绿肺"是指能吸收二氧化碳并释放出氧气的绿地、森林等，又能突出青秀山的绿色、自然、无污染、原生态风光的景点特色。

例（2）是澳大利亚著名景点悉尼歌剧院的介绍，悉尼歌剧院作为澳大利亚的一处地标性建筑，"looks like a white sail in the sea"在这里把它比作海上的白色风帆，形象生动地表现出它的建筑外观和造型特点。

二、重复

广告语言通常要求简洁明了，避免冗赘重复。但是为了对某个信息或某种情绪进行强调，英汉广告都会特意安排重复某个词语或概念，以增强广告语的韵律，连接语篇，吸引消费者的注意力，使得消费者印象深刻。

（3）A modern car for a modern driver.（宝马汽车）

（4）Maybe she's born with it. Maybe it's Maybelline.（美宝莲纽约）

（5）When you are sipping Lipton, you are sipping something special.（立顿茶）

（6）恒源祥，羊羊羊。（恒源祥）

（7）过年过节不收礼，今年过节不收礼，收礼只收脑白金，脑白金。（脑白金）

（8）不溶在手，只溶在口。（M&M巧克力）

英汉广告所使用的重复，既可以重复某个词语，亦可以重复某个句型。以上例子中，例（3）例（4）均为单词的重复，而例（5）就是句型的重复。作为出现在美宝莲电视广告中的最后一句话，例（4）用两个maybe来引导句子，强调了美宝莲的功效，它没有用非常肯定的语气，但是让人十分肯定美宝莲这个品牌，提升了美宝莲的可信度和影响力。

三、引用

引用是修辞手法的一种，援用名人的话或现成的话语，如诗歌、成语或格言等来对作者的观点加以佐证，充实文章的内容，收到言简意赅的表达效果。引用利用了读者或听众对名人以及大众意见的从众心理来增强语篇的说理性及说服力。

（9）防城港市依山傍海，拥有靓丽的颜值和良好的空气，这里海湾多，半岛多，绿树多，三岛三湾环绕港城，海湾、江湖、岛屿、丘陵、田园、海上红树林等元素浑然天成，城市各项建筑布局有序，错落有致，是一座"海在城中，城在海中，人在景中"的全生态海湾城市，可以恣意享受"推开门窗观碧海，歇坐阳台闻涛声"的优美意境。

（10）St. Mark's Basilica stands at one end of St. Mark's Square. Napoleon called the square the "finest drawing room in Europe."（Piazza San Marco）

例（9）中，"推开门窗观碧海，歇坐阳台闻涛声"和"海在城中，城在海中，人在景中"均为引用，突出了防城港的城市特色。例（10）中拿破仑曾赞叹意大利威尼斯圣马可广场是"欧洲最美的客厅"和"世界上最美的广场"，用上名人所说的话，圣马可广场的美就显得很高端、真实，有信服力。

四、拟人

拟人就是把事物人格化，将人类的形态、外观、特征、情感、性格特质套用到非人类的物品上，赋予事物人的动作或情感。在广告宣传文本中，拟人的修辞能拉近商品与消费者之间的距离，促进消费者产生对商品的好感。

（11）Why your skin drinks it down so quickly?（玉兰油）

（12）Sexify your look.（迪奥香水）

（13）蒂花之秀，青春好朋友。（蒂花之秀化妆品）

例（11）中，皮肤被拟人化，而皮肤对护肤品的吸收，则被类比成"喝水"，从而展现了玉兰油易于被皮肤吸收的特点。"性感"这一名词通常是表示唤醒一个人内心欲望的着装或动作，例（12）的广告语中，将"性感"一词拟人化，向消费者传递了使用该产品能使其更加吸引人和更有魅力的含义。以这样的方式，让商品与消费者产生共鸣，因为每个人都渴望变得更漂亮和更有魅力。例（13）的广告语中将该商品拟人化为消费者的朋友，产生出与人相依相伴、相亲相爱的温情，使得消费者对商品更加容易产生信赖之情。

五、双关

双关是一种修辞手法，指在上下语境中，利用一词多义和多词同音的方式，使得表达具有双重意义，即同一个句子可以理解成两种或多种截然不同的意思。在广告宣传文本中，双关可以达到简洁精练和生动风趣的修辞效果，使人产生深度联想，加深对商品的记忆，起到了很好的宣传作用。

（14）Make up your own language，Rimmel（芮谜粉底液）

（15）要想皮肤好，早晚用大宝。（大宝面霜）

例（14）中的Rimmel有两个含义，第一个指的是Rimmel的粉底液，第二个则是广告里的女主人公，她在广告中没有说一个字。在看完广告之后，我们会产生一种好奇：Rimmel粉底到底有多么神奇的效果。这样就使广告变得更加有趣，也让消费者对商品产生更多的好奇心。例（15）在双关上不同于例（14）的地方就在于，例（15）使用的是语法双关，例（14）使用的是语义双关。首先，"早晚"有时间状语早上和晚上的意思，同时也有作为副词迟早的意思，它不仅仅强调大宝要在早上和晚上使用，还强调了即使现在不用，迟早也要用大宝。两个广告语的使用都非常简洁，但是中文的广告语除了简洁之外，还强调了工整和押韵，更能吸引人们的眼球。

六、夸张

夸张是指故意言过其实，对客观的人或事做扩大或缩小的描述的修辞方式。夸张重在感情的抒发而不在于事实的记述。广告语中的夸张通过对人的主观心理感受、商品或服务的某些特征进行夸大和强化，突出地反应产品某一方面的特性。使产品给消费者留下深刻的印象，增强其对于产品的认可度，激发消费者的购买欲望。

（16）For all skin types, with light reflecting particles and vitamin E.（Nivea Daily Essentials Tinted Moisturising Cream 妮维雅精华保湿霜）

例（16）对肤质进行了夸张，说妮维雅精华保湿霜适合所有类型的肤质。这好像是在暗示人们说妮维雅对于每个人来说都是正确的选择，让消费者对妮维雅产生了一种认同感。

七、仿写

中华文化博大精深，有些习语、谚语、诗词、名人警句脍炙人口，为人耳熟能详，流传千古。如果广告语中运用这些习语、句式，那么广告主利用群众对其熟悉的佳句已有的美好感觉，能够驾轻就熟地将广告信息传递给大众，并让其铭记于心。这种套用谚语、诗歌、名言警句的广告，无论在英文广告、中文广告及翻译的外来广告中，都相当普遍。

（17）Wherever you are. Whatever you do. The Allianz Group is always on your side.（Allianz Group）

（18）车到山前必有路，有路必有丰田车。（丰田汽车）

（19）路遥知马力，日久见跃进。（跃进汽车）

"Wherever you are. Whatever you do. The Allianz Group is always on your side." 安联集团，永远站在你身边。读到这样的广告词，让人自动联想到：Wherever you are, whatever you do, I am always with you…这熟悉的旋律和歌词。丰田车的著名中文广告词："车到山前必有路，有路必有丰田车。"这样的广告词，会让中文广告受众群体自然地联想到中国古语：车到山前必有路，船到桥头自然直。

从以上举例的句子可以看出，在英文、中文广告的写作和翻译中，套用与模仿固有成语、习语、谚语、诗词、歌词、名人警句、格言，从句式到内容都是很常用的方法。通常广告写作手段是保留句型，精妙地替换个别字词或者语句，以承托广告的主要信息，将其传递给广告受众群体。需要注意的是，在广告语创作过程中广告中模仿古诗词、名人名言，对作者、译者的知识创作水平要求甚高，对读者的欣赏水平和领悟能力都有较高要求。若作者、译者知识水平高，博古通今，融会贯通，但广告受众群中的文化水准、知识面却与作者、译者大相径庭，这类广告很难达到预期效果，难以引起相关联想或者难以形成足够触动，广告效果大打折扣，事倍功半。因此，广告句型的大众化和通俗化是广告创作和翻译考虑的重要方面。

八、其他

除了以上列举的几种修辞手法以外，其他用于中英文广告宣传的修辞手法还有很多，如设问、通感、析名等，同样能够增强广告的效果，给人们留下深刻的印象。

（20）Wouldn't you really rather have a Buick？（Buick 牌汽车广告标题）
（21）阿尔卑斯，甜蜜如拥抱。（阿尔卑斯糖广告）
（22）津津凉，美滋滋，乐无穷。（津乐美饮料广告）

第三节　文化修辞对比

在不同民族传统文化影响下，不同民族的心理特征也不同，这些心理特征不仅影响着人们的生活和风俗习惯，也会影响着语言活动。

一、中文浮夸的渲染话语与英文简洁的含蓄用词

汉英两种语言文化的差异："汉语讲究以言感人，偏重呼唤功能，而英语表达客观具体，突出信息功能。"（顾维勇，2005）汉英表现出的上述差

异在商业广告语言风格上的反映就是，汉语广告较多使用浮夸的渲染话语来打动人，呼唤人们的情感；而英语广告的用词简洁含蓄，注重逻辑思维，以理服人。

（1）该厂能生产大衣、西装、衬衣、毛衣等不同类型服装等上千个花色品种纽扣，产品规格齐全，种类繁多，造型新颖。

译文："The factory can produce various new types of buttons in thousands of different designs for coats, suits, shirts and sweaters.

（2）皮张之厚无以复加，利润之薄无以复减。

译文：The leather shoes made here are thick enough; the profit that's obtained is slight enough.

在例（1）广告词中，"连续三个四字结构'规格齐全''品种繁多'和'造型新颖'没有依次对应译出，而是译为various new types，因'种类繁多'与句中'上千个花色品种'意思重合，故略而不译，使英译平行文本行文简洁，表达地道"。而汉语广告的传神之处就在于它所采用的对照辞格。一"厚"一"薄"，一"加"一"减"对照鲜明。"由于过于关注文本形式和修辞本身信息而忽略广告受众的文化价值观"，所以，原译拘泥于原文，照搬汉语中对仗形式，有悖于广告英语简洁通俗的语言风格。

改译："Get our thick leather shoes which profit you thick."改译的广告前后巧妙地重复使用thick一词，突出了皮张之厚和消费者受益之丰厚。此外，英译采用了英语广告惯用的祈使句，很富有感染力和煽情性，符合英文广告受众者的习惯审美。

以上英汉广告翻译实例表明：汉语广告在语言的外在形式上表现出：（1）空洞修辞的大量堆积；（2）频繁使用四字格词语。比如，在例（1）中连续使用三个四字结构词语——"规格齐全，种类繁多，造型新颖"，其中规格齐全与品种繁多属于内容重复，因此"品种繁多"一词省略不译。汉语倾向于语言的渲染叠加这一特点，在中文商业广告中尽显无疑。而英文广告相对简洁，英文广告的用词特点是"简洁明快，含蓄不露"（蔡基刚，2003）。英文广告历经百年的发展，显得较为成熟。众多的英文广告则更偏重于注重摆事实列数据，以客观的语言描述产品，创建一种务实可靠的形象。

二、中文崇尚权威与英文崇尚事实

(3)经几代技术人员的努力,吸取现代先进工艺之精华。

译文:The natural flavor is improved by years of researched state-of-the-art technology...

在中文广告中常常会看到"国内外先进技术""高科技技术"科学方法等字眼来突出产品的先进性和科学性,如将此类广告生硬地直译并不符合西方读者的文化需求。因在科技发达的西方国家,产品的科学性和先进性不需要文字来突出,产品所代表的科学性、现代的先进性是不言而喻的。所以,直译会在英文广告中显得冗长而空泛。西方文化会以事实经验为重要依据,注重收集事实和数据,经验和观察方式。中文广告中通常会引用权威机构组织对产品的评价。在中文广告中常会采用:"国家免检产品""中国驰名商标""中国消费者协会推荐产品""国家品牌计划""国家保密配方""国宴饮品""获某某金奖"等权威评述语作为广告的承诺依据。

三、中文群体意向与英文个人取向

中国人大多带有群体取向,提倡集体主义,以家庭、社会和国家利益为重。在这种以群体取向为特征的文化影响下,中国人在商务往来中注重人际关系、集体忠诚意识。

(4)五谷香酥片配以芝麻、五香、奶油、巧克力、芝麻、咖喱、海鲜等各种调料,方便即食,营养丰富,老少皆宜。

译文:Crisp Cereal Chip is nicely flavored with condiments such as hot pepper, spices, cream, chocolate, curry, and seafood extract. It is nutritious and ready to serve.

在以上例子中,如果把"老少皆宜"生硬地翻译成:suitable for both the old and young,显然忽略了年龄在西方文化中的避讳。"老少皆宜"在汉语中属于套语，实质指向是广泛的，英语中很少使用这种表达，所以可以选择省略不译或者将"老少"改译为for grown-ups and children, for both sexes of all ages或for growing children and the whole family.

在中文广告中，广告商常会采用群体意向这一文化心理，不断渲染这种群体意向文化。比如以上广告中所用"老少皆宜"，以及司空见惯的"深受大众喜爱""我们都爱喝""大家好才是真的好"。

（5）海尔，中国造。（海尔集团）

（6）中国人的生活，中国的美菱。（美菱冰箱）

这类广告定位好产品消费群体，即中国国民，激发中国国民使用国货的情怀，继而唤起大众的购买欲望。与中国文化相反，西方国家推崇个人主义，每个人都是独立体，每个人的独立是最有价值的。这一维度在广告中有很好的体现。西方广告常出现：independence/independent、equal、uniqueness/unique、privacy/private之类体现个人主义的用词，体现了西方文化中追求个性，追求差异的特点。例如：

（7）Just do it.（Nike）

（8）Fit you well.（Reebok）

（9）What sort of Man Read Playboy? He's his own man. An individualist. And he can afford to express himself with style—in everything from the girls he dates to the way he dresses.

例（7）中Nike的广告语突出了追求个性、勇往直前、唯我独尊的个人主义价值观。例（9）中Playboy广告宣传语采用individualist（个人主义者）一词，在中西方文化中有不同的理解。在中国传统文化中，人们会认为"个人主义"或"个人主义者"有自私自利的贬义。在西方文化中，individualist有对自我个性的强调、张扬个性、追求自我、敢于自我表现这一褒义。所以在处理中西文化差异较大的词汇翻译时，要具体问题具体分析，对翻译进行调适。

鉴于中英广告中语言修辞差异、文化差异的特点，在双语广告翻译实践中要以广告受众对象为导向，深入了解中英广告语言的修辞特点，带有跨文化交际意识，在充分了解双语广告文本的基础上具体分析汉语、英语语境下，对原文本文字进行调适，对中英平行文本进行增补，从而充分表达广告的艺术魅力，更好地影响和吸引消费者，进而实现产品的宣传与营销。

第四章 英汉外宣修辞对比与翻译案例

第一节 中英文企业简介修辞对比与翻译

一、引言

企业简介是企业向外界递出的一张名片，是外界了解和认识企业的重要渠道。一份成功的企业简介能够帮助企业树立良好的企业形象，并提高企业产品与服务的宣传度。在现今全球经济一体化的趋势下，越来越多中国企业积极拓展海外市场，通过英文网站来进行对外宣传，希望借此吸引顾客消费、扩大企业对外交流与合作、提升企业国际影响力。然而，现今许多企业简介的英译版本却不尽如人意，有些甚至只是对中文原文的直接翻译，忽略了中西方语言文化差异，导致英译版质量不高。

对中国企业而言，企业简介的英译版本不应该是其中文版本的对应简单翻译。企业简介的英译版本的目标读者是外国读者，尤其是以英语为母语者,因此在翻译时应当着重考虑目标读者的语言文化习惯,尽量使用外国读者容易接受的文法,而原文只作提供信息源之用。并且,由于中英两种语言之间存在差异,在翻译时,我们应在文本内容和结构上作出调整。但要调整什么,又要如何调整,还需要参考英文企业简介平行文本。因此,分析中英企业简介平行文本的异同对中国企业简介英译具有重要启示意义。

二、中英企业宣传语篇对比

(一)语料选取

本文选取的研究语料来自六家大型中国企业(包括中国电力建设集团有限公司、广西北部湾银行、美的集团、华为投资控股有限公司、珠海格力电器股份有限公司、漳州片仔癀股份有限公司)网站的中文企业简介和美国六家大型企业(包括GNC、United Health Group、Johnson & Johnson、GE Power、Wells Fargo & Company、HP)网站的企业简介。选取的中美企业均为上市公司,涉及多个行业,并且这些企业在全球范围内具有一定影响力,在企业宣传方面有丰富的经验,具有很好的代表性。

(二)文本内容

就文本内容而言,中文企业简介的信息比较全面,包括公司的性质、社会地位、地理位置、历史发展、产品特色、员工人数、服务项目、研发能力、财务状况、公司文化、公司荣誉、公司新闻,等等。因此,中文企业介绍的信息往往比较多,篇章也比较长。而英文企业的介绍信息相对比较少,篇幅也比较短。在本文所选取的语料中,中文企业简介的字数多在400字左右,其中格力的企业简介字数多达1065字;而英文企业简介的字数则为100词左右,其中GE Power的企业简介字数最少(75词),Wells Fargo & Company的字数最多(134词)。由此可见,英文企业简介更偏向于使用简短的篇幅。

例1：漳州片仔癀药业股份有限公司简介

> 漳州片仔癀药业股份有限公司是以医药制造、研发为主业的国家技术创新示范企业、中华老字号企业，现市值超1500亿。拥有1家研究院、35家控股子公司、7家参股公司。经营6大品类、470多个产品系列。在全国7个省、直辖市建立23个科研、生产和药材基地。
>
> **核心产品**
>
> 国宝名药片仔癀，为国家中药一级保护品种，处方和工艺受国家保护，传统制作技艺列入国家非遗名录，单品种出口连续多年位居中国中成药外贸单品种出口前列，成"海丝"路上"中国符号"。
>
> **片仔癀荣誉**
>
> 公司荣获中国主板上市公司价值百强、全国文明单位、全国质量标杆、国家级"绿色工厂"、全国慈善会爱心企业、福建省工业企业质量标杆、福建省劳动关系和谐企业、福建省节水型企等20多项称号，被授予（第六届）福建省政府质量奖。企业技术中心通过国家评定，研发实力居中国中药研发实力前10强（列第7位），片仔癀连续多年居"中药大品种科技竞争力"排行榜清热解毒领域第一名。品牌连续六年获评"健康中国"肝胆用药第一品牌，以566.96亿列《2020年中国最具价值品牌100强》第55位，居2020年胡润品牌榜医疗健康行业第1位。
>
> **经营业绩**
>
> 2020年，公司实现营收65.07亿元，比增13.72%；利润总额19.82亿元，比增20.53%；净利润16.94亿元，比增22.12%；上缴税收8.7亿元，比增29.33%,再创同期历史新高。全球投行Torreya发布2020年《全球1000强药企报告》，公司排名从2019年的第80位上升至第49位，位居中国前10强。

例1中漳州片仔癀药业股份有限公司简介包括了公司性质、核心产品，荣誉和经营业绩几个方面。同样为医药保健品企业，美国GNC公司的企业简介相对就简洁了许多，简介的篇幅非常短。公司的介绍更多从顾客的角度出发，着重于描述公司能为顾客做什么以及公司的目标和愿景。

例2：美国GNC公司简介

> **Our promise to everybody**
>
> Living mighty. Living long. Living fit. Every person has a different definition of what it means to live well—and at GNC—we see that as something worth celebrating.
>
> Whether you're just getting started, or you need to keep going, GNC is committed to sparking your motivation and supporting your desire to live well.

例3：美国GE Power公司简介

> **About GE Power**
>
> GE Power builds the power generation technologies we depend on today and creates the energy technologies of the future. Our innovative solutions and digital offerings help make power more affordable, reliable, accessible, and sustainable.

此外，中文企业简介几乎都强调企业所获得的各种荣誉和奖项，尤其是政府颁发的奖项。例如，在片仔癀公司的简介中提到了"公司荣获中国主板上市公司价值百强、全国文明单位、全国质量标杆、国家级'绿色工厂'、全国慈善会爱心企业、福建省工业企业质量标杆、福建省劳动关系和谐企业、福建省节水型企等20多项称号，被授予（第六届）福建省政府质量奖"。企业通过描述荣誉和奖项来表明本企业得到了官方的支持和认可，显示了企业的地位。北部湾银行的企业介绍中也提及其先后荣获"金融机构支持地方经济发展突出贡献奖""全国银行业金融机构小微企业金融服务先进单位""全国十佳城商行""全国七五普法中期先进集体""广西优秀企业"和"广西企业100强""广西服务业50强""广西地方税纳税百强""服务八桂综合贡献奖"。

英文企业简介中均没有提及所获奖项，但几乎都提到他们的领导团队，并且附有详细个人介绍，一般点击了小标题后，读者就可以进入链接，看到详细的领导人个人介绍。例如，在GE Power官网上，紧跟着About GE Power这个栏目后面，就是Leadership Team，详细介绍了公司各方面的负责人。

因此，我们在对中国企业简介进行英译的过程中，对中国企业获得的奖项部分，应该酌情删减，因为英文读者并不关心企业得过什么奖项，也不会依据奖项来判断这个企业。而领导团队的个人介绍部分，可酌情增加，领导者的行业地位和个人阅历，会增加企业的可信度。

同时，英文企业更注重企业宗旨的宣扬，更侧重于介绍企业能为顾客提供什么服务。例3中，美国GE Power公司第一句话就强调了公司的功能"builds the power generation technologies"和"creates the energy technologies of the future"，同时强调创新对于企业的重要。

（三）文本结构

在文本结构上，中英企业简介总体上都比较完整，所涵盖的信息有共通之处。但企业简介的重点部分，则因不同企业而有所不同。此外，大部分英文企业简介配有段落小标题，让读者一目了然，如Walmart企业简介包括"our business, our history, our leadership, location fact, working at Walmart"等；而Johnson & Johnson企业简介包括"Our history, Our Leaders & Leadership Approach, Our Commitment to Our People, Our Commitment to Innovation"等。这些小标题都与链接相结合，读者可根据兴趣选择点击阅读。而中文企业简介只有华为和中国电建有小标题，但无链接，如华为的小标题为"华为是谁？我们为世界带来了什么？我们坚持什么？"而中国电建的小标题为"战略定位、核心竞争力、精品工程"。

美国苹果公司的官网上没有找到关于苹果公司规模、公司历史的介绍，公司介绍的板块分为"Newsroom, Apple Leadership, Job Opportunities, Investors, Ethnics & Compliance, Events, Contact Apple"七个板块。苹果公司所宣扬的商业道德单独设立为一个板块。

例4：苹果公司的商业道德

> **Ethics and Compliance**
>
> Apple conducts business ethically, honestly, and in full compliance with the law. We believe that how we conduct ourselves is as critical to Apple's success as making the best products in the world. Our Business Conduct and Compliance policies are foundational to how we do business and how we put our values into practice every day.
>
> We do the right thing, even when it's not easy.
>
> Tim Cook

（四）修辞风格

中美企业简介呈现了不同的修辞风格。中文企业简介通常采用第三人称进行叙述，措辞正式，语气庄重，更多地向读者展示"我是谁"，在例5广西北部湾银行的企业介绍中，文本历数了银行分支机构、营业网点、职工人数、总资产、存款余额和贷款余额等数据，以及公司所获得的一系列荣誉来说明"公司实力有多么雄厚"。

而英文企业简介大多采用第一人称 We（或our）进行叙述，语气亲切自然，易于拉近企业和读者（客户）之间的距离，例6强生公司的公司简介一直使用第一人称"We"来加强读者的认同感，同时在末尾强调公司能为客户做什么"to help people everywhere live longer, healthier, happier lives"这种第一人称的角度，有利于建立与顾客的连接，树立"顾客至上"的企业形象。

例5：广西北部湾银行企业简介

> 广西北部湾银行是顺应国家实施北部湾经济区开放开发战略，在原南宁市商业银行基础上改制设立的省级城市商业银行，于2008年10月挂牌成立。目前已在南宁、桂林、柳州、北海、贵港、钦州、防城港、崇左、玉林、百色、梧州、河池等12个设区市和桂平、横县、凭祥等42个重点县域设立了分支机构，在田东、宾阳、岑溪发起设立了3家村镇银行。全行共有一级分支机构21家，营业网点超220家，职工人数超3400人。逐渐成长为总资产超3000亿元，存款余额超2200亿元，贷款余额超1600亿元，具有良好公司治理和风险管理机制的现代商业银行。2020年主体长期信用等级提升至AAA，成为广西区内第一家主体长期信用等级获评AAA的城商行……

例6：强生公司简介

> **About Johnson & Johnson**
>
> Caring for the world, one person at a time, inspires and unites the people of Johnson & Johnson. We embrace innovation—bringing ideas, products and services to life to advance the health and well-being of people around the world. We believe in collaboration, and that has led to breakthrough after breakthrough, from medical miracles that have changed lives, to the simple consumer products that make every day a little better. Our over 125,000 employees in 60 countries are united in a common mission：to help people everywhere live longer, healthier, happier lives.

（五）中文企业简介翻译启示

根据以上分析可以发现，中英文企业简介在文本内容、文本结构和修辞风格等方面有许多不同之处，这些不同之处恰恰给予了我们一些翻译启示。

1. 企业简介的翻译要以目标语为导向

中文企业简介的英译版本面向的是国外读者，因而文字编排应该符合他们的阅读习惯。在翻译时，不应逐字翻译，而应对原文本进行重新编排，不拘泥于原文本的内容、结构等，根据需要增加或删减信息，整理出外国读者关心的信息。

2. 企业简介的翻译应对内容有所选择和增减

从收集到的语料来看，中文企业简介相对于英文企业简介篇幅过长，内容陈杂，阅读起来比较费时费力，而英文简介追求简洁明了，因此在翻译时，应该对文本进行压缩，把字数减少，需要详细介绍的部分可以使用超文本链接或设立分项目，让感兴趣的读者另行点击阅读。

此外，中文企业简介喜欢提到的荣誉奖项很少出现在英文企业简介中，可以看出，外国读者并不是很关心企业曾经获得什么样的荣誉奖项，并且若企业所获奖项是国内奖项，外国人不甚了解，提了也没有多大用处，而且荣誉奖项的名称一般较长，因而容易占据较大篇幅，直接导致简介篇幅变长。因此在翻译荣誉奖项这一方面，大可以进行简化或者删减，以保证文本篇幅简短。

除此之外，英文企业简介一般喜欢提到企业愿景、领导团队，强调顾客至上，在翻译时可以酌情增加这些信息。

3. 调整文本结构，多用小标题

英文企业简介倾向于先做一段概括性的介绍，大概描述企业的基本信息，再使用小标题进行分段，从而具体描述企业发展故事、企业文化、领导团队等信息，并且外国企业的网站常常使用链接的形式让读者自行选择要不要对这些小标题之下的信息进行了解。这样做的优点在于可以让企业简介的版面变得简洁明了，信息明确，读者阅读起来省时省力。而中文企业简介则几乎没有分小标题，而是全部信息杂糅在一起，导致信息主次不明。因此在翻译时，可以对原文本进行整理拆分，先做一段概括性叙述，再用小标题分段具体描述其他信息。

4. 借鉴英文企业简介的表达方法

英文企业简介多使用"we/our"等第一人称词语来代替公司名称，有效地拉近了与读者之间的距离感，给人一种亲切感；并且英文企业简介常常使用customer等词，强调顾客至上的信念，容易使顾客或潜在顾客对企业产生好感。而中文企业简介则比较官方客观，较少出现"我们"等词，一般全文都使用公司名称作为主语，这样虽然比较正式客观，但在国外读者看来可能会有冷冰冰的感觉。因而在翻译时，根据国外读者阅读习惯，可以适当多用we/our等词来代替公司名称，以拉近距离感；适当增加customer等词表现出企业重视顾客的想法，展现出一个对顾客友好的企业形象。

（六）结语

通过收集中英文企业简介的真实语料可以发现，中英文企业简介在文本内容、文本结构和修辞风格等方面有许多不同之处，在翻译时必须注意到这些不同，借鉴英文企业简介，对中文企业简介的英译版本进行调整，使之尽量符合外国读者的阅读习惯。但现今仍有许多中国企业的简介的英译版本只是对原文本的简单直接翻译，如选取语料中的格力的企业简介，这是十分不可取的。中国企业在走向世界的过程中，向外递出的英文企业简介这一名片应当与国际接轨，翻译得体的英文简介才能实现文本功能，展现良好的企业形象。

三、互联网公司中英语篇修辞对比

（一）语料

一般来说，互联网公司是指利用互联网技术来提供产品信息或技术服务而获利的组织。近年来，我国许多著名的互联网公司纷纷赴境外上市，成为走出国门的领先者，比如京东、小米等，这直接刺激了外国顾客对于购买该公司产品或服务的需求。同时，公司中文简介的英译文本也会成为外国受众所接触的第一道关卡。如何使受众能更好地接受所宣传的企业概况，本文将会着重分析我国著名的上市互联网企业的网页，通过分析它们的中英简介版本，发现共性，提炼优点，为相关的外宣翻译实践提供一定的翻译参考。

（二）受众视角的提出

外宣翻译是企业走向国际化的重要体现。文字翻译的质量高低与修辞的运用紧密相关。从西方修辞学的发展历史看，主要分为古典修辞学与新修辞学两大学派。古典修辞学的集大成者是亚里士多德，他认为："修辞术的定义可以这样下，在每一事例上发现可行的说服方式的能力。"（Aristotle, 1954）由此可见，修辞的功能是劝服。随着翻译实践的开展，单一的说服并不被读者所接受。此时新修辞学派的代表人物肯尼斯·伯克提出了新的修辞的定义："人们使用词汇形成态度或导致他人采用行动。"（Burke, 1969: 41）"认同"又称"同一"，是新修辞学的核心。外宣是说服性的文章，其结果是需要得到译文受众者的认同。所以，外宣文献的翻译实际上是译者帮助读者认同原文的过程。由此，在新修辞的理论下，受众的视角不容忽视。公司简介的对外翻译同时作为跨文化的一种交际行为，成功与否就是要做到语言文字符合外国受众的文化习惯，至少做到能懂且易于理解。考虑到受众的接受可能，转化中英的修辞差异，增强译文的可读性及无形中劝服的话语能力。

（三）互联网公司中英简介的修辞共性

主流的互联网公司都是通过提供优质和免费基础服务赢得客户，在海量用户的使用下，在通过增值服务，满足特定客户的需求而谋取利益。因此，除去基本的规模、荣誉、运营理念、创始人、名字来由外，中英简介的最大修辞共性便是用大量的数字来强调公司各类平台下的产品和服务功能，以此来劝服受众的使用欲望及信任感。从我国十大互联网企业的简介来看，单论这一点，数字说服的意识已经增强不少。

（四）互联网公司简介的修辞差异

1. 词语修饰

汉语的修辞着重于对语言的修饰，表现在对语言材料的选择与加工之中，因此，汉语倾向于堆积繁杂的形容词、副词，用以加重文章的文采。西方修辞学更强调人文性及社会交往，强调语言的说服功能。英文句式中的词语修辞更为朴实和简洁。

2. 语篇构建

语篇是一个具有完整使用意义的语言单位，是交流过程中以某种逻辑联系在一起，以达到一定的交际功能的信息组合。韩礼德的系统功能语法把篇章意义认定为构成语言整体意义的三个有机部分之一。互联网企业简介中文中着重于宣传企业的荣誉及附属的产品服务等信息，在字词上会花费大篇幅笔墨来渲染说明，同时多用排比、分句短语等对称性短句一一列出，细分模块，呈总分结构，宏观描述；而英译简介大多缩短文字内容，突出产品的服务功能等直接与目标客户的东西，分块独列，微观呈现，用表格等数据化的形式例证。

（五）公司中英简介的翻译方法

通过对修辞语言的基本分析，可以得出互联网公司简介的翻译可以从简化修饰语、人称转化、关联突显、信息重组这四个大的方面入手，结合目标受众接受能力的思考，提升一定的翻译质量。

1. 简化修饰语

例1："百度，全球最大的中文搜索引擎、最大的中文网站。百度拥有数万名研发工程师，这是中国乃至全球最为优秀的技术团队。这支队伍掌握着世界上最为先进的搜索引擎技术，使百度成为中国掌握世界尖端科学核心技术的中国高科技企业，也使中国成为美国、俄罗斯和韩国之外，全球仅有的4个拥有搜索引擎核心技术的国家之一……"

译文：You don't need us to tell you that China's Internet space is booming. With the world's largest Internet user population—731 million as of December

2016—and a long way to go to reach Internet penetration levels of developed countries, China's Internet industry is growing in both scale and influence. And as more and more Chinese users come online, Baidu continues to innovate to meet their changing needs and diverse tastes. We aim to serve the needs of our users and customers with products and solutions that prioritize the user experience and reflect our corporate culture—simple and reliable...

这是百度简介的中英文本的开头，从中我们可以看出文本内容是不对称的。就单独字词可以看出，中文宣传喜欢用一些"虚词"，比如"最大""数万""最优秀"等，用来对公司的规模或发展成果进行修饰。"最""领先"这些烘托性的夸大词语受企业简介的喜爱，无实质意义，只是起烘托造势的作用，但是汉语普通大众对这些能够树立民族自豪感、鼓舞民族精神的修辞喜闻乐见，受到普遍认可（陈小慰，2011）。反之，外国读者会偏向朴实平淡的言语，他们认为对词语的过分修饰会冲淡本身的感染力。因此，在英译文本中，百度处理得很是巧妙，对于这些常见的赞词一律省略跳过，避免让外国读者产生误解、迷惑甚至是对公司成就的不信任感。同时，因为西方人喜欢用事实数据说话，所以翻译中还用数字例证来具体指出中国互联网用户的人数，通过国家的互联网发展趋势来引出百度的服务内容，慢慢引入，阅读起来毫无压迫感，符合新修辞理论下追求受众同一的诉求。

2.人称转化

翻译中应该"不再把文本视作无生命的符号，读者和译者也不再是被动地接受文本，而是以一种创造性的精神与之对话，从中发掘新的意义"（卢小军，2012）。在互联网公司的网页简介上，就是在介绍公司或产品，如何介绍能使读者乐于接受又与人称代词的转化有关。

例2：通过互联网服务提升人类生活品质是腾讯的使命……腾讯的发展深刻地影响和改变了数以亿计网民的沟通方式和生活习惯，并为中国互联网行业开创了更加广阔的应用前景。

译文：It is Tencent's mission to enhance the quality of human life through Internet services... The development of Tencent has profoundly influenced the ways hundreds of millions of Internet users communicate with one another as well as their lifestyles. It also brings possibilities of a wider range of applications to the

China's Internet industry.

这则英译简介全文都在用"it"第三人称来说明腾讯的发展，还用上了强调句，口吻十分地客观冷静，而且通篇重复用"it"，给人一种累赘的感觉，十分难受。对比上文的百度案例，中文文本中一直在用第三人称陈述着百度的公司或产品这个主语，语言修饰手段官方正式，但给人一种不可接近的陌生感；但是英译版本却主要以第一人称为主，偶尔伴随第二人称用于提问和加强幽默，语言修饰平淡通俗，用来拉近双方之间的距离，增进语言的亲和力，给人一种平易近人、服务至上的感觉。例如，"You don't need us to tell you that..."，从一开始落笔就赋予读者认同感，相信读者的背景知识，既可以很好地推广中国互联网事业，又不会给人一种逼迫的感觉。

3. 关联突显

企业简介可以看作一张名片，成功与否，取决于文字说明的重心。由于中西方的文化差异，在价值诉求方面会略显不同。受中国传统修辞的影响，中文文本大多会强调身兼国家天下大事的成立理念和原则，以此来提升自我的形象，吸引国内受众；但企业简介翻译的主要受众是外国人。外国文化多追求个人自由和幸福，并且他们阅读的最终目的是为了投资或者服务需求，所以在价值诉求上就会偏向你能提供给他什么或者一些他熟悉的可以被他认可接受的同类服务产品的证明。

例3："网易是中国领先的互联网技术公司，由丁磊先生于1997年6月创立，并于2000年6月在美国纳斯达克股票市场公开上市。网易公司一直秉持"匠心"和"创新"的理念，为用户提供各类优质服务。目前，网易业务涵盖游戏、电商、新闻门户、邮箱、文化娱乐、在线教育、企业服务、工具应用等，是目前中国最大的互联网公司之一，覆盖超过9亿的用户。"

译文："NetEase, Inc. is a leading internet technology company in China. Dedicated to providing online services centered around content, community, communication and commerce, NetEase develops and operates some of China's most popular PC-client and mobile games, e-commerce businesses, advertising services and e-mail services. In partnership with Blizzard Entertainment, Mojang AB (a Microsoft subsidiary) and other global game developers, NetEase also operates some of the most popular international online games in China."

英文文本中，省略了很多的原文内容，诸如"由丁磊先生于1997年6月创立""网易公司一直秉持'匠心'和'创新'的理念"等，同时又增加了一些新内容"In partnership with Blizzard Entertainment, Mojang AB (a Microsoft subsidiary) and other global game developers" "online services centered around content, community, communication and commerce"。从中可以得出，删减的内容都是依据受众的喜好而定，拓展的内容，比如跟两个国外的著名游戏公司合作都是对于公司能力的补充说明，侧面意义上可以增进受众对公司产品服务的熟悉度，增加信任感，从而提高购买诉求。

4.信息重组

简介对比中发现，中英文文本内容的翻译大多是不对称的，这也就意味着在翻译时可以通过适当对信息要素的顺序进行调整，突显要点和省略不必要的冲突信息，从受众的思维习惯和阅读习惯中进行英译活动。

例4："携程旅行网创立于1999年，总部设在中国上海，员工超过30000人……今日的携程，在线旅行服务市场居领先地位，连续4年被评为中国第一旅游集团，目前是全球市值第二的在线旅行服务公司。"

译文："As one of the world's leading online travel agencies, Trip.com is here to help you plan the perfect trip. Whether you're going on holiday, taking a business trip, or looking to set up a corporate travel account, Trip.com is here to help you travel the world with cheap flights, discount hotels, and Chinese train tickets. Looking to find great travel deals or enjoy the biggest savings on your next trip? Trip.com has you covered. With our easy-to-use website and app, along with 24-hour customer service, booking your next trip couldn't be simpler. With Trip.com, quality travel services in over a dozen languages including English, Mandarin, Japanese, Korean, German, French, and Spanish are just a call—or click—away..."

携程的简介翻译是一个很好的利用文化差异的案例。首先，中文文本中，它一直在介绍公司的发展规模、版图扩张和所获的荣誉，这显然很好地获得了中国受众的信任感；但是换成英文受众，他们很不喜欢这类很强的企业文化侵略性，反而认为一个在简介中将企业的发展壮大看得比为客户提供优质产品还要重要的企业，如何能取得客户的信任？（崔建立，2012）因此，携程对信息进行了改编重组，全文描述酒店服务和机票信息，并用一系列的超链接来取代取得的版图扩展，满足顾客的服务需要，同时避免了文化因素的冲突和尴尬，可以获得受众的信赖，发展壮大公司的业务。

（六）对中国公司企业简介英译的分析

综合以上翻译启示对美的集团企业简介的中英版本进行分析。

例10：美的是一家消费电器、暖通空调、机器人与自动化系统、智能供应链（物流）的科技集团，提供多元化的产品种类，包括厨房家电、冰箱、洗衣机及各类小家电的消费电器业务；家用空调、中央空调、供暖及通风系统的暖通空调业务；以库卡集团、安川机器人合资公司等为核心的机器人及工业自动化系统业务；以安得智联为集成解决方案服务平台的智能供应链业务。美的坚守"为客户创造价值"的原则，致力创造美好生活。美的专注于持续的技术革新，以提升产品及服务质量，令生活更舒适、更美好。美的于1968年成立于中国广东，迄今已建立全球平台。美的在世界范围内拥有约200家子公司、60多个海外分支机构及12个战略业务单位，同时为德国库卡集团最主要股东（约95%）。

Established in 1968, Midea（SZ：000333）is a publicly listed and, since July 2016, Fortune 500 company that offers one of the most comprehensive ranges in the home appliance industry. Midea specializes in air treatment, refrigeration, laundry, large cooking appliances, large and small kitchen appliances, water appliances, floor care and lighting.

美的集团的英译企业简介对原文本信息进行了整合编排，将众多信息整理成了一段概括性的介绍，比较简洁，但后面的段落还是同原文一样，没有分小标题，只是直接叙述，看起来不够清晰明了，建议在后面的段落前加上business、brand promise、innovation等小标题，让读者一目了然，也便于读者阅读。

（七）结论

基于对我国著名互联网企业的公司简介中英文本分析，我们得出在新修辞学理论的驱动下，受众的接受能力才是翻译质量好坏的重要标准。而受众的认同又受到目的语的文化背景的影响，因此在翻译实践中，需要在有关修饰语、人称、关联突显、信息等方面进行适当的改写和调整，直译或省略法，从受众的角度去考虑，真正地做到忠于公司形象却又避免文化冲突的合理的跨文化传播活动。

四、中英食品企业简介修辞对比

（一）引言

随着经济全球化的不断发展，各国之间联系越来越密切，企业在经济全球化这一浪潮中占据重要地位，企业简介亦是企业走向世界市场的重要名片，主要包括介绍企业历史、发展状况、企业文化、企业目标、产品、经营性质和目的等方面内容，让读者对企业有一个清晰的认识、良好的印象。因此企业简介是对外宣传，树立企业形象的重要手段，也是让市场充分了解自己的重要途径。良好的企业简介翻译有助于企业产品顺利进入国际市场，树立良好的企业形象，提高企业声誉，赢得消费者喜爱。随着企业的国际化，随之而来的是企业简介的国际化：配备中英文企业简介。越来越多的跨国企业将企业简介翻译成英文，大多是直接按照原版语言特点翻译成英语，虽然语法上没有错误，相关意思也能够准确表达出来，但译文往往不够简明，忽略了目标读者的不同而达不到其效果。翻译目的论指出，翻译过程的最主要因素是整体翻译行为的目的。诺德提出译者应该遵循"功能加忠诚"的指导原则，因此我们在翻译过程中应该做到有针对性，让企业简介无论是对内对外都能够起到有效的作用。在前人的研究中，部分学者从语用学角度出发，提出相应的翻译原则与策略。本文尝试从翻译目的论出发，通过类比、对比分析食品汉英企业简介的异同点，为食品类企业"走出去"的名片翻译提供有效的翻译建议。

在经济全球化日益发展的当今社会，企业简介尤为重要。无论是国内还是国外，无论是买方还是卖方都需要经过详细的了解，才能达成促销或交易。因此树立良好的企业形象是每个企业发展不可或缺的战略。企业简介是对企业基本情况的总体概括，主要包括企业历史、发展状况、企业文化、企业目标、产品、经营性质和目的等方面的内容。企业简介的目的主要在于向广大消费群众介绍企业相关产品，树立良好的企业形象，提高企业信誉与知名度，从而达到诱导消费者消费的目的。不同的民族受不同文化的影响，表达方式与接受方式会有所不同，因此汉英企业简介会存在一定的差异：中文企业简介多用四字词语，文章务虚不务实；英文企业简介则注重事实，务实不务虚。下文通过具体对比分析今麦郎面品有限公司、伊利企业中英文简介、雀巢、北京御食园食品股份有限公司以及卡夫亨氏公司的企业简介来说明翻译企业简介存在的差异，根据这些差异译者需要在坚持"功能加忠诚"的原则下，翻译出适合读者文化需求的企业简介，以达到良好的宣传效果。

（二）话语内容的差异

受不同价值观、不同文化观念的影响，中英企业简介在内容上有所差别。以下选取片段文字进行分析。

例1：北京御食园食品股份有限公司始终坚持"食以民为天"的品牌理念，依托怀柔山区得天独厚的生态环境优势，成功开创了"公司+基地+农户+市场"的干鲜果品加工一体化经营之路，自主研发、自主生产和销售北京特产食品、中华名小吃、特色休闲食品和绿色原生态食品四大品类两百多种产品，年销售额超过3亿元，堪称北京特色食品行业的一面旗帜。公司的板栗系列、营养小甘薯系列受到市场的一致欢迎。御食园牌冰糖葫芦、北京果脯、茯苓夹饼、怀柔甘栗、驴打滚、小甘薯、京八件等20种产品被中华烹饪学会授予中华名小吃称号。

例2："Nestlé is the world's largest food and beverage company. We have more than 2,000 brands ranging from global icons to local favourites, and we are present in 189 countries around the world."

通过这两个片段的对比发现，中文企业简介的内容较长，采用两个独立的分句描述企业所获得的主要成就与荣誉称号，如"年销售额超过3亿元，堪称北京特色食品行业的一面旗帜""成功开创了""自主研发、自主销售""受到市场一致欢迎"以及"被中华烹饪学会授予中华名小吃称号"等，用权威认证与一些所获成就来提高企业的形象。此外描述内容时会有一些套话官话相随，一系列成就描述读下来让读者有一种该企业为"优秀企业"之感，内容上虽从事实出发，但一路加以渲染，有时给读者留下夸大现实的印象；英文企业简介内容则较短，多注重企业的整体形象，列举真实的信息，无夸大事实的倾向，传达给读者的信息明确简洁。如雀巢（Nestlé）用"largest""more than 2,000 brands""in 189 countries around the world"这一系列数据事实说明了其规模之大、子公司数量之多以及遍布的国家数量之广。雀巢与北京御食园食品股份有限公司相比，两者企业简介的相同点都是为企业打造良好的形象，内容都是与企业相关并有助于提高形象的信息。

（三）行文结构的差异

中英企业简介不仅在内容上不同，在行文结构上也存在着一些异同点。接下来这部分是对比分析伊利公司中英文简介在行文结构上的差异。

例3：2017年7月12日，在荷兰合作银行发布的2017年度"全球乳业20强"中，伊利集团蝉联亚洲乳业第一，位居全球乳业8强，连续第四次入围全球乳业前十，体现了企业在亚洲乃至全球全方位的综合领先优势。在发展历程中，伊利始终坚持"国际化"和"创新"两个轮子，固守"质量"和"责任"两个根本，以高品质、高科技含量、高附加值的多元化产品，赢得了消费者的高度信赖。每天，1亿多份伊利产品，到达消费者手中，每年，有将近11亿中国消费者享用到营养美味的伊利产品。

例4：Inner Mongolia Yili Industrial Group Co., Ltd, a provider of healthy and nutritious dairy products, is China's largest dairy producer with the most complete product lines, and the only dairy product sponsor of Beijing Olympic Games and Expo 2010 Shanghai. In 2015, Yili reported a double-digit growth in its operating turnover and net profit：the Company achieved a main operating turnover of 60.36 billion RMB, the first ever in domestic dairy sector to have an operating turnover exceeding 60 billion RMB, and a net profit of 4,654 million

RMB, continuing to lead in Asian dairy sectors. So far, Yili has opened its first major overseas dairy factory in New Zealand...

通过对比发现，在行文结构方面，伊利公司简介注重意合，不追求文本的形合，两句话之间可以没有必然的联系：第一句话"……体现了企业在亚洲乃至全球全方位的综合领先优势"描述的是伊利公司在全球的地位。第二句话：伊利始终坚持"国际化"和"创新"两个轮子……是伊利的发展历程中所坚持的信念。最后一句话："每天，1亿多份伊利产品……，则是伊利的消费者数量。通过三句话读者能够对伊利公司有一个地位、信念以及销售量上的整体理解，前后不用任何连词，行文也能顺理成章；这样的行文结构有利于读者对伊利产生信赖感；在伊利公司英文简介中则是比较注重形合，行文结构逻辑严密，多使用连词与复合句与上下文衔接，整个文本层次分明。文中a provider of、and、so far等连词使得文章结构严密；伊利公司英文简介按照时间顺序言简意赅的传达了三件事：企业地位、企业利润以及企业"走出去"，以时间顺序进行描述加以连词连接，使得行文层次分明，逻辑严密。

（四）语言风格的差异

中英企业简介存在的最明显差异为语言风格上的差异。因文化背景的不同，语言风格上也存在着不同。美国语言学家莱昂斯（John Lyons）指出语言与文化具有历史的联系，语言是打开文化宝库的钥匙，离开语言天然的文化背景，难以充分地理解语言本身。最后这一部分则是对比分析今麦郎食品有限公司与卡夫亨氏公司（The Kraft Heinz Company）的简介片段在语言风格上的不同。

例5：今麦郎面品有限公司是全国方便食品行业的龙头企业，本部位于河北省邢台市，以方便食品为主业，是集生产、销售、研发于一体的现代化大型综合食品企业集团。今麦郎面品有限公司的前身是河北华龙面业集团，创建于1994年3月，是一家股份制企业。以公司董事长兼总裁范现国为首的决策者，将"产业报国，造福社会"作为企业的崇高理念，凭借得天独厚的资源优势、领先水平的专业优势、门类齐全的配套优势、优越的产品性价比优势、国内高覆盖率的市场优势，创造了企业超常规、跨越式的发展模式。

例6：The Kraft Heinz Company（NASDAQ：KHC）is the fifth-largest food and beverage company in the world. A globally trusted producer of delicious foods, The Kraft Heinz Company provides high quality, great taste and nutrition for all eating occasions whether at home, in restaurants or on the go. The Company's iconic brands include Kraft, Heinz, ABC, Capri Sun, Classico, Jell-O, Kool-Aid, Lunchables, Maxwell House, Ore-Ida, Oscar Mayer, Philadelphia, Planters, Plasmon, Quero, Weight Watchers Smart Ones and Velveeta. The Kraft Heinz Company is dedicated to the sustainable health of our people, our planet and our Company.

通过对比可看出中文企业简介的用词比较华丽，多用四字成语，内涵丰富，以排比或拟人等方式加强语言表达的气势，体现出一定的程式化；如今麦郎食品有限公司简介中的用语"集……于一体"表现了其企业的类型，"产业报国，造福社会"阐明了其企业理念，"得天独厚""门类齐全"说明了其发展优势，"超常规、跨越式"突出其发展模式的优点。相比之下英文简介用词则比较平淡直白，无太多的修饰，词语通俗易懂，"is the fifth-largest food and beverage company in the world"，用简单的单词来描述卡夫亨氏在全球中的地位，"provides""include""is"三个动词将企业产品质量、子公司以及发展目标简洁明了地传达给广大的读者。由比较可知，中文企业简介用词多辞藻华丽，注重"雅"，符合中国读者的文化倾向；而英文企业简介多用词简洁平实，注重陈述事实，符合英文读者的文化需求。

（五）结语

通过三个方面对五家不同的食品企业简介的分析，我们可以看到中文企业简介与英文企业简介文本在话语内容、行文结构以及语言风格方面确实存在着一定的差异。在内容方面，中文企业简介注重荣誉称号与发展成就，这样有利于使读者信赖该企业，这符合中国读者的心理需求；而英文企业简介则是比较注重实在性的数据，用数据来说服读者与消费者。行文结构方面，中文注重意合，即想表达的含义不用通过语言手段来表达，不追求语言结构的严谨，汉语句子之间有意义上的联系，无需一定的衔接词；而英语则是注重形合，句子的含义需要通过句子与词语间的紧密相连来表达出来。在语言文字方面，因中英文化存在着一定的差异，语言风格上也存在着差异：中文企业简介文字辞藻华丽，多为被动以及静态的词语，而英文中则多为主动性词语，并且多为动态的词语。因此在翻译过程中应遵循"内外有别"原则，根据读者群体的不同分别在内容、结构、语言方面做出相应的调整。

翻译目的论的观点是：翻译过程的最重要的因素是翻译的目的，译文必须具有可读性与可接受性，能使读者理解和接受交际语境中的意义。译者应遵循"功能加忠诚"的指导原则。因此，在翻译目的论的指导下，中英企业简介的翻译可以使用省译法、增译法以及结构整合与重组的翻译方法。省译法即在把企业简介翻译为英文时，可以适当省略掉一些过分华丽的辞藻与过分赘述的内容，以符合外国读者的习惯；增译法即在把企业英文简介翻译为中文时可适当增加一些话语，以期与中国读者对中国文字的表达习惯相符；结构整合与重组的翻译方法是根据汉语与英语思维的不同，根据各自的特点来重组，如中文简介多是含蓄隐晦最后才得出结果，而英语多是开门见山直接切入主题，因此在翻译过程中将中文简介翻译为英文则需先将重点提到前面，再进行翻译，将英文翻译为中文时可适当将重点信息往后放置。

综上所述，在翻译企业简介的过程中，译者需要根据读者需求来对译文进行调整，在翻译的过程中需要充分了解中文与英文企业简介的特点，根据各自的特点进行整合翻译，以期使译文达到能够让读者对企业介绍的信息明了、不困惑的程度，并且能够让企业简介真正起到良好的宣传效果。

第二节　中英产品手册修辞对比与翻译

产品手册是常见的解释性文本，由制造商编写，旨在为消费者提供有关产品名称、用途、性质、性能、原理、结构、规格、用法、维护、注意事项等的全面而清晰的介绍，以便人们可以识别和理解产品。产品手册的基本属性是宣传产品以唤起消费者的购买欲望，从而实现购买并促进商品流通。

本文将以化妆品的产品手册为例，对比和总结中英文产品手册的修辞特征。随着经济全球化的发展，越来越多的国外化妆品进入中国市场，中国的化妆品也流入海外市场。作为产品的介绍工具，化妆品说明书对产品的销量，以及对顾客的吸引度起着非常重要的作用。因此，准确地翻译化妆品说明书，对化妆品产业的发展具有重要的意义。

一、英汉化妆品说明书的共性

由于中西方的文化差异以及产品种类繁多，因而化妆品的说明书具有各式各样的特点。但是商品说明书的性质决定了各种说明书的共性。一般说来，商品说明书内容由四部分组成：（1）化妆品的特征功能和成分；（2）使用的方式；（3）注意事项；（4）主要的指标和规则。

在语言特征上，英汉化妆品说明书上都具有专业性的特点。两者都包含化妆品相关的专业术语。例如梵蜜琳自然防护隔离BB霜的说明书中的产品介绍部分：

例1："Refreshing and breathable texture, fresh and not greasy, waterproof and anti-sweat, can effectively block the UV."

译文："质地清爽透气，清爽不油腻，防水防汗，可有效阻隔紫外线。"

该产品是一款化妆品，因而"refresh，fresh"不应翻译为"新鲜"，而是具有化妆品语言特色的"清爽"。再者，"UV"作为一个专业术语，中文有其对应的专业名词"紫外线"。因此，英汉互译的过程中不可自我臆想，仍需仔细查阅相关资料，运用恰当的词汇，使其具有可读性，便于受众理解和接受，达到介绍产品和促进营销的效果。还有，介绍产品的使用类型时会使用到类似facial cleanser/face wash（洗面奶）；toner/astringent（爽肤水）"；moisturizers and creams（护肤霜）；moisturizer（保湿）；sun screen/sun block（防晒）等以及在介绍化妆品的主要成分时会用到甘油（glycerin）、甘油硬脂酸酯（glyceryl stearate）、Dual Target Vitamin C（双效修护维他命C）、plant extracts（植物精华）、clarifying agent（净化成分）、biological gum（生物糖胶）、Hyaluronic acid（玻尿酸）。

与其他产品说明书相似，中英文的化妆品说明书在使用方法以及注意事项方面，多使用简单句以及祈使句。

例2："Usage: Please use it every morning and wash it off at noon; please use it on evening and wash it off before bedtime; for those career women who need make-up at daytime, please use it once on every evening and wash it off before bedtime."

译文："使用方法：早上使用，请中午洗掉，傍晚使用，请睡前洗掉；白天需要化妆的职业女性，傍晚使用一次，请睡前洗掉。"

在英文的介绍中，多次使用"please"的句型，加强句子的语气，表明一种谦逊的语气，拉近与读者的距离，令读者感受到商家亲切的态度和体贴的服务。句子较为简单，简洁明了，令读者一目了然，能够快速获取有效信息。再者，简单句型能集中读者注意力，令读者对产品的印象更加深刻。

例3："Caution: Please drink less during usage, eat less spicy food, get enough sleep and keep away from ultraviolet light or strong light exposure for a long time."

译文："注意事项：使用本品期间应少饮酒，少食辛辣等刺激性食物，保持充足睡眠，避免紫外线或强光的长时间照射。"

注意事项中多使用"please, drink, eat, get, keep away from"，以及中文版本中的"少饮、少食、保持和避免"，无主语，动词开头的句子，动词起到强调的作用，起到警示读者作用，做到提醒读者，进行积极的引导消费者正确使用产品，避免不良后果，提升消费者的使用感。

二、中英化妆品说明书修辞差异

由于中西方文化的差异，中西方语言的表达方式和运用之间存在着巨大的差别,语言运用的差异使得中英化妆品说明书之间各具特色。

在产品描述方面,中文会运用一些夸大的词语和语气,吸引消费者的眼球,提高消费者的购买欲,从而促进产品的销售,增加生产者的利润收入。请看例4中雅诗兰黛密集特润修护精华露的介绍。

例4:"内涵突破性配方,拥有5倍浓度的神秘修护复合物,彻底改善肌肤状况。强力聚合三种创新科技,集中作用于21个夜晚,大幅度加强了肌肤自我修护功能,使之能够对抗更多压力伤害,重获健康新生。"

该产品的中文描述中为了突出精华液的非同一般,使用了"突破性""神秘""大幅度"等词语令消费者眼前一亮,但是我们不免看出,这只不过是一种夸张的描述。以及其中提到"彻底",使得说法过于绝对,表明该介绍为了追求广告的效果,而忽视了客观事实。

但是在英文说明书介绍方面,更注重中立和运用中肯的语气,表现英文产品描述更加追求真实的态度。比如例5中百合防晒中的描述,其中使用"reduce"表示该防晒霜只是拥有一定的功效,并非如上文中"彻底"描述的那么扩大化产品的效果。

例5:"...provide the skin with double protection, reduce the damage of UV&UVB to the skin and prevent the skin from sunburn, suntan and the occurrence of fine veins; moisturize and nature the skin, make it soft, smooth and delicate."

在词语特点选择方面,中英化妆品的说明书也各不相同。英文化妆品说明书倾向于使用复合词。比如block-flaw(遮瑕)、block-pore(控油)、anti-aging(抗衰老)等相关复合词,而汉语中多使用四字结构,类似于"色泽持久、色彩时尚、粉质细腻、均匀服帖、质地舒适"等四字结构,使得句子整齐,而且通俗易懂,朗朗上口。

英语中语法比语言的节奏重要。汉语则恰恰相反,语音和节奏受到高度重视(胡德龙,2005)。例6 CLINQUE COLOR SURGE IMPOSSIBLY GLOSSY(倩碧丝滑恒润唇彩)的化妆说明,英文采用"unbelievable"以及light给予人无限的遐想。汉语中采用"方、光、放"的押韵手法,使得句子读起来气势连贯,意思表达清晰,并且达到音韵美、节奏美和形象美的统一。

例6："Unbelievable shine and comfort. Light moisturizing formula."

译文："富含闪亮恒润配方，夺目唇光，精彩绽放。"

英语语言较为平凡朴实，而中文辞藻华丽。有时为了突出产品的效果会采用一些修辞手法，使得产品形象化，给予消费者更清晰的印象。例7中，英文直接表达block和strengthen the resistivity，表明防晒霜的阻隔作用。然而，中文中使用比喻的修辞手法，将"防晒霜形成的膜"比喻为"一层保护伞"，形象生动地描述该产品的功效，使得抽象且令消费者困惑的事物变得具体，消除消费者困惑的同时，也加深了他们对产品的印象。倘若直接用"阻隔"，此类直白的词语，就达不到这样的效果。在产品特点方面，中文经常使用"晶莹亮白、水凝通透、光彩动人"等华丽的词语，使得句子抑扬顿挫，读起来顺畅，同时极具感染力，赋予句子一种节奏美。

例7："Being refreshing, it slows the oxidation caused by free radicals and blocks kinds of radiation to strengthen the resistivity of the skin."

译文："缓解皮肤暗沉等肌肤问题带来的尴尬，打造清新裸妆的同时给肌肤提供一层保护伞。"

在英汉翻译过程中，译者很容易掌握两种语言的相似性。译者可直接将英文直译成中文。然而，译者很难处理两种语言的差异性。因此，译者翻译过程中需要遵守一些翻译的原则，以至于在翻译过程中实现功能对等（刘银屏，2011）。

三、英汉化妆品说明书的翻译原则

（一）忠实原则

无论是怎样的翻译，我们都必须做到忠于原文，不可随意更改原文意思。作为化妆品产品介绍的重要工具，化妆品说明书对产品的发展起着十分重要的作用。而化妆品说明书作为产品介绍的科技类文体，必须保持客观性和中立性，否则就会误导消费者，从而引起消费者的反感，导致销量下降。

上文我们对比出西方国家的产品说明介绍，大多持有一种中肯的态度，而有些中国产品为了扩大产品的功效，带有些许夸张的语气，但仍然可以被消费者所接受。因此在汉译英的过程中，切忌使用"完全""彻底""一定"等过于绝对的词语，以免引起消费者的误导，影响产品和公司的形象。

（二）准确性原则

翻译的作用就是将一种语言转换成为另一种语言，使得不同语言的人进行有效的沟通交流。只有准确地进行翻译，才能够有效地传达信息。在化妆品说明书的翻译过程中，要格外注意产品的专业词语。比如"firm"（紧致），在化妆品领域中，要使用其专用词，才不会让消费者困惑，使其快速获取和理解信息。因此"firm"在化妆品上，大多数译为"紧致、紧肤"，不应翻译为其常用的意思"坚固"。在翻译的过程当中，要做到充分了解化妆品行业的相关术语，遇到翻译障碍，要及时查阅资料和寻求相关人士的帮助，切勿使用非专业词代替专业术语。错误性的翻译会给消费者带来阅读性障碍，降低消费者了解产品的兴趣和欲望，无法吸引潜在客户的注意力，因而达不到宣传产品的效果。

（三）可读性和感染力原则

中英文化差异使得英汉语言表达方式迥异，使得译者在英汉互译时，要遵循英汉语言各自的习惯，精确了解产品信息。由于说明书往往同时具备广告功能，因此其语言具有较高的可读性，因而在翻译时请注意适当控制和使用目标语言。既要通俗易懂，也要适度地运用文学性语言，以达到广告的效果（冯庆华 & 穆雷，2008）。中文偏向于使用四字词语，使得文字更加灵动而具有美感。但是，在英文中却没有相对应的词语与之匹配。例如，"give natural and lovely colors with a glossy shine."（增添双唇如珍珠般的淡淡色彩，自然亮丽），"自然亮丽"四个字就囊括整句英文所要传达的信息，而四字结构的用法符合中文习惯，既做到简洁明了，也做到通俗易懂。前面的"增添双唇如珍珠般的淡淡色彩"采用增添的译法，英文中并没有与之完全对应的句子，增加词语的译法是为了使得句子更加通顺，也是对产品进一步的阐述，使得产品形象更加鲜明。此处，还采用了比喻的修辞手法，"如珍珠般的淡淡色彩"，突出唇膏透亮的特点，进而吸引消费者，增加其购买的欲望。由此可见，化妆品说明书的翻译，尤其是对产品功效和特点描述方面，译者要充分理解原文，适当地增加或者删减词语或者短语，做到表达清晰和简洁通顺。英译中时，也可适当地使用一定的文学性描述，使得意思明了，还能通过文字表现出产品的一种美感和鲜明的特征。

四、总结

充分了解英汉化妆品说明书的语言特点以及英汉互译原则，有利于翻译工作的顺利开展。在往后的化妆品翻译工作中，首先我们要熟悉化妆品领域的相关知识，以及中英文语言特点，在遵守翻译原则的基础上，翻译出准确而地道的中英文说明书，才能吸引更多消费者，进一步推动化妆品产业的发展。

第三节 中英网站修辞对比与翻译

一、中英高校网页"学校简介"的平行文本分析

在中国高校开展国际化办学、扩大学校国际对外交流与合作的过程中，高校的网页起到了越来越大的作用。许多有意来中国留学的外国学生会通过浏览学校的官方网站来了解学校概况和办理相关事务。网页中的高校简介作

为宣传文本，是树立高校形象、对外宣传、吸引海外学生与建立国际合作的重要渠道。然而，目前大多数广西高校英文网页中的"学校简介"都是按照中文的简介逐字翻译而来，没有考虑到英文读者的文化差异、认知差异和审美差异，在很大程度上降低了译文的跨文化宣传功能。因此，本文将运用平行文本对比的方法，对比广西地方高校与美国高校"学校简介"，以找出广西高校对外宣传中存在的问题并提出对策建议。

（一）平行文本的定义和研究样本

平行文本的对比在翻译研究中具有独特的作用，翻译是一种跨文化的交际活动。虽然在不同文化中的平行文本具有相似的信息及功能，但往往在文本内容、表达方式及文化意识方面存在着一定的差异。近年来，不少学者比较了不同类型的使用文体文本，如旅游文本、企业外宣、酒店文宣、学校简介、广告文本和博物馆概况等。

平行文本可以分为两类。在语料库翻译中，平行文本指的是由原文和对应译文构成的语料。而另一种定义是"在语言上彼此独立，但是在相同（或相近）的情境下产生的不同文本"（House, 2007）。这一类平行文本的研究亦可用于翻译学的研究，目的是检验不同的语言如何表达相同的事实材料。本文研究的平行文本是第二类，本文将选取中国大学的中文学校简介和美国大学的英文学校简介进行对比。就文本的功能而言，中国高校和美国高校官方网页上的学校简介文本具有相似的文本功能，包括介绍高校的办学历史、展示高校的教学和科研实力、吸引来该校学习的学生、求职的师资和有意与该校进行学术合作的机构等，但是中国高校和美国高校官方网页上的文本在内部构成规则上具有较大差别。

为此，文章首先构建了可比语料库——广西高校网页英文简介语料库和国外著名高校网页英文简介语料库。广西高校为广西大学、广西民族大学、广西师范大学、广西医科大学和桂林理工大学，涵盖综合类、理工类、师范类和医学类高校；国外高校覆盖美国排名在前10以内的5所美国顶级名校，包括普林斯顿大学、哈佛大学、芝加哥大学、耶鲁大学、哥伦比亚大学和斯坦福大学，同时还包括英语作为官方语言的新加坡和马来西亚的高校：南洋理工大学、马来亚大学和博特拉大学,文本的选取具有一定的代表性和说服力。

(二)文本信息特点对比

文本内容。在文本信息内容层面,广西高校的学校简介篇幅长,信息全面,信息涵盖内容基本相似。如表4-1所示,在所收集的简介文本中,广西医科大学的简介篇幅最长,达6337个字,桂林理工大学的简介篇幅最短,为2648个字,5个中国高校简介的平均篇幅为3946个字。

表4-1 广西高校简介字数

广西高校	简介字数
广西大学	3807
广西师范大学	3810
广西民族大学	3128
广西医科大学	6337
桂林理工大学	2648

美国高校网页"学校简介"则简洁得多,各个高校之间介绍的内容差异性也比较大,往往在"About XXX"的栏目中设小标题或分栏,用超链接的形式把与学校相关的介绍放在小分栏中,小分栏的设立各个学校并不相同,但每个小分栏的内容都比较简单,篇幅最大的是耶鲁大学的历史介绍,有267个字,而最简短的信息介绍则不使用文字,仅仅使用图片和数字。例如表4-2中斯坦福大学介绍自己的学生人数、教工人数、校园面积等数据的时候,都没有文字叙述,仅仅把数据进行简单罗列,简单明了,一目了然。

新加坡和马来西亚高校的简介也比较简洁,新加坡南洋理工大学的英文简介有210字。美国高校网页大量使用图片进行信息的视觉呈现。相对而言,中国高校网页里字多图少,国外高校网页图多字少,注重使用图片和视频等更为直观的媒介进行信息的呈现,吸引读者的注意力,新加坡南洋理工大学的主页首页基本都是视频和图片,文字很少。

表4-2　美国斯坦福大学对基本数据的简介

> **Student Enrollment**
> - **6,366** undergraduate
> - **8,791** graduate
>
> **Faculty**
> - **2,279** faculty members
> - **19** Nobel laureates are currently members of the Stanford community
> - **5:1** student to faculty ratio
>
> **Campus**
> - **8,180** contiguous acres
> - Nearly **700** major buildings
>
> **Research**
> - **7,700+** externally sponsored projects
> - **$1.93 billion** total budget

文本结构。从文本结构来说，中国高校中文网页"学校简介"文本结构完整，信息力求面面俱到。行文顺序一致，各个高校简介所涵盖的信息基本相同。基本都遵循了线性的推进方式，开篇往往是学校的地理位置或历史发展，中间依次介绍学校的师资力量、学生人数、学科分布、课程建设、学术成果、国际合作等具体内容，最后以学校的政治立场、发展愿景与发展目标结尾。

广西大学的简介，在第一段中陈述了广西大学的地位，第二、三段描述学校发展历史，中间的段落列数了学校的学科建设、办学条件、师资力量、学生人数、辉煌成就和荣誉称号等，在最后两段中陈述了广西大学的发展得到中央和广西壮族自治区党委和政府的关怀和支持，并表明学校的政治立场和发展目标："学校将以习近平新时代中国特色社会主义思想为指引，深入贯彻党的十九大精神，坚持社会主义办学方向……为实现中华民族的伟大复兴做出新的更大贡献！"

美国高校网页中"About XXX"的栏目也包含了读者所需的重要信息，但是篇幅往往比较短小，依靠小标题和分栏等超链接形式来展示学校的历史沿革、学术成就、著名校友、事实数据、校园环境等具体细节，在分栏的设置上各个学校不尽相同。例如，在"About Yale"的栏目中，分为了"Leadership & Organization""Yale Facts""Tradition & History""Yale & the World"和"Visiting"五个板块。在芝加哥大学"About"栏目链接了"History""Associates""Breakthroughs""University Leadership"和"News"板块。而普林斯顿大学网页中介绍学校的板块为"Meet Princeton"，下设"In Service of Humanity""Facts & Figures""History""Honors & Awards""Contact Us"和"Visit Us"五个部分。

以下的表4-3至表4-7展示了耶鲁大学简介的各个链接板块，表4-3耶鲁大学简介中"Leadership & Organization"板块为58字，表4-4耶鲁大学简介中"Yale Facts"板块仅仅使用数字来罗列出学生和教师的人数，不使用文字表述。表4-5中"Traditions & History"板块共123字，提到了耶鲁是一个具有300多年历史的高校；表4-6中"Yale and the World"板块共127字，介绍了耶鲁大学为当地机构和国际机构提供的服务与课程，但文本中并没有直接介绍耶鲁大学提供了什么面向国际的课程，而仅仅提供了相关的链接供感兴趣的读者进行进一步了解。表4-7中"Visiting"板块简单介绍了耶鲁大学的地理位置"耶鲁大学位于康涅狄格州纽黑文市，距纽约90分钟车程"，表示欢迎大家来参观，同时提供了其他的链接信息，包括学校地图、学校的校车时间、学校的导游服务、学校所在地的介绍等。

表4-3 耶鲁大学简介中"Leadership & Organization"板块

Leadership & Organization

Yale is overseen by President Peter Salovey and the university's board of trustees, who comprise the governing and policy-making body known formally as the Yale Corporation. The institution is also led and supported by the University Cabinet, an advisory body convened by the president, which consists of the deans, vice presidents, and other senior academic and administrative leaders.

表4-4　耶鲁大学简介中"Yale Facts"板块

Yale Facts

By the Numbers

Data provided by the Office of Institutional Research

6,057	7,517	2,789	21%
UNDERGRADUATE STUDENTS	GRADUATE & PROFESSIONAL STUDENTS	INTERNATIONAL SCHOLARS	PERCENTAGE OF INTERNATIONAL STUDENTS
120	4,869	10,374	3,149
COUNTRIES REPRESENTED BY INTERNATIONAL STUDENTS	FACULTY MEMBERS	STAFF MEMBERS	STUDENTS RECEIVING SCHOLARSHIPS/GRANTS (YALE SOURCES)

表4-5　耶鲁大学简介中"Traditions & History"板块

Traditions & History

　　Yale has grown and evolved for 300-plus years, passing many milestones and forging traditions along the way.

　　The university traces its roots to the 1640s, when colonial clergymen led an effort to establish a local college in the tradition of European liberal education. In 1701 the Connecticut legislature adopted a charter "to erect a Collegiate School." The school officially became Yale College in 1718, when it was renamed in honor of Welsh merchant Elihu Yale, who had donated the proceeds from the sale of nine bales of goods together with 417 books and a portrait of King George I.

　　Take a stroll through Yale's three centuries of history, and learn about the traditions that have become part of the fabric of our university.

表4-6　耶鲁大学简介中"Yale and the World"板块

Yale and the World

Since its founding in 1701, Yale has been dedicated to expanding and sharing knowledge, inspiring innovation, and preserving cultural and scientific information for future generations.

Yale's reach is both local and international. The University partners with its hometown of New Haven, Connecticut and engages with people and institutions across the globe in the quest to promote cultural understanding, improve the human condition, delve deeper into the secrets of the universe, and train the next generation of world leaders.

View the timeline of Yale's history

The Yale and the World (YATW) website provides a comprehensive directory for the myriad of internationally oriented programs at Yale. These programs are housed in virtually every school, department, and center across Yale.

Read more about Yale's Global Strategy

表4-7　耶鲁大学简介中"Visiting"板块

Visiting

Yale University is situated 90 minutes from New York in the city of New Haven, Connecticut.

Whether you're in town for an admissions information session or simply want to join one of the many activities happening here, we invite you to explore our campus and community. Take a guided tour, attend a concert, or stroll through our scenic and historic Old Campus.

修辞风格。中国高校中文网页"学校简介"通常采用第三人称视角，行文正式，文体庄重，带有浓重的汉语修辞风格，大量使用四字词语或成语，起到突出强调、增强文章感染力的作用，并使行文朗朗上口。每个高校的网页首页都列出了学校的校训，校训往往都是以四字词语的形式出现。广西大学的校训为"勤恳朴诚，厚学致新"，广西民族大学的校训为"厚德博学，和而不同"等；同时，网页板块的名称也往往以四字词语的形式出现，如"机构设置""科学研究""学科建设""招生就业""队伍建设""公共服务""校园服务"等。在简介的行文中，也使用了大量四字词语，例如下文中广西桂林理工大学的简介。

例1：学校全面贯彻落实党的教育方针，遵循"厚德笃学、惟实励新"校训，传承和弘扬"艰苦创业、敬业奉献、团结协作、开拓创新"的桂工精神，坚持"育人为本、质量立校、人才强校、科技兴校"办学理念，以立德树人为根本。

美国高校网页的英文"学校简介"通常采用第一人称叙述视角，使用"we"或"our"来指代学校，建构身份认同感，行文亲切自然。例2中芝加哥大学的介绍就使用了"our commitment"和"our global campuses"来缩短与读者的距离。例3耶鲁大学的介绍中，使用第一人称"we"来指代学校，同时使用第二人称邀请参观耶鲁校园，语气亲切自然，拉近了学校和读者之间的距离。

例3：The University of Chicago is an urban research university that has driven new ways of thinking since 1890. Our commitment to free and open inquiry draws inspired scholars to our global campuses, where ideas are born that challenge and change the world.

例4：Whether you're in town for an admissions information session or simply want to join one of the many activities happening here, we invite you to explore our campus and community. Take a guided tour, attend a concert, or stroll through our scenic and historic Old Campus.

相对而言，新加坡和马来西亚高校的英文介绍语篇语言比较简洁和中规中矩，较少使用修辞手法，但很少使用第一人称的视角，和中国高校相似，基本都是客观列举和陈述事实。

例5：Universiti Malaya, or UM, Malaysia's oldest university, is situated on a 922 acre (373.12 hectare) campus in the southwest of Kuala Lumpur, the capital of Malaysia.

意识形态与文化传统。中国高校中文网页的"学校简介"和美国高校英文网页的"学校简介"体现了中西方不同的意识形态和文化传统。广西高校网页"学校简介"中普遍存在体现政治意识形态的文本内容。比如强调学校发展的政治方向、国家领导人对学校的重视和政府颁布的荣誉称号等。

例6的内容出自广西大学的学校介绍的最后一段，文本强调学校的发展是在国家和党的领导下，发展方向符合政府的规划，培养的人才是为国家为社会服务的。例6强调了国家级领导人和自治区领导人对学校的关心，同时罗列广西民族自治区各个部门为支持广西大学出台的文件。例7出自广西民族大学的学校介绍，同样强调各级领导对广西民族大学的建设和发展的重视和支持。

例6：面向未来，学校将以习近平新时代中国特色社会主义思想为指引，深入贯彻党的十九大精神，坚持社会主义办学方向，落实立德树人根本任务，服务"建设壮美广西 共圆复兴梦想"的目标任务，按照建校"百年目标、三步实施、五个一流、六条方略"的规划思路，努力培养新时代有社会责任、有法治意识、有创新精神、有实践能力、有国际视野的"五有"领军型人才，加快推进"双一流"建设和内涵式发展，为实现中华民族的伟大复兴做出新的更大贡献！

例7：近年来，广西大学的发展得到中央和广西壮族自治区党委政府的关怀和支持。1998年10月，时任中共中央总书记、国家主席江泽民为广西大学题词："百年大计 教育为本 团结奋斗 努力办好广西大学"；2018年12月，中央政治局常委、全国政协主席汪洋到广西大学视察慰问；贾庆林、宋平、尉健行、李岚清等多位党和国家领导人曾到广西大学视察，教育部和广西壮族自治区党委政府主要领导到校指导工作、解决问题。自治区党委政府先后批准印发《广西大学综合改革试点方案》《广西大学推进一流大学和一流学科建设方案》和《"部区合建"广西大学实施方案》，与教育部签署《教育部 广西壮族自治区人民政府关于"部区合建"广西大学的协议》，学校进入了以"双一流"建设和"部区合建"为主要目标的内涵式发展新阶段。

例8：党和国家历届领导集体始终关心和重视广西民族大学的建设和发展。1958年，毛泽东主席在南宁人民公园接见我校师生代表；1990年11月，江泽民总书记来学校视察时，称赞说："这里的环境很美，是读书做学问的

· 63 ·

好地方。"2006年11月，国家主席胡锦涛出访越南时，亲切接见了我校在越南讲学、留学的师生代表；2010年5月，时任中央政治局常委、中央书记处书记、国家副主席习近平到学校考察工作，勉励师生要倍加敏于求学、学有所成、锻炼成才，成为社会主义事业的建设者和接班人。2013年10月，中央政治局常委、全国政协主席俞正声来我校视察调研。朱德、班禅额尔德尼·确吉坚赞、帕巴拉·格列朗杰、陈毅、阿沛·阿旺晋美、赛福鼎、司马义·艾买提、尉健行、周铁农、李铁映、李兆焯、陈至立、罗豪才、司马义·铁力瓦尔地、刘延东等党和国家领导人先后来学校视察。

同时，中国高校也非常重视各种荣誉称号，典型的高校简介文本充斥着政府颁发的各种荣誉称号。例9和例10分别介绍了学术期刊和学校教师队伍，在例子中都以所获得的荣誉称号来证明学校的实力。

例9：《广西民族大学学报（哲学社会科学版）》先后获得"国家期刊奖百种重点期刊"（2003年）、"中国百强报刊"（2013、2015、2017年）、全国高校社科名刊（2019年）等荣誉称号；入选教育部名栏、名刊建设工程入选期刊（2004、2006年），"国家社科基金资助期刊"（2012年），"国家社科基金资助优秀期刊"（2014年）；系中文社会科学引文索引（CSSCI）来源期刊（南京大学）、中文核心期刊（北京大学）、中国人文社会科学核心期刊（中国社会科学院）、中国人民大学书报资料中心"复印报刊资料"重要转载来源期刊。

例10：学校有国家级、省部级高层次人才约160人次，其中有国家"万人计划"科技创新领军人才、哲学社会科学领军人才、国家"万人计划"百千万工程领军人才、国家"长江学者"特聘教授、国家百千万人才工程人选、全国文化名家暨"四个一批"人才、国家级教学名师等国家级人才20多人次，国家级各类人才称号已经齐全（包括双聘院士）；有广西院士后备人选、广西八桂学者、广西特聘专家、广西优秀专家、广西十百千人才工程人选等省部级人才约140人次。

相比之下，国外高校网页"学校简介"中几乎不出现此类政治或政策性的表述，而会比较强调学校的使命。例如在普林斯顿的学校简介中，就强调了普林斯顿的非正式座右铭"Princeton in the nation's service and the service of humanity"（为国家服务，为人类服务）。同时，用具体的数据和事实来介绍学校的教学水平、学术水平和发展状况。例12是马来西亚博特拉大学的愿景，"To become a university of international repute"（成为国际化的大学），要致力于"wealth creation, nation building and universal human advancement"（创建财富，建设国家和促进人类进步）

例11：Princeton University has a longstanding commitment to service, reflected in Princeton's informal motto — Princeton in the nation's service and the service of humanity — and exemplified by the extraordinary contributions that Princetonians make to society.

Christopher L. Eisgruber

President of Princeton University,

Class of 1983

例12：As a premier institution of learning, widely recognised for leadership in research and innovation, UPM continues to strive for excellence. In order to motivate the entire university community towards achieving excellence, it ensures that all the members, both students and members of staff, share the responsibility of strictly adhering to the demands of the University's vision, mission and goals.

（三）结语

本文采用平行文本比较模式，从文本信息、文本结构、修辞风格和意识形态等多个层面对广西高校和美国国家高校网页的"学校简介"进行对比分析，对比结果显示，广西高校中文网页中的简介和美国高校英文网页中的简介存在较大差异。在进行高校外宣文本的英译时，译者可参考和借鉴国外高校简介的平行文，以提高国外受众的文本信息接收度。具体的翻译策略为：其一，缩减高校"学校简介"文本的篇幅，中文简介太长，不利于读者的网络浏览，可适当压缩长篇大论的介绍，多增加介绍的层次和超文本链接，做到信息按读者需要来提供，读者感兴趣的信息可以凭借搜索或链接功能得到，不必统统放到简介中。其二，在高校宣传文本的英译中，恰当地处理政治化或文化专有的信息，并改进文本组织结构。中文读者能理解但英文读者因缺乏相应背景知识无法理解的信息可以淡化甚至删除，不翻译成英文，因此类信息对英文读者的意义不大。

二、中英旅游网站对比研究

随着人民生活水平的提高，旅游业也得到了空前的发展，旅游网站具有信息量大的特点，在促进旅游业发展、文化交流、增进游客对景点的了解等方面发挥着举足轻重的作用，因此旅游网站文本的翻译质量不容忽视。本文旨在从修辞角度，在结合实例的基础上，就汉英旅游网站文本的各自特征和差异展开讨论并分析其原因，并提出相应的翻译策略和方法，以推动旅游网站文本的翻译达到更好的效果。

在互联网时代，旅游网站是世界各地旅游爱好者获取旅游信息的重要工具。旅游网络提供旅游信息和文化，宣传旅游目的地，吸引了潜在的游客，极大地促进了旅游业的发展。作为一种修辞形式，旅游网站的文本通过语言符号来说服读者，影响并最终传递给旅游消费者。然而，不容乐观的是，广西各个旅游网站英文版的文字质量鱼龙混杂，影响着广西旅游的对外宣传效果。本文通过对比分析中英文旅游网站平行文本的接受者意识，探讨旅游网站的文本英译问题。

旅游网站文本是人们旅游过程中必不可少的辅助工具，同时也起着对外宣传的作用，因此其翻译的好坏影响十分重大。本文在介绍旅游网站中语言文字翻译特点的基础上，从当代修辞理论角度对比分析汉英旅游网站文本在话语内容、诉求策略、话语建构方式和美学手段上的差异，并以青秀山旅游网站文本翻译为案例进行具体探讨分析，提出旅游网站的翻译应以受众为转移，对文本进行调试和呈现，最后达到宣传和营利的目的。

本文所选用的平行文本来自对南宁和伦敦旅游景点的宣传网站，具体选取了南宁青秀山景区官网（http: //www.qxsfjq.com/）和伦敦景点介绍官网London Attractions（https://tickets.london/）。

（一）英汉旅游网站文本的修辞共性

当代新修辞不再把修辞局限于演讲范围或者修辞格，一切传播和文化过程乃至社会、政治运动都成为修辞运动，不但修辞格、文采，还有修辞的参与者（传播者和受传者）、话语结构以及效果都要在修辞分析中得到说明。汉英旅游网站均以图片和语言文字为主，其文字对景区作总体说明，并附加图片来达到最优宣传效果，主要包括旅游景点的介绍和旅游服务信息。总体来说都以加强宣传效果和说服潜在游客，以实现盈利的主要目的。

旅游网站的中英文版存在许多共性，例如景点介绍的相似性。两个版本都提到了青秀山的地理位置、占地面积、景点特色和历史发展等信息，都属于介绍文本的文体，为正式的商务文体，遣词造句较为严谨，语言简洁流畅，通俗易懂，没有使用复杂或生僻难懂的措辞或句法，易于读者理解。

（二）英汉旅游网站文本的修辞差异

受东西方文化的影响，中英文旅游网站表现形式有许多的不同之处，我们将从话语内容、诉求策略、话语构建方式和美学手段这四个方面来进行比较。

（1）话语内容。因为东西方社会文化、思维方式和语言的差异，使得英汉旅游网站在话语内容方面也存在着一定的差异，这种差异不光表现在文本信息量不一样，还表现在其传递信息时的侧重点不同。总的来说，青秀山中文网站信息量大，文字信息较多；相对而言，英文网站的信息量相对较少，也更侧重图片形式的介绍和报道。如例3和例4所示，中文网站的导航条包括首页、5A专栏、景区简介、认知之乐、青山花历、景点介绍、虚拟景区、摄影专区、山民之声、景点咨询、旅游服务、电子商务、在线留言和最新公告等栏目。同时，还有不时更新的景点咨询栏目，以及酒店预订与旅游纪念品购买等服务的链接，附加滚动的公告。而英文网站中的导航条仅仅出现了Home、Introduction、Photograph 和 Attraction 四个栏目。中文网站内容明显更为丰富。

例3：青秀山官网中文版

图片来源：http://www.qxsfjq.com/

例4：伦敦景区官网英文版

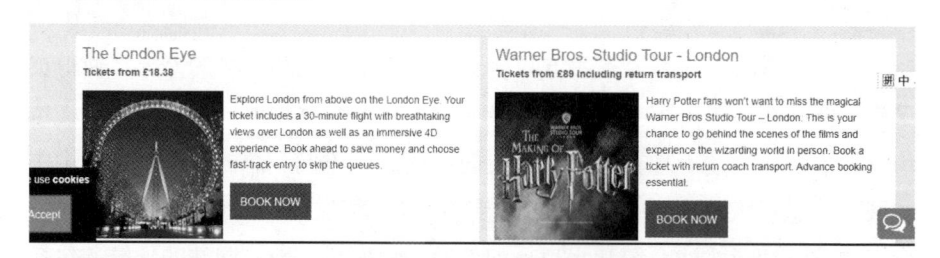

图片来源：https://www.visitlondon.com/

汉语旅游简介更加着重突出旅游景点的价值和社会身份特征，例如该景点的历史地位和社会影响等。同时，中文旅游景点语篇喜欢突出景点的权威性，如例5和例6所示，"最"字被频繁地使用，非常符合中国人尊重和信任权威的特点，相对而言，此类表达相应的英文文本中出现次数比较少。

例5：青秀山旅游风景区是集旅游观光、休闲娱乐、文化交流、科研科普为一体的著名风景旅游区，拥有……全国最大的自然生态兰花专类园——

兰园……

例6：青秀山千年苏铁园面积达100余亩，有树龄千年以上的苏铁近百株。<u>最大</u>年龄的"苏铁王"距今已有1360余年高龄。园内已收集苏铁种类50余种，总株数上万株。是全国<u>最大</u>的篦齿苏铁、叉叶苏铁、德保苏铁、石山苏铁迁地保护育种基地之一，是全国"<u>景观最好、树龄最老、胸径最大、植株最高</u>"的苏铁专类园。

此外，在描述某个景点时还喜欢引用一段喜闻乐见的俗语、名人名言或者中国古诗，刺激游客的观赏欲望。例7中引用了"山不高而秀，水不深而清"等名句来进行景点景色的描述。写意性的景点描述能带来强烈的代入感，提高感性认识。

例7：寻百年古道、访千年古寺、游万亩森林、赏亿年苏铁，"山清水秀、花美林奇、山旷谷幽、物欢人乐""山不高而秀，水不深而清"，这就是生态旅游景观独特，全国省会城市市中心罕见的大型综合生态景观绿地——青秀山旅游风景区。

与汉语旅游文本描述和评价性文字比较多不一样的是，英文旅游文本更注重信息具体实在，突出个性，很少使用过于抽象的描述。因此在中译英的时候，英文文本会更侧重客观信息的传递，而简化或省略描述性信息。例8是关于温莎城堡的介绍，语言使用朴实无华，体现了英文文本崇尚简单明了的文本审美要求。

例8："Windsor Castle is the oldest and largest occupied castle in the world. A royal home and fortress for more than 900 years, the castle remains a working palace today."

青秀山景区网站的英文版是如何的呢？与中文网站相比，青秀山英文网站中的导航条仅仅出现了Home、Introduction、Photograph 和 Attraction 四个栏目，英文文网站内容明显进行了简化，仅仅保留了英文读者可能感兴趣的内容。青秀山景区景点的英文介绍语言风格也相对简练和翔实。

例9：Also mentioned as Sino-Thai Friendship Park. Covering land area of 7.2 mu, the park is a joint-built park attraction described in the cultural exchange project signed between Naning and Khon Khan Thailand in 1993. It's a park full of foreign country charms in the park. Thailand park was designed by Thai designers and consists of Buddha hall, wood tower, stupa and wood clock groups, showing strong Thai charms and representing architectural styles of south, north and middle Thailand.

（2）诉求策略。诉求策略指的是宣传文本为激发受众产生认同感所使用的语言策略。

为了获得认同，吸引游客，网站内容的诉求策略也因为东西方的差异而迥乎不同。汉语属于汉藏语系，英语属于印欧语系，由于两地的生活习性、地理环境、生产方式、历史条件以及社会结构都不相同，因此形成了不同的思维方式。在诉求策略上，汉语旅游网站往往表现讲究文采和口彩，大量使用修饰性和比喻性语言，甚至使用口号来造势和渲染气氛，从而达到激发受众情感的目的。如例7使用了召唤性信息"寻百年古道、访千年古寺、游万亩森林、赏亿年苏铁"来邀请游客游览青山，语言表达朗朗上口，节奏鲜明，增强了行文的气势，提高了语言表达效果，极易激发游客一睹为快的兴趣。

此外，英语旅游网站文本多从游客的角度出发来，更多的话语建构策略在于给读者提供信息，为读者提供服务。英文文本常常使用第一人称we或者our，构建一个与受众对话的氛围，以缩小与受众之间的距离，让游客置身其中，产生认同感。如：

例10：Visitors of all ages love the 59ft (18m) high Treetop Walkway, which soars into the tree canopy offering a bird's-eye view of the gardens. Enjoy a stroll along the Great Broad Walk Borders, home to more than 60,000 plants, and step into history at Kew Palace, the former summer residence of King George Ⅲ. Plus, relax with refreshments in one of our inviting cafes. Kew Gardens is less than 30 minutes from central London, and easily reached by road, rail, and London Underground.

在青秀山景区的英文翻译中，译者也使用了这一策略：

例11：It's the landmark of QingXiu Mountain, climbing to the top of the tower, you can have Yongjiang River, distant mountains and hills and urban and rural landscapes within ten miles into your eyesight.

（3）话语构建方式。话语建构方式是指为取得最佳修辞效果对话语信息进行的安排。英语语言的逻辑思维严谨，在话语建构中更擅长由总至分的演绎法，而中文逻辑往往习惯由分到总的归纳法，把最重要的总结性信息放在段落的后面。

例12：青秀山旅游风景区位于广西首府南宁市中心，坐落在蜿蜒流淌的邕江畔，规划保护面积13.54平方公里，核心保护区面积约5.86平方公里，森林植物园区面积约7.68平方公里。青秀山群峰起伏、林木青翠、岩幽壁峭、泉清石奇，以南亚热带植物景观为特色，常年云雾环绕，具有高浓度的负氧离子，形成一个独特的天然休闲氧吧，素有"城市绿肺""绿城翡翠，壮乡凤凰"的美誉，是南宁市最靓丽的城市名片之一。

译文：Nanning Qingxiushan Scenic Spot（hereinafter mentioned as the Scenic Spot）lies in the heart of Nanning downtown and neighbors to the north shore of the winding Yongjiang River. The Scenic Spot enjoys planning area of 13 square kilometers, in which, 6 square kilometers have been built and open to the public. The Scenic Spot has numerous peaks rising high and low, green and prosperous trees, quiet rocks and steep cliffs, clean springs and rare stones. Featured with South Asia tropical plant landscape, the Scenic Spot is endowed with rich negative oxygen ions and a unique natural relaxation oxygen bar forms here. Famous as an attraction where "the mountain is not high but graceful, the water is not deep but clear", "the Scenic Spot is reputed as the Green Lung of Nanning and the Emerald of the Green City, Phoenix of the Zhuang Region."

例12中的中文对青秀山旅游风景区的描述是徐徐展开的，先说了风景区的位置和面积，再说风景区的景点特色，最后总结青秀山风景区的地位。而英文逻辑更喜欢把重点信息放在前面。因此，我们应该在英文翻译中做出相应的调整，把"是南宁市最靓丽的城市名片之一"这一信息放到英文段落的开头，再展开其他信息。

话语建构方式除了体现在话语信息的段落逻辑上，还体现在行文方面。汉语行文重意合，句型松散，句与句之间的逻辑关系靠意义来连接，而不依赖于某种语言连接手段。而英文重形合，句子间的逻辑关系依靠语言形式手段来体现，多使用长句和复合句，名词代词、介词短语和独立主格结构等语法手段来凸显逻辑，使句法紧凑。

（4）美学手段。美学手段是指为添加语言美感而使用的修辞手法，美学手段的使用，能给受众留下更深刻的印象，打动受众从而激发认同感的建立。汉语旅游文本传递信息时往往凝练含蓄、词藻华丽，讲究声律对仗和音韵和谐，强调语言的朦胧美，大量使用四字词、叠词、排比句来强化表达，更多地强调一种主观感受。

在以上例子中，"群峰起伏、林木青翠、岩幽壁峭、泉清石奇""城市绿肺""绿城翡翠，壮乡凤凰"均为四字成语，对仗工整、朗朗上口，四字成语的使用，使得汉语的修辞凝练含蓄、词藻华丽。

例13：Discover beautiful glasshouses including the iconic Palm House and its exotic rainforest; the Princess of Wales Conservatory which invites you to explore 10 of the world's climatic zones; and the Waterlily House with its amazing, giant lily pads.

例14：Step on to authentic sets, discover the magic behind spellbinding special effects and explore the behind-the-scenes secrets of the Harry Potter film series.

在例13和例14的英文景点介绍中的叙述都比较朴实，没有太多修辞。英语旅游宣传平行文本信息往往比较平实，多以名词、动词、副词、非谓语动词为主要成分的结构特征，并用叙述说明的方式来提供实在、有效的景点信息。在英译汉的过程中，我们往往需要弱化修辞，使用各种连接手段来整合原有的中文信息。

（三）英汉旅游网站文本的翻译策略

旅游景点的翻译是向外国游客宣传和介绍本国、本地的人文和自然风光的重要方式，译者不仅要忠实于该景点的自然特点和人文内涵，让外国游客在有限的文字介绍中准确、全面地了解该景区特点，而且还要让译文对外国游客有良好的接受度。因英汉旅游景点文本有其自身的语篇特点，而且还受各国游客特定文化背景、阅读目的和欣赏水平制约,因此在文体风格上需要进行调整,以符合不同受众的口味。

1. 因地制宜

在汉译英之前,译者必须弄清楚译文是给谁使用、怎样使用、想达到怎样的效果,才能更好地达成翻译效果。需要考虑中西文化差异,采取不同的翻译策略。比如景点介绍的详略程度方面,汉语旅游网站景点需要提供详尽的信息,全面介绍该景区的自然风貌和历史沿革,而且还需要运用优美的文字,使读者心向往之。英语旅游网站需要进行更加客观的描述,因此在英译过程中需要删繁就简,特别是一些对于外国游客来说不知所云的描述,需要适当地进行增删,运用简单明了的语言进行介绍。

2. 信息重组

由于东西方文化背景、思维方式、审美习惯的差异,旅游网站文本的篇章结构上也差异巨大。为了获取最佳的翻译效果,在把旅游网站简介英译的时候,就必须按照英语行文习惯重新组织原文,除了适当进行增删外,必要时还需要调整原文的顺序,使逻辑更加紧密,中心更加明确。此外,还可以适当运用代词、连词、省略、替代等,使得文本前后连贯,首尾衔接。

3. 透彻理解

在汉译英的过程中,由于汉语句子受东方重辩证逻辑的影响,是语义的,而英语句子受西方文化重形式逻辑的影响,是语法的,因此,句子形态方面差异巨大。有时汉语句子由好几个短句组成,翻译时需要重新分析句子之间的功能和层次重新断句,原文中没有关联词语的,在译文中可以根据需要适当增加关联词。

(四)结语

鉴于英汉旅游网站文本不同的修辞特点,译者应以翻译效果为重,以受众为转移,注重话语修辞性,运用受众所熟悉所认同的方式激发其潜在的游览兴趣。除了要遵循图文一致这一基本原则外,译者需要深入了解并把握英汉旅游网站的修辞差异,从而有针对性地对文本进行调试,使其更好地说明和补衬图片内容,使其相得益彰,更好地说服游客,最后达到宣传和盈利的目的。

三、中国—东盟博览会网站中英版对比

博览会作为一个重要的展示平台，对经济发展具有重要意义和促进作用。在广西南宁举办的中国—东盟博览会既是东盟商品进入中国的通道，也是中国企业投资东盟国家的平台。中国与东盟之间这十多年商贸规模的迅猛发展，充分证明了中国—东盟博览会的重要作用。随着博览会参展单位和参会人员的逐年增加，为了方便东盟和其他域外国家参展单位和参会人员对中国—东盟博览会的了解，一个信息准确、便于理解的英文外宣网站是必不可少的宣传平台。本文将通过对中国—东盟博览会网站的中英文版本的功能结构、网站内容和文本内容等方面进行分析对比，来分析展会网站的中英文表达方式的不同和探究其中的外宣翻译方法。

（一）网站功能结构

首先，从网站结构来看，中国—东盟博览会网站英文版比中文版功能结构更为清晰，体现了对国内外服务侧重点的不同。虽然中英文版本都概括了关于博览会的重要信息，但是英文版网站主要以服务国外参展商和参会人员为主，而中文版除了相关的服务外，侧重于展现各种商业合作信息和政务信息。比如首页的各个选项按钮当中，中文版的分为"参展商、专业观众、展商目录、项目撮合、新闻中心、关于我们"这六个选项，英文版对应的是"Exhibitors, Visitors, News, Services, About CAEXPO"五个选项。从中英文选项对比中我们可以发现，除去相同部分的参展商（Exhibitors）、专业观众（Visitors）、新闻（News）、关于我们（About CAEXPO）外，中文版的重点在于"展商目录"和"项目撮合"两个选项，英文版的重点在于"Services"选项上。

此外，在中文版网站中，与英文版相比，还多了一个"商贸投资服务

窗"选项，主要提供"商贸""投资""海关""税务"这几项与跨境投资、商品进出口紧密相关的信息服务。而英文版中，出现在相同位置的则是中国和东盟各个国家商业部的联系方式。

因此，从结构功能来看，中英文版本都给参展商和参会人员提供基本服务。但中文版的网站功能侧重点在给国内客户提供相应展商资料，并且促进相关商业合作，而英文版则侧重给国外客户展示展会相关服务，如餐饮服务（Food Service）、酒店服务（Hotel Information）、交通服务（Traffic Service）、票务服务（Ticket Service）等。这种结构和功能上的不同是由服务对象的不同来决定的，因为国内参展商和参会人员注重的是寻找相应的合作商家和合作机会，而且由于相对熟悉本国情况，因此不用太注重饮食、住宿、交通等情况。对于国外客户来说，由于对中国并不太了解，因此在英文版网站上必须要简单明了地展示相应服务和信息，以便他们更好地过来中国参展。

（二）网站内容

从网站内容丰富程度来看，中文版网站主页内容更丰富，信息更密集，英文版内容相对比较简洁明了。如首页最大的循环播放窗口，中文版共有七个宣传页面，分别是"展会公告""投资活动介绍""林木展""商贸投资服务窗""祝福语征集活动""新闻中心""专题回顾"，而英文版的只有"展会公告"（The 15th China-ASEAN Expo Bulletin）、"林木展"（China-ASEAN Expo Forest&Wood Products Exhibition 2018）和"专题回顾"（The 14th China-ASEAN Expo Review）三个页面。从中可以看出，中文版网站包含的内容更丰富，信息更密集，而英文版侧相对简洁，突出重点。

从内容分类情况来看，中文版和英文版展现的内容也不一样。以网站新闻页面为例，中文版页面主要展示的是中国东盟博览会的贡献、发展情况等新闻，而英文版的更多是展示中国与东盟各国的合作情况。这也说明了在外宣网站上并不能只是中英文内容的直接翻译和复制，而是要针对国内外不同情况来特定展现。

此外，从二级页面来看，以同一选项"关于我们"（About CAEXPO）为例，中文版这个选项里面包括了"领导寄语""人事信息""统计信息""规划计划""文件资料""信息公开""调查征集"等13个选项,而英文版只有"Overview""Organizers""Functional Organization""Comments""Contact Us"这5个选项。从中可以看出,中文版网站内容丰富,除了有关中国—东盟博览会基本信息外,还有相当一部分是用来展示相关政务信息。英文版网站则是内容精简突出,主要展示博览会相关概况、博览会相关机构、各个机构的功能,还有重点展现了各国领导人和官员对博览会的评价。

从这些对比我们可以发现,在网站内容的展示上,中文版和英文版的不同体现了国内外参展人员关注点的不同。由于国情的不同,国内参展商和网站浏览者在参展时必须查阅相关政务信息和相应商业资料,而且会通过各种资料来寻找商业投资机会,因此在网站中文版会展示相应政务信息。对于外籍人员来讲,他们最需要知道的并不是博览会有关的政务信息,而是这个博览会的基本资料,办相应的手续应该找哪个机构,还有他们自己国家官方政府或发言人对这个博览会的态度。

(三)文本内容

从文本内容来看,中文版和英文版并不是简单的直接翻译,而是适当地使用了增补法和修辞方法。以首页滚动窗口的"第15届中国—东盟博览会参展参会公告"为例,中文版只有包括时间地点简单的一句话。

英文版是"The 15th China–ASEAN Expo Bulletin The China–ASEAN Expo(CAEXPO)is co-sponsored by ministries/department of commerce or industry and trade of China and the 10 ASEAN member states as well as the ASEAN Secretariat, and is organized by the People's Government of Guangxi Zhuang Autonomous Region."从中可以看出,英文版的公告增加了对这个展会的补充说明,以增加其官方性质和展示其规模。

从公告具体文本内容来看,中文版的内容为:

第15届中国—东盟博览会展览以"创新升级"为主旨,以信息化、智能化与制造业的深度融合为重点,以技术创新推进产业提质升级为目标,进一步加强中国与东盟的国际产能和装备制造合作,更加注重出口产品科技含量和附加值,大力发展服务贸易,有效引导、支持企业"走出去"开展产能与越来越多的中外展商将会通过东博会网站去了解有关展会的相关信息。希望展会网站也能不断完善，更好地为广大中外参会人员服务。

第四节　会展致辞的修辞对比与翻译

随着全球化的快速发展，区域合作经济显得尤为重要，各国多种形式的经济论坛、投资峰会等也备受关注。中国—东盟商务与投资峰会就是其中一个意义突出的重大会议。修辞作为一种能够更好表达语言文字意思的手法，在语言表达和文字表达中尤为重要。本文主要选取该峰会中的几个典型的开幕式致辞为研究材料，并从排比、明喻、暗喻、引用等修辞中对比分析中英文翻译中的不同之处。从修辞对比分析，更好地了解中英两种语言的特点，对以后的翻译学习和翻译工作都有重要的意义。本文主要选取中国—东盟与投资峰会的几个典型的国家领导人的开幕式致辞作为材料，对中英翻译中几种常见的修辞进行对比分析，以求开拓思路、抛砖引玉。

一、排比修辞对比分析

通过对中国—东盟商务与投资峰会中几个会议致辞的材料分析，笔者发现中国领导或者发言人用到排比修辞的频率很高。排比的运用使得文章更加气势磅礴、震撼人心，具有很强的感染力。由于中英排比都有结构匀整、句式相似、意义相关、排列紧凑、语气一致等共同特点，使得中文和英文都有一种语言的均衡美和气势美。但是，在中英的排比翻译中，往往要用到直译、意译、减译等方法，才能既把意思完整地传达出来，又能够保持文章的均衡美和气势美。比如：

例1：李克强总理在第十届中国东盟商务与投资峰会的开幕式致辞中，使用了多重排比句："我们应当坚持经济优先、发展优先、民生优先的大方向，把焦点聚集在这里，继续发扬团结协作、同舟共济的精神，携手应对可能发生的和不可预见的风险和挑战，努力保持经济平稳运行和健康发展。"（选自李克强总理致辞第六段）

译文：We should adhere to the guideline of giving priority to the economies, development and people's well-being. We should focus our attention to those three aspects and keep advocating the spirit of unity and cooperation, as well as helping each other. We should also join hands to deal with possible and unforeseeable risks and challenges, and strive to keep the economy running smoothly and healthily.

例1出现的排比是四字格形式，通过理解"经济优先、发展优先、民生优先"是排比，重复词语"坚持"。中文行文中倾向于重复，而英语忌重复，所以在中译英中，要考虑是否应该把一些词语省略掉以免造成赘余。另外，在例子中，"坚持""聚集""发扬""应对"和"保持"这几个动词也是并列的词组，这也凸显了中文致辞中经常出现的不规则排比句的特点，这些排比句通常意义上呈排比，但排比形式不是很明显，在翻译中我们要对这些不规则排比句有足够的敏感性。

例2：习近平主席在第九届中国—东盟商务与投资峰会上的致辞，也使用很多排比句："中国是世界上最大的发展中国家的国际地位没有变，中国独立自主的和平外交政策没有变，中国走和平发展道路和实行对外开放的基本国策没有变。"

译文：China's international status as the world's largest developing country, China's independent foreign policy of peace, and China's basic state policy of peaceful development and opening to the outside world all remain unchanged.

例2中，三个"没有变"被重复使用在句子中以增强句子的气势，但是如果把这三个词全部翻译出来，就不符合英语的表达习惯，而且显得累赘多余。因此，在翻译中要适量删减一些词组以保证英语语言的简洁性。

二、比喻修辞对比分析

（一）明喻修辞对比分析

比喻修辞分为明喻和暗喻。明喻是将具有某种共同特征的两种不同事物加以对比，通过联想更形象地去了解事物，以达到可以更鲜明、更简洁、更生动地描述事物的目的。明喻的结构主要分为三部分：喻体，指作者欲描述之主题；喻依，指的是用来说明喻体的事物；喻词，指用来连接喻体和喻依的补助词。在商务峰会致辞中，为了更好地把意思完整地表达出来，同时又不失华彩且形象生动，发言人也经常会用到明喻修辞。比如：

例3：我们共同见证了中国—东盟友谊之花盛开绽放，多领域交流根深叶茂，经贸合作硕果累累。（马飚在第六届中国东盟博览会上的讲话）

译文：We have witnessed the flourished of China-ASEAN friendship, more frequent multi-field exchange, and more fruitful economic and trade cooperation.

例3中，中文词藻略显华丽，包含着比喻的修辞，发言人把中国与东盟国家的友谊比作盛放的花朵，表明中国与东盟国家的友谊正在蓬勃发展，经贸合作也取得迅速发展，但是在翻译成英文时，只需要把核心意思翻译出来就可以了，并不需要一字一句原原本本地译出来。

（二）暗喻修辞对比分析

暗喻是把一个事物的名称用在另一个事物的名称上，用来表示两种不同事物之间的相似关系。暗喻往往是用生动、具体、浅显、简单的、人们所熟悉的东西来比喻干涩、抽象、深奥、复杂的陌生事物，从而更形象、更深刻地说明事理，力求达到贴切、新颖、创新的表达效果。暗喻这一修辞手法也是商务峰会中发言人致辞中常用到的一种修辞手法。比如：

例4：实践证明，中国和东盟既是唇齿相依、患难与共的好邻居，又是平等互利、合作共赢的好伙伴。（选自温家宝总理在第八届中国东盟投资峰会上的讲话）

译文：Facts have shown that China and ASEAN are both good neighbors sharing weal and woe and good partners for win-win cooperation based on equality and mutual benefit.

例4中，"唇齿相依"和"患难与共"翻译为"good neighbors sharing weal and woe"其实就运用了暗喻的修辞手法。温家宝总理把中国与东盟的关系比喻为人的嘴唇和牙齿一样不可分离，更加形象生动地说明了中国与东盟国家的友好合作关系对双方都非常重要。

例5：中国和东盟各国人民之间的传统友谊源远流长、历久弥新。（选自温家宝总理在第八届中国—东盟投资峰会上的讲话）

译文：The traditional friendship between Chinese people and the people of ASEAN countries has run a long course and is poised to become even stronger.

例5中，用"源远流长"比喻中国与东盟国家的友谊像流水一样源源不断，友谊非常深厚，永远长存，也展现了中国与东盟国家的友谊通过中国—东盟投资峰会这一大平台取得了可喜的成就和进步。

例6：区域合作方兴未艾，国与国相互依存日益密切。（选自刘奇葆在第四届中国—东盟商务与投资峰会上的讲话）

译文：The regional cooperation is upward surge and the relationship of interdependence between countries is becoming increasingly closed.

例6中，"方兴未艾"意思是事物正在发展，尚未达到止境。由于"方兴未艾"这个词在英文中有对应的词组"upward surge"，因此，在翻译中，遇到这种情况，要先了解是否有相对应的词组，再做进一步的翻译。"方兴未艾"比喻中国与东盟国家的区域合作正在蓬勃发展，也将继续往更好的方面发展。

三、引用修辞分析

引用也是开幕式致辞中发言人常用的修辞手法。发言人常常引经据典，一方面显示自己的博学，另一方面让众所周知的人或事来帮自己说话，能使听众更好地理解自己的观点。在对商务峰会领导人的致辞分析中发现，引用这一修辞也常被用到。比如：

例7：路遥知马力，患难见真情。中国和东盟的友好关系历经考验、历久弥坚。（选自习近平主席在第九届中国—东盟商务与投资峰会开幕式上的致辞）

译文：As distance tests a horse's stamina, so time reveals a person's heart. China-ASEAN friendship has stood the test of time and emerged even stronger.

例7中，习主席引用了中国古诗《事林广记》中"路遥知马力，日久见人心"这一诗句，原意是指路途遥远才知道马的脚力好赖，日子长了才能看出人心好坏。表示中国与东盟国家的友好关系是经得起时间的考验的，也将会共同努力应对困难和挑战。"日久见人心"与"患难见真情"这两句诗意思相近，因此在翻译时可直接引用"日久见人心"这个原句翻译，以便更好地传达发言人想要表达的意思。

例8：中国有句古话叫作：感恩知福，饮水思源。广西的发展离不开在座各位工商精英的大力支持，离不开大家的才智和心力。（潘琦在第三届中国—东盟商务与投资峰会上的讲话）

译文：As an old Chinese saying goes, "Feel grateful and know where the happiness comes; when drinking water, think of its source." Development of Guangxi cannot be separated from the support, wisdom and intelligence of your business elites present here.

例8中，引用了中国古话"感恩知福，饮水思源"来表达广西政府对各位商界精英对广西经济发展做出的贡献表示感谢。在翻译的时候，首先要了解清楚原句的意思，看英文是否有与之相对应的话语，若没有，再把核心意思翻译出来。一些谚语或俗语也经常被引用到会议演讲或致辞中。例9—11这三条俗语都表达了中国与东盟国家不仅在地理位置上非常接近，在合作关系上也非常亲密。

例9：中国人说：割不断的亲，离不开的邻。

译文：Chinese also like to say：close family cannot be separated, and good neighbors cannot be parted.

例10：远亲不如近邻。

译文：A good neighbor is better than a brother far off.

例11：远水难救近火。

译文：Distance water cannot put out a fire close at hand。

综上所述，多种修辞手法的使用给中国—东盟商务与投资峰会的会议致辞增添了五彩斑斓的色彩，让致辞更具感染力。但是经过对中英商务致辞中修辞手法的对比发现，在翻译过程中，中文与英文的运用存在很大区别。比如中文表达中多运用排比语言气势，加强表达效果，把所要阐述的东西描述得更严密，更透彻。而在翻译中，如果逐字翻译，则不符合英文的行文习惯，也显得累赘啰唆。因此，为了更好地进行中外经济文化交流，作为一名译员，要了解清楚中英翻译时的修辞运用差别，从而才能更好、更确切地传达作者的本意。

第五节　中英城市形象宣传片的修辞对比和翻译

"城市形象宣传片"指的是对城市的形象进行宣传的影片，其目的是树立城市形象，提高城市的知名度。当前城市形象宣传片大致可以分为：城市宣传资料片、城市旅游形象片、城市招商形象片、与大型活动相配合的城市形象宣传片。

城市形象宣传起初是单纯对一个城市的景色样态进行拍摄和宣传，但是发展至今，城市形象宣传片已经很好地融入了城市的原有的特色文化、经济、科技等元素。这些元素使得城市宣传片与自然纪录片有着很大的区别，如今的城市纪录片不仅展示了一个城市的外在形象，也对外展示了该城市的发展潜力及其综合实力，使外界人对被宣传的城市有敬佩和向往之情，潜移默化之中，越来越多的人也会更加愿意投资该城市，由此城市的发展是必然的。

一个城市的成功不只在于看它的经济有多发达，科技有多进步，文化有多先进，政治有多稳定，还要看这个城市的宣传力和影响力。在如今这个科技网络高速发展，旅游业成为重要的发展行业，而宣传带来的影响力是不可估量的。如果宣传做得好，一个城市的旅游和投资行业就会迅速发展，其影响力就会得到大大提升，政治、经济、文化方面自然而然地也就被带动起来。因此，城市宣传片不仅仅是一个普通的广告，它关乎的是这个城市的发展和未来。

一旦一部宣传片让人观看之后有向往该城市之心，有想深入了解的欲望，那么这就说明这部宣传片是起作用的。旅游业也是这样带动起来的，正如我国的著名景点杭州西湖，其实本质上就是一个很宽敞的湖，绕着湖边走边观赏，走到最后无非就是走到脚酸了口渴了，而获得的无非就是一些留念的照片。但是为什么每天还有这么多游客挤破头地去观看呢？其中一个很重要的因素就是因为西湖闻名遐迩，而它闻名的一个很大的原因就是宣传得好。从古代开始，人们就以口头、文字等形式对西湖进行宣传，因此大多数人对西湖的印象大概会是"欲把西湖比西子，淡妆浓抹总相宜"吧。相似地，城市形象宣传片具有吸引游客、招商引资等功能，在对外宣传城市的同时，使城市的文化、习俗等得到宣传，带动了城市经济的快速发展。

一、中英城市形象宣传片的修辞共性

中英城市形象宣传片的内容以视频和语言文字为主，其视频就是对城市的自然风光、人物、建筑、习俗现象等进行拍摄，而其中带有的中文或英文的字幕或者简单解释文字则是使人们更好地了解视频的具体内容或介绍某些特殊的景点或人物。

总的来讲，中英城市形象宣传片的共性均是提升城市知名度、吸引商人投资、促进城市经济发展。而且宣传片中均会重点提及被宣传城市的著名景点，例如南宁中文宣传片子中重点提及了中国东盟博览会，并且描述博览会是如何的重要，对促进中国和东盟国家之间的经济文化等交流起到很大的作用，这些描写也从一定程度上提升了南宁的魅力；又例如成都英文宣传片中也重点拍摄了都江堰，作为受过教育的中国人几乎都知道都江堰这个水利工程在我国历史上起着重要的作用，也由此都江堰自然而然也成了一个著名的景点，它既起到防洪抗灾的作用，同时也能够以它的"英名"来吸引游客，带动沿线经济的增长。

此外，中英城市形象宣传片不得不提的一个明显共性就是片中常常提及被宣传城市获得的头衔，这些头衔往往是国家级别的或者国际级别的，由此来证明该城市获得的认可和美誉。例如，南宁，地处中国西南疆，素有中国绿城的美誉，被评为"全国文明城市""国家卫生城市"和"国家生态园林城市"，获得了"联合国人居奖"。Nanning, located in the southwest of China, is well-known as "Green City of China" and honored as "National Culturally Advanced City", "National Recognized Clean City" and "National Ecological Garden City". It is also a winner of UN Habitat Scroll of Honor Award. 又如，Chengdu, the "Best City to Visit in China" named by the UNWTO.成都被世界旅游组织评为中国最佳旅游城市。

中英城市宣传片使用的最明显的一样的修辞手法就是利用引用手法和较多的排比手法对城市进行描述。排比手法如，"南宁面向东南亚，东邻粤港澳，南临北部湾，背靠大西南"。排比手法常常由三个或三个以上结构相同或相似、内容相关、语气一致的短语或句子组合而成，给人一种整齐对仗的舒服感，运用排比可以加强语势，强调内容，加重感情，使要表达的观点得到进一步强调，给人印象深刻。宣传片中常见的就是引用手法，常常引用著名诗人、词人或作家的名句来描述被宣传的城市，而这些名人往往是和被宣传城市有一定的相关性。例如，Out of the Ninth Heaven Chengdu was born, where thousands of households looked as pretty as a picture.（九天开出一成都，万户千门入画图）这是唐代大诗人李白用来形容成都这个天府之国的自然美景，其诗给人以开阔的感觉，并且表达了成都的自然风光正如一幅画一样美妙。引用手法不仅给人以深刻的印象，而且也增强了该城市的文化力量，对城市起到了很好的宣传作用。

二、中英城市形象宣传片的修辞差异

　　由于考虑到观众的文化背景、思想习俗等，中英城市形象宣传片的修辞或多或少都会存在较大的差异。这些差异都是为了让不同文化背景的观众能够更好地了解被宣传的城市，树立一个高尚、优秀而又质朴的城市形象。

　　为了吸引潜在的游客和商人，中文城市形象宣传片中不乏会看见一些使用夸张手法的词语，常常使用"最"或"第一"等来形容城市的某个特点。例如，"哈尔滨，一座雄踞中国疆域最北最东的特大城市。冬季，这里拥有世界最美的冰雪；每天，这里迎来中国最早的曙光"。这种使用极端形容词的方式虽然说会在一定程度上说明彰显其地方地位的重要性，但是出现得多了难免会让人觉得其可信度下降。正如，《重庆》宣传片和《成都》宣传片中都各自说是"最具幸福感的城市"，然而我们都知道"最"字就应该形容独一的、至高的东西。

　　在中文的城市宣传片中，一些浮华、优美又对偶的描写常常出现，其目的是为了表现其风景的美，然而这些描写都是相似且无实际意义的，有时还让人有点摸不着头脑。例如，"赋予哈尔滨迷人神韵，万千气象，金源故地，千年文脉，滨江关道，百载沧桑"。

　　英文宣传片中的用词则比较贴近实际，没有夸大宣传，符合了外国人要求的准确、明了。诸如，Qinhuai river that flows through the city is not only the mother river of Nanjing, but also one of the first rivers to be known for its culture and history in China.句子中直说秦淮河是中国著名文化历史名河之一，而并没有说是第一，这种委婉的表达更加接近实际，更能让人接受。而且英文宣传片中的句子之间不会重点讲究对仗，只是把意思和内容简单客观地表达出来，让人易于接受和明白，这点上中英的宣传片是很不同的。

三、中英城市形象宣传片的翻译

中英城市形象宣传片中存在着诸多的差异,翻译就必须考虑到两种语言文化背景的不同。为了让翻译出来的句子既符合原文的意思,又要使其简单易懂,翻译的时候我们往往会运用一些基本的翻译技巧来完善翻译。

首先经常用到的一个翻译方法就是"对应翻译",其实一些简单表达的陈述句是可以完全对应或通过大部分对应来翻译的。例如,"一条邕江穿城过,一座青山城中坐,青山伴着绿水转,绿水青山都是歌。The Yongjiang River runs through the city. A green mountain stands in the city. The river winds along the mountain. They inspire the creation of songs."这个句子就属于部分对应,其中前面两句我们一读便知道它是对应翻译的,对应翻译更能符合原文中文的表达习惯,只不过为了考虑它的深层含义有时候不得不对句子的翻译进行一些调整。"绿水青山都是歌"翻译成了"They inspire the creation of songs."非常精妙,突出了这些青山绿水如此优美,能创造出自然之歌,能够激发人创造出优美的曲子。

"增译"(addition/amplification)和"减译法"(deletion)也是常常用到的翻译方法,例如这个句子,"龙舟竞渡,焰火闪亮,舞姿曼妙,糍粑甜香"译为"The regional elements, such as dragon boat race, shining fireworks, graceful dances and sticky rice cakes."为了解释清楚这些四字词的意思,译者把"The regional elements"这个添加上去,使外国观众一看就知道原来这些词是用来描述这个城市的文化现象,属于这个地区的元素特征。这种增译看似微小,实际上起着过渡、衔接甚至是解释的作用。

"词序调整法(inversion)"是中英城市宣传片中最常见的翻译方法,对语序进行相应调整可以使译文读起来更加顺畅,更加符合英文的表达习惯。例如,《南宁》宣传片中的"处在华南经济圈、西南经济圈与东盟经济圈,三大经济圈的交汇点"译成了"It is significantly located at the junction of three major economic circles namely South China Economic Circle, Southwest China Economic Circle and SASEAN Economic Circle."

城市形象宣传片中,特别是接近结尾部分,一般会有一些带有号召力的一两个句子作为整个宣传片的精华。而这一两个句子往往短小而精悍，通常采用"意译"的方式进行翻译。比如南宁的城市形象宣传片的结尾"光荣与使命同在，魅力与风采卓然。Nanning, a city with honor and mission!"中文句子凸显文化内涵，表达方式是明显地中国号召类型的句子，其意思实则有些指代不明；而其英文翻译非常清晰明确而且简洁，很好地将真正要表达的意思体现了出来。

由于现实生活中城市形象宣传片所起的作用非常明显，很大限度地影响了城市的发展，因此在宣传片制作过程中不仅要表达出城市的价值和优势，也要关注宣传的不同版本里面使用的修辞和翻译。作为大众的我们也不能只看宣传片里面的美好事物作为娱乐，也应该关注里面的用词和翻译，进行积累和学习；更要关注宣传片里面未提及的存在于现实中的一些事物，从而才能真正地了解那个城市。

第六节　中国—东盟商务致辞的修辞比较及翻译

中国—东盟博览会是中国唯一一个由许多政府联合组织并在一个地方长期举办的展览。以展览为中心，开展多种类多层次的交流活动，搭建中国与东盟国家交流与合作的平台。通过东盟，参与的成员国可以进行经济、政治和文化交流。2003年，中国—东盟博览会由温家宝总理首次发起，是发展与东盟国家和平与繁荣的战略伙伴关系的重要举措。

基于东盟的背景，亚洲许多国家可以利用这一平台进行更多的商业交流与合作。商务礼仪在现代商务和政治活动中发挥着重要作用。作为商务礼仪的重要组成部分，商务演讲对这些活动的影响不容忽视。本文阐述了中国与东南亚国家在政治、商业交流和翻译中的礼仪致辞表达的特点。更重要的是，找到它们之间的共同点。此外，挖掘礼仪致辞的积极方面，促进政治和商业活动的顺利发展。

一、中国与东盟十国礼仪致辞中称谓和问候的表达

礼仪致辞是社交场合中人们用来表达礼仪以维护和发展人际关系，人与组织群体之间以及组织与组织之间相互关系的文书。中国与东盟国家相互交往的礼仪致辞包括一般礼仪致辞的基本内容、特点和要求。在提点方面，首先是礼貌：尊称、客套话不能省略，但要恰到好处。接下来是真挚亲切：专注于情感交流。第三，简洁：为了礼节，所要表达的内容是点到为止。最后，委婉：只讲相关事项的基本要点和原则，不涉及或直接与双方的争议观点和意见相关。在要求方面，语言应该是热情和礼貌，使客人有宾至如归的感觉。

大多数东盟国家以英语作为官方语言。因此，许多东盟国家的礼仪致辞与一般英语国家的礼仪致辞相同。重要人物和参与者的称呼是"尊贵/尊敬（客人），（你/他/她）陛下，（你/他/她）殿下，（你/他/她/）阁下，女士们、先生们"。他们的中文翻译是"贵宾们，陛下，殿下，阁下，女士和先生们"。但是，在大多数中国的仪式致辞中，并没有多少称谓有意地将重要的参与者与一般的参与者区分开来。如果会议中有特别重要的人，他们会在礼仪致辞的开头提到。其他人将被称为"女士们，先生们，同事或朋友"。

当一些东盟领导人在重要会议上发表仪式致辞时，他们将以参与者为主体表达他们的问候。例如，菲律宾领导人使用了"Greeting from the Philippines！"（来自菲律宾的问候！）作为他在中国上海世博会上的礼仪致辞的开始。在这里，没有使用姓名或称谓来区分重要参与者和普通参与者的现象，但仍可以实现参与国家向东道国表达友好问候的作用。

这是在语言表达上，汉语强调抽象思维，用词概括性强，而英语强调具象思维，用词具体明确。由于中国人感情含蓄，通常直接将称谓作为称呼语，西方人往往感情外露，所以会在称呼上用不同的搭配体现对方的身份。英语和汉语在语言学上最重要的区别就是形合与意合的对比，这一特点在英汉两种语言的礼仪致辞上表现也尤为明显。汉语注重意合，语言组织主要取决于语言本身的语义手段，句子与句子之间的连接依靠语境和语义，连接词的使用较少，句型短小简洁；英语强调形合，英语语言组织主要依赖于

语言本身的语法手段，使用各种语言连接手段来连接，以表示句子的结构关系。以表达喜悦心情为例，汉语往往使用比较简单的词汇和句式就可以传递出丰富的情感，常常以"很高兴""很荣幸"作为句子开头，往往省略主语，而英语则必须加上主语，或者使用人称代词如"I'm pleased /delighted /honored/proud to..."，或者使用形式主语如"It's a great pleasure / privilege ..."，只有使用比较复杂的用词和句式变化才能体现出同样的情感。

二、中国与东盟十国礼仪致辞中的引用

在许多中国与东盟国家交流的仪式致辞中，引用了中国和其他国家的谚语和名人名言。不仅因为中国综合实力的不断发展和壮大，还因为历史文化的认同感。2015年11月20日，中国国务院总理李克强11月20日在当地出版的《星洲日报》发表的《历史的航道、崭新的坐标、扬起的风帆》一文中引用了中印两国的诗句谚语——李白有诗云，"相知在急难，独好亦何益"，马来西亚亦有谚语，"遇山一起爬，遇沟一起跨"。与此同时，李克强总理在致辞中还提及中印两国交往的历史渊源，"中马是隔海相望的近邻，友好交往历史源远流长，最早的商贸往来可以追溯到公元纪年之前。中国明代航海家郑和曾七下西洋，五次到访马六甲，在中马两国史书上留下丰富的记载，三宝山、三宝井和许多美丽的故事广为流传"。基于两国在历史上长期友好的交往以及儒家文化的影响，李克强首次访问马来西亚，并出席东亚合作领导人系列会议时，在发表礼仪致辞中使用中国和马来西亚的名言，不仅可以得到马来西亚各界的认可，同时可以增强双方国家文化相同之处的认同感。李克强总理在第20次中国—东盟领导人会议上的发言中引述了菲律宾的谚语，"扫帚之所以结实，是因为棕榈叶被拧在了一起"；在澜沧江—湄公河合作首次领导人会议上的讲话引用东南亚的谚语——"微风聚在一起，就有台风的力量"；在泰国国会的演讲中提到"中国有句谚语说，种瓜得瓜，种豆得豆。泰国也有句谚语，撒什么种子结什么果"（As a Chinese saying goes, "You reap melons if you plant melon seeds, and beans if you sow bean seeds." I understand there is a similar saying in Tailand: "you reap what you saw.")。

除此之外，东盟国家领导人和世界其他国家的领导人在对中国的会议以及活动中，也会引用本国和中国的名言和谚语。2010年上海世界博览会上，菲律宾领导人在致辞的结尾用菲律宾语"Mabulay"（中文翻译为：祝您长寿，生活愉快）表达对中国、与会者的美好祝福。美国第67任国务卿希拉里·克林顿在2011年5月9日晚设宴招待中方代表团时引用邓小平名言"摸着石头过河"（A person crosses a river by feeling his way over the stones.），并且在第三轮中美战略与经济对话期间，希拉里国务卿和财政部长盖特纳分别引用中国名言和成语"逢山开道，遇水架桥"（When confronted by mountains, one finds a way through. When blocked by a river, one finds a way to bridge to the other side.）和"有福同享，有难同当"（Share fortunes together, meet challenges together.）这不仅是对自身和他国文化元素的自信，更是对自身和他国文化的善用，形成了言近旨远、明晰机智的文风和思维方式。

三、结语

中国和东盟所有邻国陆上毗邻，隔海相望，享有长久的友谊关系。虽然语言不同，但文化上有相通之处，诗句和谚语的含义相似，它们的理解可以通过翻译实现，以增强彼此的理解和感情联系。加上以儒家文化为主的中华文化不断走向世界，孔子学院不断发展，越来越多的东盟国家和世界各国开始学习中华文化，对日益频繁的各种政治和商业活动礼仪致辞中出现的中国名言和谚语能够更好地理解和认同。

不难看出，各国领导人在发表礼仪致辞时常见的修辞手法为引用，引用本国或他国的名人名言或者谚语。中国的名言及谚语大多采用的是对偶、比喻和反问，当他们被其他国家领导人引用时，往往是通过意译的方法按它们的原文的大意来翻译，不作逐字逐句的翻译。

中国领导人在引用他国名言及谚语时，会采用对偶和象征的手法，意译和直译的方法相结合。不论是何种方法，翻译的目的都是为了在更能够体现出本民族的语言特征的同时，加强国家之间的文化交流和感情联系。

第七节 中英演讲中元话语标记劝说功能的跨文化比较

元话语是用于组织话语、表达说话者立场和观点、涉及读者反应的一种话语方式。任何话语或语篇都是由基本话语和元话语构成。基本话语侧重于表达概念意义，元话语侧重于表达语篇意义和人际意义。

政治演讲是国家领导人正式表达观点的途径之一，为了准确清晰地表达意见，说服听众，演讲语篇使用了大量的元话语来实现语篇的劝说功能。

比较元话语标记在美国和中国政治演讲中的使用，能帮助我们探索中美文化中政治演讲不同的修辞偏好，以及不同文化对劝说策略的影响。

一、元话语与劝说功能

亚里士多德在《修辞学》中提出，演讲中的劝说有三种手段：人格诉求（Ethos）、逻辑诉求（Logos）、情感诉求（Pathos）。人格诉求（Ethos）指的是演讲者本人的品格或素质所产生的说服力，简单地说，演讲者应该努力塑造树立可信、自信、权威的公众形象来增强演讲的效果。逻辑诉求（Logos）指的是逻辑论证所产生的说服力。演讲者对论据做出一定的选择和安排，使其论点更具说服力。情感诉求（Pathos）指的是表达情感的诉求，演讲者需要思考和理解听众的心理需求，缩小心理距离，说服他们同意自己的论点。

1959年，Zellig Harris首次提出元话语的概念。其后，很多学者在这一领域不断探索,赋予了元话语不同的定义与分类(Williams, 1981; Lautamatti, 1978; Vande, 1985; Crismore, 1989; Crismore et al., 1993; Hyland, 1998, 2005)。一些学者研究了元话语的劝说功能。例如,Crismore和Farnsworth(1989)研究了元话语如何通过语码注释语、情态标记、态度标记和评价标记建立《物种起源》中的人格诉求(Ethos);而Hyland(1998)则以CEO信函为语料,研究元话语如何通过建立信誉诉求(Ethos)、逻辑诉求(Logos)、情感诉求(Pathos),增强信函的说服性。研究表明,模糊语、强调标识和关系标记有助于建立信誉诉求;文本元话语和语码注释语的使用有助于建立逻辑诉求;而关系标记、态度标记、模糊语和人称代词的使用,有助于实现情感诉求。从这些研究中,我们可以得知,元话语能帮助实现话语的劝说功能,同时,亚里士多德劝说三种手段,人格诉求、逻辑诉求和情感诉求,是通过不同类别的元话语标识而得以实现的。

还有不少学者对不同语言中元话语的使用进行了跨文化比较研究。例如,英语和芬兰语(Markkanen等人,1993; Mauranen, 1993)、英语和西班牙语(Dafouz Milne, 2008; Emma, 2008)以及英语和汉语(胡光伟和Geng Gao, 2011)等等。研究的结果表明,元话语在不同的文化中都有使用,但元话语的使用因文化差异而有所不同,不同语言中元话语的使用频率和说服功能的修辞偏好都存在一定的差异。先前的研究多使用书面材料作为研究素材,例如论文、作文、研究报告等,对口语语篇的研究偏少。

Hyland(2005)把元话语分为交际和互动两大类。交际类元话语有助于引导读者,注重组织话语的方式,包括过渡标记(transition markers)、框架标记(frame markers)、回指标记(endophoric markers)、言据标记(evidentials)、语码注释语(code glosses)。互动类元话语包括模糊语(hedges)、增强语(boosters)、态度标记(attitude markers)、自称语(self-mention)和介入标记(engagement markers)。

以Hyland的元话语人际模式为基础,本研究结合演讲的特点和亚里士多德的劝说理论,建立了一个元话语劝说模式,如图4-1所示。这一模式涉及了演讲沟通中的三个主要因素,即说者、听者和论述内容,同时把元话语标记的子类型与其对应的劝说功能加以对应。因回指标记很少在演讲中出现,因此不放入此模式中。

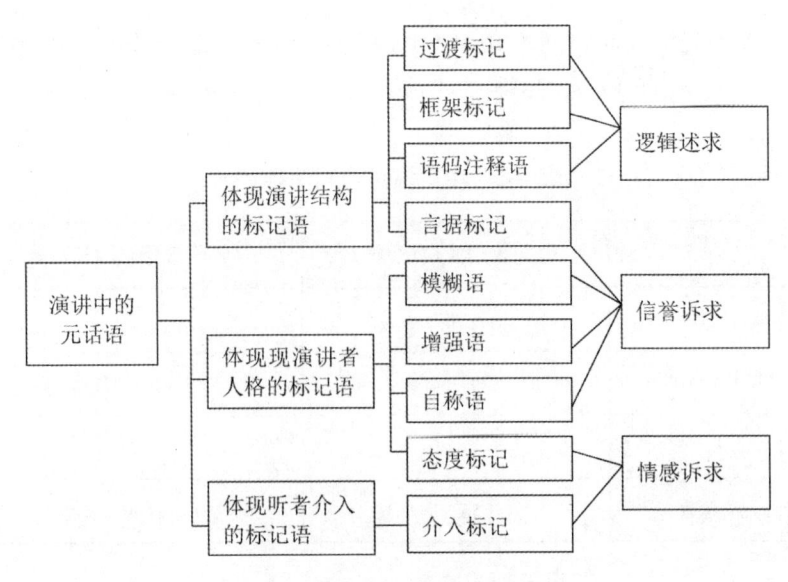

图4-1 演讲中的元话语劝说模式

二、研究方法

（一）研究问题

本研究拟解决的研究问题是：

（1）元话语标记是如何通过政治演讲中的人格、逻辑、情感诉求来实现劝说功能的？

（2）元话语标记在中美政治演讲中的具体使用上一般有什么偏好？

（3）文化因素如何影响劝说策略的选择？

（二）语料的收集

政治话语通常包括选举演说、就职演说、会议辩论、集会演说和外交演说等。本研究所有收集的语料均为会议演讲，包括中国和美国演讲稿各

30篇，源于美国政府官网（https://www.whitehouse.gov）和中国政府官网（http://www.gov.cn）。演讲语料库具体数据如表4-8所示。

表4-8　中美演讲语料库描述

	美国政治演讲语料库	中国政治演讲语料库
演讲次数	30	30
文本字数（范围）	870—5495	916—3271
平均演讲字数	1876	2264
标记语总数	56291	67913

（三）元话语的界

根据亚里士多德的三种劝说方式及它们在劝说功能上的分布，我们把所有的元话语可分为三类。表4-9向我们展示了所涉及元话语的分类和定义，所有定义参照Hyland的元话语模式。

表4-9　元话语的定义和分类

体现逻辑诉求的元话语
过渡标记：表明语段间的内在逻辑。这类标记包括附加、对比和连续标记语。 **框架标记**：标记文本分界或文本结构示意图。 **语码注释语**：用于表示解释或举例的词语，确保读者或听者能够知道作者的意图。
体现信誉诉求的元话语
增强语：强调确定性元话语。增强语表明作者或演讲者承认不同立场的存在，但还是选择缩小这种可能性，表达他们对所说内容的确定性。这类元话语不留有与听众协商的空间。

> **模糊语**：表达保留意见的元话语。强调所陈述的内容基于演讲者的推理，而不是确定的事实。这类元话语保留与听众协商的空间。
>
> **言据标记**：指明信息来源的元话语。能建立主题的权威性，引导读者对话语的解析。
>
> **自称语**：指作者在文本中的自我称呼。
>
> **体现情感诉求的元话语**
>
> **态度标记**：表达作者或演讲者对命题的情感评价。
>
> **介入标记**：明确针对读者，引起他们注意或邀请他们参与话语共建的元话语。

Hyland的元话语模式对元话语的每一类别都给出了明确的定义。但是，对某些词语进行元语篇识别和限定仍然是不容易的。当面临不清楚的情况时，元话语的分类须依据上下文意思及词语在文中的具体功能而界定。

（四）研究步骤

本研究采用了定量与定性试验相结合的研究办法。首先，建立一个中英文元话语列表。英文列表可参照Hyland编制的元话语列表，中文列表中的元话语大多来自英文翻译，同时依据元话语定义从中文演讲稿中进行补充。其次，搜索中英文元话语列表中的所有词汇，并进行标记和统计。在上下文中仔细分析检索到的词汇，进行人工标识，然后使用Ant Conc 3.2.2 统计语料中每个元话语标识出现的频率，并使用统计分析软件SPSS将中美两个演讲语料库中的每类元话语进行比较（独立性样本t试验），当P值小于0.05时，两组数据存在差异。最后，对子语料库中的中美典型例子进行比较。运用亚里士多德的经典修辞学，来阐述元话语中的每个类别是如何通过人格、逻辑、情感诉求等手段来达到劝说目的，分析中美两国政治家在元话语方面的使用差异，阐述中美文化对语篇说服风格的影响。

三、研究结果及分析

表4-10是中美两个语料库中元话语标记使用情况的描述性统计。总体来说，美国演讲语料库中元话语标记的使用频率明显高于汉语演讲语料库（1151.8/10000：572.8/10000），这说明美国政治演讲话语拥有更多的演讲者与听众间的互动。同时，数据显示，美国演讲中，表达信誉诉求的元话语使用频率最高（715.9/10000），其次是表达情感诉求和逻辑诉求的元话语。而排在中国演讲首位的是表达情感诉求的元话语（286.4/10000），然后才是表达信誉诉求和逻辑诉求的元话语。简单地说，在劝说过程中，美国演讲更注重追求信誉诉求，而中国演讲更注重情感诉求。我们将在下文中从逻辑、信誉、情感三个方面对中美元话语的使用进行进一步比较。

表4-10 具有说服功能的元话语标记的使用频率

	美国政治演讲语料库		中国政治演讲语料库	
	出现次数	每万字频率	出现次数	每万字频率
逻辑诉求	2454	435.9	487	71.7
信誉诉求	4030	715.9	1458	214.7
情感诉求	3081	1151.8	2134	286.4
总数	9565	1151.8	4079	572.8

（一）有助于理性诉求的元话语

理性诉求指的是演讲论述的各个要素之间是否有合理联系，使得读者或听众能够理解和接受演讲者的观点。通常为了使得演讲的内容通顺易懂，演讲者往往使用关联性的话语来表明论点间的关系，这类词语包括过渡标记、框架标记和类语码注释语。

表4-11 有助于理性诉求的元话语

	美国政治演讲语料库		中国政治演讲语料库		Sig.
	出现次数	每万字频率	出现次数	每万字频率	
过渡标记	2032	361.0	261	38.4	.000
框架标记	322	57.2	146	21.5	.000
语码注释语	65	11.5	28	4.1	.001
总数	2419	429.7	435	64	.001

1. 过渡标记

过渡标记是指表示话语之间内在逻辑的元话语标记，过渡标记的使用可以使话语流畅连贯，同时强调演讲中的某些部分。数据表明，美国语料库中的过渡标记的频率几乎是中国语料库的十倍（361/10000：38.4/10000），这个结果在一定程度上是由于英汉两种语言的结构特点造成的。英语重形合而汉语重意合，英文句子或短语间的逻辑关系必须通过连接词明确地表达出来，而汉语语篇中的句子或短语之间能通过内在含义连接，不需要使用连接词。

2. 框架标记

框架标记通常用于组织文本、标记文本结构，以便分清正在讨论或将要讨论的话题。框架标记又可分为话题标识和顺序标识。话题标识指的是提供论述的框架信息，提示听众即将论述的内容，如"I argue here, my purpose is, well, right, now, OK"等。

顺序标识词是指以线性、渐进的方式连接话语各个部分的言语标记，以便于读者解读文本的目的，如"first, second, next, finally"等，使用顺序标识词能点明文本框架，指引读者有序地理解演说者的观点。

在以下的例子中，例1和例2属于话题标识，例3和例4的序数词都属于顺序标识。

例1：Now, North Korea is calling for dialogue.

例2：在此，我谨对研讨会的成功举行表示热烈祝贺，向参加本次研讨会的两国各界人士和涉农部门人士，表示诚挚的欢迎和由衷的敬意。

例3：And here's what you need to know. First, I will not sign a plan that adds one dime to our deficits- [...] Second, we've estimated that most of this plan can be paid for by finding savings within the existing health care system,[...]

例4：推动文明交流互鉴，需要秉持正确的态度和原则。我认为，最重要的是坚持以下几点。第一，文明是多彩的，人类文明因多样才有交流互鉴的价值。[……]第二，文明是平等的，人类文明因平等才有交流互鉴的前提。[……]第三，文明是包容的，人类文明因包容才有交流互鉴的动力。[……]

数据显示，美国演讲使用框架标记的频率高于中国演讲（57.2/10000∶21.5/10000）。而中文演讲中出现的顺序标识词比英文演讲中出现得多，在30篇演讲中，有24篇中文政治演讲使用了顺序标识，而仅有9篇英文政治演讲使用顺序标识。

主题标识词和顺序标识词都点明了大致的文本框架，并提供话语论述的概要信息。两者的不同之处则在于顺序标识词是以明显的线性方式组织全文。美国演讲比中国演说中更喜欢使用主题标识语，为听众提供理解演讲的框架梗概，而中国演讲更偏向于使用线性思维进行篇章组织。

3.语码注释语

语码注释语指的是表示解释或举例的元话语，通过解释说明所述内容来提供额外的信息，确保读者或听者能够知道作者的意图。演讲者使用语码注释语时为了确保信息能被听众准确理解，以达到话语的理性诉求。语码注释语的使用如例5和例6所示。

例5：With regard to maritime disputes, it's critical that all nations have a clearly understanding of what constitutes acceptable international behavior. That means no intimidation, no coercion, no aggression, and a commitment from all parties to reduce the risk of mistake and miscalculation.

例6：2013年与2005年相比，中国碳排放强度下降28.5%，相当于少排放二氧化碳25亿吨。

在例5中，为了引导听众理解什么是"acceptable international behavior"，句中应用了语码注释语"that means"，引导出更详细的解析。例6中的中文例子"相当于"也有类似的功能，演说者随后给出了一个更具体的数字来说明碳排放的减少。因为比起模糊的百分数，人们往往能够通过精确的数字获得更直观的了解。

语码注释语的使用频率在英语演讲中比中文演讲中更高。（11.5/10000：4.1/10,000）。英语演讲似乎在语篇中为听众提供了更多的解释说明，这或许受到了中英文化不同修辞风格的影响，英文语篇"以读者为中心"，而中国语篇则"以作者为中心"。"以读者为中心"的语篇通常需要作者增添更多的解释说明，使得两个语料库中语码注释语出现频率产生差异。

（二）有助于信誉诉求的元语言

除了理性的诉求外，信誉诉求是影响说服功能实现的另一个重要因素。如果演讲者能让听众觉得他是一个诚实、可信和权威的人，演讲的劝说力度会增强，而有助于信誉诉求的元话语包括模糊语、增强语、态度标记和自称语。统计数据表明，增强语和态度标记的使用频率没有显著差异，但美国政治演讲中模糊语的使用频率远远超于中国政治演讲（176.6/10000：7.4/10000），自称语的使用情况也相似（433.8/10000：121.8/10000）。统计数据还显示，为了增强可信诉求，美国语料中模糊语的使用频（176.6/10000）比增强语（99.3/10000）高，而中国语料中，增强语的使用频率（77.9/10000）比模糊语（7.4/10000）高。

表4-12　有助于实现信誉诉求的元话语

	美国政治演讲语料库		中国政治演讲语料库		Sig.
	出现次数	每万字频率	出现次数	每万字频率	
增强语	559	99.3	529	77.9	.227
模糊语	994	176.6	50	7.4	.000
自称语	2442	433.8	827	121.8	.013
言语标记	35	6.2	52	7.7	.203
共计	4030	715.9	1458	214.7	.776

1. 增强语

增强语的作用是表达作者论点的确定性和保证性，并强调正在讨论的内容。在政治演讲中，虽然演讲者通常是名人，但在演讲过程中，他们仍然需要重新树立信誉。我们来看下面的例子。

例7：There's no question in our view that every nation must protect its citizens against crime and attacks online, as well as off. But we must do it in a manner that's consistent with our shared values.

例8："海阔凭鱼跃，天高任鸟飞。"我始终认为，宽广的太平洋有足够的空间容纳中美两个大国。中美双方应该加强对话，增信释疑，促进合作，确保中美关系始终不偏离构建新型大国关系的轨道。

在例7中，演讲者使用"There's no question"来表达他在保护美国公民免受网络犯罪袭击的决心，使用"must"来表达一种坚定的态度。演讲者通过增强语的使用来树立一个自信满满的领导形象，以赢得听众的支持。

例8则运用了"应该""确保"和"始终"来强调演讲者对中美关系的态度。这些增强语的使用明确表达了中国政府的友好立场，增强了听众对中国政府政策的信心。

在这两个例子中，通过使用增强语，演讲者都树立了一个强势、自信的形象，获得了听众的信任感。数据表明，美国演讲和中国演讲中都大量使用了增强语（99.3/10000：77.9/10000），T检验的结果并无显著差异。增强语可以表决心，给承诺，帮助演讲者树立一个自信的形象，这一点在中国文化和美国文化中都很重要。

2. 模糊语

与强势语相反，模糊语表示话语的不确定性。演讲者通过表达自己的不确定性，给予了听者更多的协商余地，通过树立一个谨慎、谦虚、体贴的形象来增强话语的可信度。

数据表明，美国演讲中模糊语（176/10000）的使用频率要远高于中国（7.4/10000），这是英汉演讲语料库使用频率差异最大的元话语之一。除此之外，两种演讲语料中使用模糊语的目的侧重点也有所不同。美国演讲语料库中最常用的模糊语是情态动词，如"would"和"could"，而中国语料库中最常用的模糊语是副词和形容词，如"较""确定"。让我们看以下例句：

例9：And I will say again, we would not have gotten to this point and I think our colleagues in Iraq would acknowledge were it not for their staff, whose work is often done under trying conditions—and I might add, Mr. Secretary, I think their work remains as important as it ever has been.

例10：目前，中国除了大豆有一定缺口、需要进口弥补以外，小麦、稻谷、玉米三大品种产需都实现了基本平衡。

在例9中，通过使用情态动词"would"和"might"，搭配"I will say again"和"I think"等表达主观意志的表达，演讲者把话语限定为自己的判断，把话语确定性的判断权力交给了听众。而例10中的"一定"和"基本"是表示程度上的缓和。

以上例子表明，美国演讲中通常使用模糊语来表达对听众的尊重，在话语中留有协商的余地。而在中国语境中，模糊语更多地用于调整话语的确定性，使话语更加客观。美国演讲者使用模糊语来强调观点的主观性，中国演讲者更偏向使用模糊语来避免绝对化的表达。在中国文化中，为了获得更强的公信力，中国政府官员作为政府的代表，往往会在演讲中树立一个自信和权威的形象，不需要使用太多的模糊语。而在美语的语境中，美国政府官员却需要使用大量的模糊语来削弱语言中的强迫力，树立谦逊、体贴的形象。

3.自称语

自称语是演讲者的自我称呼，它明确提及了演讲者在文本中的存在，在实现演讲的信誉诉求方面发挥着重要的作用。自称语往往和增强语、模糊词相结合，强调了演讲者对论点的个人责任。

表4-13 自称语的单数形式和复数形式

	美国政治演讲语料库		中国政治演讲语料库	
	出现次数	百分比	出现次数	百分比
复数形式	1689	70.10%	773	93.50%
单数形式	722	29.90%	54	6.50%
共计	2411	100%	827	100.00%

统计数字显示，美国演讲者使用的自称语（433.8/10000）频率高于中国演讲者（121.8/10000），差距显著。自称语可进一步分为单数和复数形式。单数形式包括"I""my""mine"，和"我"等代词，用于提及演讲者在话语中的存在；而复数形式往往指代演讲者所代表的政府或机构，包括"we""our""ours""America""我们"和"中国"等。在演讲中，演讲者会在单复数之间进行切换，改变自己在演讲中的角色。

从表4-13可以看出，在两个语料库中，自称语复数形式的使用频率均高于单数形式，这意味着在中美两种文化中，演讲者在演讲中都更倾向于展示自己的公众角色，而不是个人角色。但在中国的政治演讲中，单数的自称语尤其少，只占了所有自称语使用的6.50%，说明中国的政治发言人几乎很少在公众演讲中使用"我"这一称呼。让我们分析以下例子，探究这两类自称语是如何帮助建立演讲者公众形象的。

例11：I love Australia — I really do. The only problem with Australia is every time I come here I've got to sit in conference rooms and talk to politicians instead of go to the beach.

例12：中方建议，推动亚信成为覆盖全亚洲的安全对话合作平台，并在此基础上探讨建立地区安全合作新架构。中方认为，可以考虑根据形势发展需要，适当增加亚信外长会乃至峰会频率，以加强对亚信的政治引领、规划好亚信发展蓝图。

在例11中，"I"出现了三次，被用于表明演讲者热爱澳大利亚是出于个人立场，而不是政治家立场，拉近了与听众的心理距离，使听众更容易接受其观点。

中国的政治演讲很少使用单数形式的自我提及语，"我"通常只在演讲开头使用，演讲者在进行自我介绍和欢迎观众的时候使用，自称语在政治话语中更典型的应用是"中方"或"我方"，在例12中，"中方"这一自称语的使用清楚地表明，发言者只是中国政府的代表。句中提出的建议是出于国家的立场，从而使得声明更加严肃和正式。

复数自称语可以代表机构或国家，可使话语的表达更官方和正式；单数自称语代表演讲者自己，有助于缩短演讲者与听众之间的心理距离。中美演讲中都使用了自称语，从总体来看，美国演讲中使用的自称语频率高于中国。同时，我们发现与美国语料库相比，中国政治演讲语料库中单数自称语使用频率极低，这可能是因为在中国文化中，政治演讲需要一个更为正式和权威的演讲者形象，而美国文化中，演讲者相对而言更关注自我的人格形象塑造，更注重拉近与听众的心理距离。

4.言据标记

言据标记指的是标明信息来源的元话语。言据标记帮助演讲者将演讲的信誉与已被承认和接受的观点联系起来，通过外部的资源来支持自己的观点，提高演讲的可信度。

表4-14 引用来源

	美国政治演讲语料库		中国政治演讲语料库	
	出现次数	百分比	出现次数	百分比
历史/经典作品中的名人	4	12.5	38	73.1
当代名人	22	68.8	12	23.1
普通人	6	18.8	2	3.8

表4-14的统计数据显示，言据标记的使用频率都不高，差距也不大。但我们发现其引证的来源有些不同。为进行进一步研究，我们把引证的来源分为三类：历史/经典作品、当代名人和普通人，并分别进行统计。表4-14显示，在美国政治演讲中，大多数的言据标志的引用来自当代的名人或官方统计数据（68.8%），而中国政治演讲中，言据标志的引用更多来自包含中国传统价值观的古诗或谚语（73.1%）。以下为包含着言据标记的中英文例子：

例13：As my predecessor, President Bush, once put it: "They are a part of American life."

例14：中国有句谚语："只要功夫深，铁杵磨成针。"美国诗人摩尔说："胜利不会向我走来，我必须自己走向胜利。"构建中美新型大国关系是一种使命和责任。"合抱之木，生于毫末；九层之台，起于累土。"让我们用积土成山的精神，一步一个脚印，携手推进新型大国关系建设，努力开创中美关系更加美好的明天。

例13来自奥巴马关于移民问题的讨论。奥巴马在讲话中引用了前任布什总统的话。例14引用了一句中国古话、一首美国诗和中国古代哲学家老子的话来表达建立新的中美关系模式并不容易，需要付出时间和努力。

简单地说，言据标记在中美政治演讲中并无数量上的差异，但是引用来源的偏好却不同，中国政治演讲更喜欢引用具有权威性的古诗名言，来体现演讲者的知识储备和个人素质，增加演讲的信誉诉求。美国演讲者的引用会引用同级别的官员或自己家人的观点，来缩短演讲者和听众间的心理距离，这种引用来源在中国政治话语中很少使用。

（三）有助于实现情感诉求的元话语

在公共演讲中，演讲者可以使用参与标记语和态度标记语来获得听众的情感支持，从而实现说服功能。

表4-15 实现情感诉求的元话语

	美国政治演讲语料库		中国政治演讲语料库		Sig.
	出现次数	每万字频率	出现次数	每万字频率	
参与标记语	2499	443.9	1540	226.8	.001
态度标记语	582	103.4	442	65.1	.000
共计	3081	547.3	2134	291.9	.000

1. 参与标记语

参与标记语是使听众参与到话语中来的元话语。演讲者能否让听众参与到演讲中，将极大地影响演讲的说服力。演讲者通过使用参与标记语，把听众放到和自己一起的阵营中，从而获得听众情感上的支持，实现演讲中的情感诉求。

参与标记语包括人称代词、提问和指令。数据显示，美国政治演讲语料库中的参与标记（443.9/10000）的使用频率语高于中国语料库（226.8/10000字）。我们来看看参与标记语在例子中的使用。

例15：Every day, we should ask ourselves three questions as a nation：How do we attract more jobs to our shores? How do we equip our people with the skills they need to get those jobs? And how do we make sure that hard work leads to a decent living?

例16：女士们、先生们、朋友们！中国人民正在努力实现中华民族伟大复兴的中国梦，同各方一道努力实现持久和平、共同发展的亚洲梦，为促进人类和平与发展的崇高事业做出新的更大的贡献！

公共演讲中的人称代词指包容性的"我们"，以及第二人称代词的"你"和"你们"等。在例15中，"we""our"和"ourselves"暗示所提出问题是所有听众需要面对的共同问题。在例16中，"女士们""先生们""朋友们"用于吸引读者注意，使其参与到演讲所讨论的话题中。因为人们往往更关心与自己密切相关的事情，所以参与标记语的使用能帮助获取观众的情感支持。

提问也是一种吸引读者注意力，让观众参与探讨问题的手段。在例17中，演讲者提了三个问题，引导观众去思考。问号在美国演讲语料库中共出现了54次，但在汉语子语料库中没有出现，相对而言，提问这种元话语手段在中国政治演讲中使用得较少。

参与标记语的另一种形式是指令。指令包括祈使句，表义务和责任的情态动词（必须、应该），以及表达判断必要性的形容词等。在政治演讲中，指令往往用于演讲的结尾来激励听众采取行动。例18中的中文"同各方一道努力实现持久和平、共同发展的亚洲梦"呼吁观众响应演讲者的号召，从而使演讲者与观众的心愿达成一致。相对而言，这种元话语手段在中国演讲中的使用更常见。

2. 态度标记语

根据Hyland（2005年）的定义，态度标记语指作者用来表达惊讶、同意、重要、挫折感等情感态度的元话语。美国演讲语料库中的态度标记语（103.4/10000）使用频率比中国演讲语料库中的要多（65.1/10000），这表明美国政客在演讲中掺杂了更多的个人情感。

例17：And I was—it's terrible being dated. I was—I did speak the first year that the Center for American Progress was inaugurated, and here I'm speaking at the 10th anniversary. And the amazing thing is they're still going; that's having me speak there first.

例18：我们希望美方始终恪守中美三个联合公报精神，坚持一个中国政策，以实际行动反对"台独"，支持两岸关系和平发展。我们也希望美方切实履行承认西藏是中国一部分，反对"西藏独立"的承诺，慎重妥善处理涉藏问题。

例17通过态度标记"terrible"和"amazing"强烈表达了演讲者个人的好恶，通过分享演讲者的感受来与观众建立融洽关系。中国政治家在公开演讲中很少表达自己的个人感受来影响观众。例18中的两个"希望"，有表达演讲者的态度，但将态度融入期望中，让观众感受到他们未来的行动对实现这种期望具有重要意义。相对而言，美国演讲者在政治演讲中用更多和更强烈的态度标记语来追求情感诉求，而中国的政治演讲的态度表达要保守和委婉得多。

四、结论

上文的数据分析表明，与中国的演讲者相比，美国的演讲者使用更多的元话语标记来获得逻辑诉求、信誉诉求和情感诉求。这一结果与之前的跨文化研究所得的结论是相似的（Mauranen, 1993a；Valero Garces, 1996；Dafouz, 2003, 2008）。其原因之一是英汉两种语言的结构特点不同，英汉两种语言在语法规则上的差异，造成过渡标记、自称语等部分元话语标记的使用差异。同时，美国演讲中元话语标记的频率较高也受其社会文化背景的影响。元话语标记在演讲中是表达立场和观点的显性信号，元话语标识越少，演讲话语中信息的关系就越不明确，听众所需付出的努力就越大。Hinds'（1987）曾指出中美文化中作者与读者关系的区别，美国文化更倾向于作者/演讲者负责的风格，而中国文化更倾向于读者/听众负责的风格。也就是说，在中国文化中,演讲者并不需要详细解读话语中的信息来确保听众的理解,但美国文化在这点上是相反的。本研究的另一发现是,在三种劝说手段中,美国演讲者使用最多的是表达信誉诉求的元话语,而中国演讲者使用最多的是表达情感诉求的元话语,这也深受两国文化的影响。

在表达逻辑诉求方面,与汉语演讲相比,英语演讲在语境中使用更多的元话语标记(过渡标记、框架标记及语码注释语)来构建话语,引导听众。逻辑诉求中,唯一在中国演讲中出现频率比在美国演讲中高的元话语是顺序标识,这意味着与美国演讲者相比,中国演讲者在引导演讲时,更倾向于采用顺序法来建构他的话语,期待观众一步一步地接受和遵循他的观点。美国演讲中演讲者与观众之间的互动更多,这解释了美国演讲者较少使用序列词的原因。

用于表达信誉诉求的元话语标识包括增强语、模糊语、言据标记和自称语。增强语用来表达说话人的确定性,而模糊语则试图避免确定性。英语演讲中使用的增强语比模糊语多,而汉语演讲中使用的模糊语比增强语多。总体而言,美国演讲中使用模糊语的频率要比中国演讲高得多,而且在使用模糊语时,大家的偏好也有所不同,这可以用美国和中国流行的文化实践来解释。模糊语是一种反省式的语言表达,用于表达认知情态,调节言语行为的言外之力。(Holmes, 1982,1988)中国演讲者用外证来支撑论据时,往往引经据典,以树立权威形象。研究还发现,美国子语料库中使用自称语的频率高于汉语子语料库,这可能表明,建立个人形象并非汉语演讲中建立可信度的首选方式。众所周知,美国文化崇尚个人主义,而中国文化崇尚集体主义。中国文化不鼓励在政治话语中过于凸显个人观点。相反,中国政治家更常提他们的国家或所代表的政府。在美国演讲中,演讲者更倾向于表达自己的情感,以塑造个人形象。综上所述,在中美两国的政治演讲中,元话语中的模糊语、增强语、自称语和言据标记都被用来塑造说话人的信誉,但在美国文化中,观众期待看到的是自信而谦逊、可以包容不同意见的演讲者,而中国观众则更希望在政治演讲中看到一个自信权威的领导者。

为了达到情感诉求,美国和中国的政治演讲都试图唤起观众的共鸣,但美国演讲者使用的介入标记和态度标记更多。研究还发现,美国演讲者使用态度标记来表达对共同态度、价值观及信息反应的态度和假设的频率更高。

第五章　英汉外宣修辞对比与翻译启示

广西壮族自治区地处边疆，拥有着丰富的人文自然景观和独特的地理位置，然而，由于各方面的原因，长久以来广西的知名度不高，很少为外界所了解。在国家的战略部署中，广西是中国与东盟诸国相联系的桥头堡，是21世纪海上丝绸之路与丝绸之路经济带有机衔接的重要门户。随着中国—东盟自由贸易区的发展，广西已经成为中国"一带一路"发展战略中的重要一环。

加强广西的对外宣传力度，提高对外宣传质量，对促进广西经济发展，发挥广西的"桥头堡"作用，具有举足轻重的作用。因此，广西的对外宣传翻译研究引起了不少学者的兴趣。王永泰（2007）以"桂林山水甲天下"之英译为例，主张在外宣翻译时应体现语言的艺术美，提出旅游广告语的翻译中"简练、押韵、节律规整"三个适用原则。杨琳和刘怀平（2013）提出在广西边疆地区民俗文化的翻译中，译者应灵活采用多种翻译策略，彰显与传播标识民族身份的异质性语言。梁美清（2018）以广西三江侗族的旅游外宣文本为例，以文化翻译观作为理论指导，探讨了旅游文本的外宣翻译策略。

方梦之（2003）认为它"包括人们日常接触和实际应用的各类文字，涉及对外宣传、社会生活、生产领域、经营活动等方方面面，但不包括文学及纯理论文本"。张健（2013）认为，外宣翻译"包括各种媒体报道、政府文件公告、政府及企事业单位的介绍、公示语、信息资料等实用文体的翻译"。笔者通过对广西部分旅游景点、企业简介、产品手册、形象宣传片等进行了实证调查之后，发现广西目前的外宣翻译整体处于比较混乱的状态，提高广西对外宣传文本的英译质量，成为亟待解决的问题。

第一节 广西外宣翻译中存在的问题

一、宣传文本中的低级错误

由于广西为少数民族地区，英文教育的普遍水平还是比较弱，因此，在各种公示语或产品宣传手册中存在着大量的英文拼写错误和语法错误。

公示语中的英文拼写错误比较普遍，例如把最简单的"禁止吸烟"（No Smoking）中的"Smoking"误写作"Smaking"；"不可回收垃圾"（Unrecoverable Rubbish）中的"Rubbish"写成"Rubish"；"自行车停放处"（Bicycle Parking）居然翻译成"Parking Fog Biycle"。不仅"Bicycle"拼写错误，而且还莫名其妙的多了一个"Fog"，等等。

在各种产品宣传手册中，成段文字的语法错误也屡见不鲜，下文将用"纯正桂花糕"和"壮乡桂圆糕"的翻译例子加以说明。

纯 正 桂 花 糕
SWEER-SCENTED OSMANTHUS CAKE

桂花糕采用传统工艺，加以科学方法精制而成。该产品具有桂花独特清香神怡的风味，口感醇香柔和，是居家旅游休闲自享馈赠亲友之佳品。

Sweet-scented osmanthus cake using traditional refining process, the product has a unique flavor of sweet osmanthus fragrance and pleasant. Delicate taste, mellow and refreshing, that is the entrance, ages, is the home of tourism and leisure to enjoy the gift of Jiapin relatives since.

例1：桂花糕采用传统工艺，加以科学方法精制而成。该产品具有桂花独特清香怡神的风味，口感醇香柔和，是居家旅游、休闲自享、馈赠亲友之佳品。

译文：Sweet-scented osmanthus cake using traditional refining process, the product has a unique flavor of sweet osmanthus fragrance and pleasant. Delicate taste, mellow and refreshing, that is the entrance, ages, is the home of tourism and leisure to enjoy the gift of Jiapin relatives since.

其中的第一句话中"osmanthus cake"后跟了一个定语"using traditional refining process"，整个句子缺乏了谓语动词。而最后一句的表达更是错误连篇，不知所云，"居家旅游休闲"居然被翻译成了"the entrance, ages, is the home of tourism and leisure"。

壮乡桂圆糕
Zhuangxing Longan Cake

壮乡桂圆糕采用桂林特产为主要原料，经过现代工艺精制而成，该产品具有清香、口感柔和的特点，老少皆宜，是居家旅游休闲自享，馈赠亲友之佳品。

Zhuangxing Longan Cake is made mainly from the specialty of Guilin with the modern technology. The product is sweet and delicious. It is suitable for anyone, young or old, to take at home or on traveling; and good to give the relatives or friends as a gift.

例2：壮乡桂圆糕采用桂林特产为主要原料，经过现代工艺精制而成，该产品具有清香、口感柔和的特点，老少皆宜，是居家旅游、休闲自享、馈赠亲友之佳品。

译文：Zhuangxing Logan Cake is made mainly from the specialty of Guilin with modern technology. The product is sweet and delicious. It is suitable for anyone, young or old, to take at home or on travelling； and good to give relatives or friends as a gift.

此段的翻译中，首先，"Zhuang"本身就可以表示"壮"这个少数民族了，原译文用了拼音"Zhuangxiang"来表达，而且拼音还拼错了。整句话英语句法非常混乱，出现了缺乏主语、搭配不对等语法错误现象。

二、专有名词翻译的规范性、统一性有待提高

广西有着丰富多彩的民俗文化资源，如民俗博物馆、展览馆及各地的民俗文化节等等。这些民俗文化活动以及文化设施中所提供的英文翻译资料，成为外国人了解广西的重要媒介。而广西的民俗文化内容丰富多彩，有民俗风情、生活习惯、生产方式、居住样式、节庆典礼、宗教信仰、传统服饰、民间艺术、烹调技艺、工艺特产、音乐歌舞等。这些领域有许多富有文化特色的专有名词，民俗词汇在英文中的文化缺失，给其英译带来了不少难度。例如，有资料把"长命锁"翻译为"a long lived lock"，此后并未加任何的文字说明。英文读者看了只会认为此物是用来锁门的东西，也许会解读成此锁质量上乘，坚固耐用，而不会想到它是用来祈求小孩平平安安长命百岁的一件信物（马慈祥，2009）。而"肚兜"被翻译成"woman bra"，也实属无奈之举。"bra"指的是承托起胸部的文胸，一般里面带钢线，外面装饰有法国蕾丝花边，与古代中国妇女所穿戴的肚兜相差甚远。

广西民俗文化词的翻译存在着多个翻译版本。在文化领域，五色糯米饭是广西壮族地区的传统食物，因呈黑、红、黄、紫、白五种颜色而得名。单单是"五色糯米饭"一词，就有好几个不同的英译版本：Multi-colored Glutinous Rice, Five-color Glutinous Rice, Colored Sticky Rice 和 Five-color Steamed Sticky Rice。糍粑是一种很有名的特色小吃，主要食材就是糯米，先将糯米蒸熟，放入石臼中捶打至黏稠状，蘸上芝麻糖汁等即可食用。糍粑的英文版本有两个："Ciba Cake"和"glutinous rice cake"。龟苓膏是家喻户晓的一种药膳，一般呈膏状，有清热祛湿、凉血解毒等功效，老少皆宜。这个民俗文化词的翻译版本有以下四个版本："Guiling Jelly" "Tortoise Jelly" "turtle jelly"和"guilinggao"。风雨桥是侗族的又一大特色，因为行

人过往可以避风雨，所以故命名为风雨桥。"风雨桥"英译版本有："Wind and Rain Bridge""Wind Rain Bridge"和"Fengyu Bridge"三种。三月三是广西多个民族的传统节日，每年农历三月三都会举办盛大庆祝活动，其主要形式为山歌对唱等。"三月三"英译版本有"March 3rd Festival""Sanyuesan Festival"和"Double Third Festival"。

表5-1　广西民俗文化词的多个英译版本

广西民俗文化词	英译版本
五色糯米饭	Five-color Glutinous Rice
	Multi-colored Glutinous Rice
花炮节	Fireworks Festival
	Firecracker Festival
	Firecracker-Grabbing Festival
百家宴	Feast Entertaining a Hundred Families
	Banquet for Hundreds
背带	Strap
	Babycarrier
	Baby-carrying Bag
糍粑	Ciba cake
	Glutinous rice cake
风雨桥	Fengyu Bridge
	Wind-and-Rain Bridge
花婆	Huapo
	Flower God
干栏民居	Stilt House
	Pile-dwelling House
	House on Stilts
三月三	March 3rd Festival
	Sanyuesan Festival
	Double Third Festival
侗族花炮节	Dong Nationality Fireworks Festival
	Dong Ethnic Group's Firecracker Festival
	Firecracker-Grabbing Festival of Dong Ethnic Group

而在经济领域，乱译的现象也不少见。例如，在第12届中国—东盟博览会中，我们发现许多参展小企业的英文名翻译存在许多不规范的现象。

（一）滥用拼音

在企业名字中使用一些拼音是可行的，但过多的拼音会使公司名字拖沓冗长，难以理解。如：Shen Zhen Yu Fu Zhi Long Iot Technology Co., Ltd，第一眼看过去感觉就是满眼的拼音，中国人要看懂都非常吃力，换上不懂拼音的英文读者，读出来更是费劲。这个公司的中文名是"深圳宇富智龙物联网科技有限公司"，其中物联网的英文为"Internet of Things"，简称IOT。深圳为城市名，应该拼写成一个词，"宇富智龙"为字号，也可拼为一个词。因此名字可简化成"Shenzhen Yufuzhilong IOT Technology Co., Ltd"。北京国电智深控制技术有限公司被翻译成"Beijing GuoDianZhiShen Control Technology Co., Ltd"，这个名字也因拼音多而显得冗长，我们可以把"国电"翻成China Power"，全名可翻为"China Power Zhishen Control Technology Co., Ltd，Beijing"。

（二）信息错漏

公司名的结构通常是"行政划分+字号+行业类别+组织形式"，随意省缺会造成信息的不完整，深圳市华讯方舟科技有限公司翻译成"China Communication Technology Co., Ltd"，其中缺失了行业划分和公司字号；惠州市雷士光电科技有限公司翻译成"NVC Light Technology Corporation"，其中的行政划分也被随意省略掉了。Management Committee of Wanggao Industrial Estate, Hezhou, Guangxi（广西贺州旺高工业区）这个英文名则增添了"Management Committee"这个原文中没有的信息。

（三）结构混乱

公司名的结构通常是"行政划分+字号+行业类别+组织形式"，因此，在翻译前弄清公司名字中哪些部分是行政划分，哪些部分属于字号非常重要。如果这个简单的问题没弄清楚，翻译出来的名字就会错得离谱。如"深圳市和丰互联电子科技有限公司"被翻译成"Shen Zhen City AND FENG Electronic Technology Co., Ltd"，广西伟正新材料有限公司被翻译成"Guangxi Wei Is the New Material Co., Ltd"。

以上仅仅列举了民俗文化词和企业名称翻译作为例子，但其他领域专有名词的翻译也同样存在类似的问题。专有名词的不规范，影响了译文的质量，造成读者认知上的混乱，也影响了广西的对外宣传。专有名词翻译的标准化是确保文化对外宣传成功的重要因素，是外宣翻译人员努力的目标。专有名词的统一化和规范化是地方外宣翻译中亟须解决的问题。

三、宣传文本中跨文化意识的缺失

莫红利和金美兰（2009）提出，在旅游宣传文本的翻译中，有四种意识是译者必须重视的，包括"读者意识、文本意识、跨语篇意识和跨文化意识"。宣传文本中的低级错误稍加注意即可避免，但由于跨文化意识缺失而造成的译文硬伤，而往往被忽视。英汉两种语言属于不同的语言结构体系，在文化、思维模式和修辞习惯上存在着极大的差异，英汉宣传文本在内容、语言表现及行文结构上也有所区别。这一点，如译者缺乏对两种文化中不同审美和修辞习惯的了解，在翻译过程中缺乏跨文化交际的意思，往往造成译文文本生搬硬套，而无法达到有效交际的目的。

中文宣传文本喜欢引经据典，高频使用描述性套话，辞藻华丽，讲究工整对仗，多用排比结构，整体更具渲染性和号召力。句子各成分之间的逻辑关系靠上下文和事理顺序来显示。

而英文宣传文本整体语气正式而平和，使用明显的形式标记来表现逻辑关系，在行文上具有形式化和逻辑严谨的特点。让我们来看看以下例句。

例1：寒山峰绿茶千年来享有"醒目茶""耳灵茶"美称。其茶依峻峨之高山而植，托天擎之雾露为养。培以富硒之天然沃土，育就了色翠味香、回甘无限的天然云雾茶。吟寒山峰绿茶能消脂、降三高、抗辐射、增免疫、防癌、化瘀、通心脑畅血脉，益寿年。绿茶之王？寒山峰也。

译文：Hanshan mount green tea famous as refresh tea, quick eared tea for a thousand of years. The green tea planted in a cloud and mist's high mountain, grow with the rich natural selenium fertile soil. And the natural green tea taste sweet. Often drink green tea has good effect on disappear fat, lowering blood pressure, Glu, hyperlipidemia, radiation resisting and immune increasing, cancer prevention, blood stasis removing, cardio-cerebral, life prolonging.

中文原文使用了大量对称工整的语句来描述茶叶，如"依峻峨之高山而植，托天擎之雾露为养"和"色翠味香，回甘无限"，同时，给茶叶赋予了一堆的保健功效"消脂、降三高、抗辐射、增免疫、防癌、化瘀、通心脑畅血脉，益寿年"，作为中文的茶叶宣传，本无可厚非，但作为英文宣传文本，此处的信息有夸大茶叶功效之嫌。茶叶变成了无所不能的"神药"，这样的修辞偏好，如原样翻译过去，翻译效果并不佳。原翻译不仅错漏百出，多处语法错误，同时也忽略了中英文修辞偏好的不同，无法有效传达信息和达到使用英文有效宣传推广茶叶的功能。

例2：王城景区由明靖江王城和独秀峰组成。王城为全国重点文物保护单位。位于桂林市中心，著名的独秀峰就屹立在王城的正中位置。元顺帝妥懽帖睦尔继位前曾在独秀峰前的大圆寺修行。朱元璋称帝封藩时，将其侄孙朱守谦封藩于桂林，称靖江王。王城就是靖江王的王府。

译文："Solitary Beauty Peak & Prince's City Scenic Area consists of Jingjiang Prince City and the Solitary Beauty Peak, which is the national key cultural relics protection unit. It is located in the center of Guilin city and the Solitary Beauty Peak is in the middle of scenic area. An emperor in Yuan Dynasty was living under the peak and the Emperor Zhu Yuanzhang of Ming Dynasty granted his grandson Zhu Shouqian as a feudal vassal under the name of 'Jingjiang' and placed his mansions here. Then this area became the Jingjiang Prince City."

在这句话中，译员将"靖江王城"翻译为"The Prince City"，这将导致文化上的误解，Prince 是王子的意思，"Prince's City"则表示"王子居住的宫殿"。但是中国历史上的"藩王"不一定是皇帝的儿子，战场上的英雄也可以被授予"藩王"的头衔。而"City"是城市的意思。因此，这个翻译带有文化上的误导。

我们再来看看另外一个译文的例子：

例3：独秀峰素有"南天一柱"的美誉，史称桂林第一峰，是靖江王府后花园里的天然靠山。山峰突兀而起，形如刀削斧砍，周围众山环绕，孤峰傲立，有如帝王之尊。登山306级可达峰顶，是鸟瞰桂林全景的最佳观景台。

译文：The solitary peak, which backs up the prince city, is praised as "Southern Sky Pillar" and regarded as the No.1 peak in Guilin.

此段中文文字来自桂林名胜独秀峰的景点介绍，中文中称独秀峰为"靖江王府后花园里的天然靠山"，此句涉及中国的风水理念，"山峰突兀而起，形如刀削斧砍，周围众山环绕，孤峰傲立，有如帝王之尊"也涉及了文化理念，在中国的封建王朝中，帝王具有至高无上的地位，"高处不胜寒"，往往无法拥有真正的新朋好友，以至于成为"孤家寡人"。因此，中文文本把独秀峰比喻成了古代的帝王，来形容它山形的"突兀而起"。这种文化信息在翻译中很难处理，译者在英翻中的过程中做了简化，但简化得有些过度了，仅仅保留了中文景点介绍中的第一句，其他信息统统丢失。

广西对外宣传文本的来源多为本地资讯，部分信息带有浓厚的民族特色。译者必须应该提高自身的理解力和表达力，具备广博的背景文化知识，对源语言与目的语言的文化差异和修辞偏好有所了解，才能够跨越语言和文化障碍，避免跨文化交际上的误解和歪曲，从而使译文获得良好的宣传功能。

第二节 平行文本语料库的建设与应用

由于文化的多元性，广西外宣文本的英译尤其复杂。广西对外宣传资料的英译具有大量少数民族文化的特有词汇，在汉语和英语中都无对等词语，如红喜、白喜、哭嫁等。无少数民族文化知识背景的译者手中若无可参考的文本，无法在翻译中处理相关词汇，即使翻译出来，由于译文版本的不统一，也会混淆读者的认知。译者水平的参差不齐，也造成译者对外宣材料的翻译望而生畏，即使翻译，译文翻译的质量也不高，无法达到良好的宣传效果。因此，我们应该建立英汉平行语料库，给广西的外宣译者提供一个可靠的翻译参考工具。借助语料库完成的译文，在专业术语的统一性和准确性方面比仅仅使用词典等传统的参考资源效率更高，译文质量也更好（Bowker，1998）。因此，有不少学者极力主张把能否有效地使用语料库以及语料库分析工具软件看成衡量当代翻译能力和翻译实际水平的重要标准之一，而且应把学会创建适用不同翻译目的的各类语料库并能熟练使用语料库解决翻译中的实际问题作为翻译课程设置中必不可少的部分（杨晓军，2007：52）。

平行语料库由大量的平行文本（parallel text）组成，通常是两种或多种语言放在一起，原文和译文对齐放置。双语平行语料库中主要分为两种类型，翻译语料库（translation corpus）和对比语料库（comparable corpus）。翻译语料库广泛由一种源语言文本及其他语言的翻译文本构成，广泛应用于机器翻译或机辅翻译，译者可以在翻译过程中对句子进行拆分、合并、删除或重新排列。翻译语料库也可以借助大量的目标语言文本，通过电脑程序自动生成翻译文本。而对比语料库所收录的文本都是同种题材和内容，但不是互相翻译的关系，对比语料库更多地运用于语言学的对比研究，通常会运用到注释，例如，对广告语篇或演讲语篇的内容进行注释或是词性标注。广西外宣平行语料库应该同时包括翻译平行语料库和对比平行语料库这两种类型。

广西外宣平行语料库可以为译者提供可靠的参考系统，提高其译品的质量。中英双语平行语料库是由中文源语文本及其具有词、句或段级平行对应关系的英文文本组成，可以为译者提供词、短语或语句的对译样例。译者在遇到翻译困难的时候，可通过语料库查询相关的内容辅助翻译，能有效提高翻译的速度和翻译的质量。相对于传统的翻译参考工具来说，平行语料库检索功能强大，语料更新快、针对性强，而且可供译者在不同语境下同时使用，能对英汉双语搭配、英汉对译等进行全面搜查，因而具备更全面的应用价值。

广西外宣语料库的建设,包括了语料库设计、中英双语语料的选取、语料的收集整理、语料的标注和检索等步骤。广西外宣语料库的设计,根据外宣材料的特点分为政治、经济和民俗文化三个子库,每个子库又分为词库、句库和语篇库。

广西外宣中英语料搜集选取包括收集中国—东盟博览会的产品手册、政府官网和旅游景点的对外宣传资料,收集有代表性且质量高的英汉语篇,将选取材料保存为电子文本文档格式。语料库使用XML标记语言,将中英文语料配对放在一起,进行标注和人工的文本对齐。语料库的检索软件可使用Concordance或Antcon,这些软件既能够分析和处理文本,方便地查看关键字的具体语境,也可以生成词表、词频表、词语搭配,进行各种数据统计。随着广西外宣中英文语料库的规模不断扩大,其使用价值会不断扩大,语料库还可以把少数民族语言和使用较多的日语、德语等也包括进来,为更多的译者提供便利,为不断提高广西外宣翻译的质量提供保障。

第三节　平行文本的修辞对比对外宣翻译的启示

何为外宣翻译?换句话说,应如何定义外宣翻译?最直观的理解是中国对外宣传材料的翻译。在全球化的背景下,中国需要走向世界,世界需要了解中国,翻译是向其他国家介绍和传播中国的桥梁。外宣的途径包括互联网、传统媒体、各类会议,而外宣的对象主要是境外读者。外宣质量的好坏直接影响到一个国家或一个地区的形象,从而影响到该地区获得投资的机会。

在外宣翻译的过程中,平行文本的应用可让译者详细学习原语言文本的修辞偏好,给译者提供语言支撑和参考,帮助译者产出功能等效的翻译。平行文本的比较可验证不同语言如何表达相同的事实材料。在表达原始文本的内容时,翻译要根据目标语言(即原始英文文本)的规范来表达,以使翻译的组织策略符合读者对目标语言的愿景,并达到与原文预期的交际目的相似的目的。英汉宣传平行文本的比较给广西外宣研究带来了以下启示。

在广西外宣翻译中,译者必须具备"受众意识"。从翻译的角度来看,"受众意识"指的是译者在翻译和翻译过程中的自我意识,并以读者(听众)身份来关注和理解自己的翻译活动。无论在翻译的哪个阶段,翻译的"受众"都是值得关注的重要因素。实际上,"受众"应该成为翻译行为的焦点。因为翻译的目的是影响受众,而这一目的的实现,有赖于"受众"对翻译的认可。因此,外宣翻译必须考虑受众的需求、兴趣、信念、价值、价值、阅读和视听习惯,对翻译内容和修辞加以选择,使得译文具备更强的文化适应性。中文宣传材料常出现的套话和官话,与国外观众习惯于简介具体的话语习惯大不相同,如果我们不进行相应的改动,就会影响译文的传播效果。平行文本比较和分析有助于最大限度地提高译文与英语的融合程度,满足目标受众的阅读期望,阅读习惯和文化需求。通过平行文本的比较和分析,译者可调整文本顺序,使得语篇更符合目标读者的阅读习惯;可借鉴平行文本中的术语来提高译文表达的规范性;还可以借鉴平行文本的文化规范来对不合适对外宣传的文本内容进行删减。因此,平行文本的比较对外宣翻译有着重要的指导作用。

在广西外宣翻译中,译者必须具备跨语篇意识和跨文化意识。平行文本的修辞对比结果表明,英汉两种语言的修辞习惯相差甚远,因此,在外宣翻译中,译者必须把如何实现跨语篇和跨文化交际的因素考虑在内。面对东盟国家的外宣翻译,必须把东盟国家的文化背景考虑在内。也就是说,在面对东盟国家的广西外宣翻译中,译者应考虑东盟各国的文化背景,如果不了解相关国家的政治、经济和文化特点,译文会因为跨文化交流上的障碍,无法达到应有的交际功能。

由于历史原因,东盟国家很多都曾经是殖民地,英语在东盟国家占有极其重要的地位,在东盟十国中,新加坡、菲律宾、马来西亚和文莱都把英语作为官方语言使用,其他国家的英文教育普及率也极高。但是东盟国家的英文与英美国家的英语并不完全相同,经过近百年来与当地语言文化的接触和融合,东盟英语的地域特征显著。中国—东盟商务区的规划与建设,使广西获得了极其珍贵的发展机遇。在这一背景下，如何宣传广西，扩大广西在东盟地区的国际影响力，是广西的外宣翻译必须考虑的因素。

第四节　外宣翻译策略的使用

外宣翻译要追求良好的翻译效果，译者就必须以目标语与目标语受众为重，在翻译的过程中考量读者的阅读习惯与修辞偏好。张健教授认为，译者应该在翻译中善于"变通"，即"译者必须有意识地根据译文读者的特殊要求，采用编译、改写等'变通'手法，改变源语文本的内容和结构，乃至风格，以方便目的语读者接受，使目的语文本更通顺、更清楚、更直接，更好地实现交际目的。"（张健，2013：20）简单地说，就是在翻译的过程中，由于源语言与目标语言的语用修辞和政治文化差异，译者应该利用适当的增补、删减和转换等翻译策略对宣传文本中的信息进行适当的加工，以实现对外宣传的预期效果。

一、增译法

"增译法"指的是在目标语中增加一些必要的语言单位，以达到衔接语义或填补语义空缺的功效，使得译文合乎目的语的习惯表达，达到和原文相似修辞效果的翻译策略。外宣翻译中的"增译法"常常用于源文文本中的文化信息在目的语中有所缺失的语境。译者需要采用某种补偿手段，明示原文词汇的文化内涵或提供理解原文所必需的背景信息（张健，2013）。增译不是随意地增加语言单位，而是为了使译文更加通顺达意，增加原文中虽无其形但有其意的一些语言单位。所增补的语言单位必须是不可或缺的，同时，增译必须尽量保持最小的文本篇幅，切不可增加过多而把翻译变成了阐释。

在广西的对外宣传文本中，难免会出现一些地方性民族、文化特色的词汇，例如民俗文化词或地方特色词汇。这些词汇对于缺乏背景文化知识的英文读者来说是难以理解的。因此，在将这些地方文化负载词翻译成英文时，应使用增译补充的方法，来填补文化差异所致的认知空白，达到良好的宣传效果。例如：

例1：打籽绣是古老的制绣基本针法之一。俗称"结子绣""环籽绣"，民间叫"打疙瘩"。打籽绣的方法是用丝线缠针缠绕圈形成颗粒状，绣一针成一籽，构成点状纹样，多用于表现花蕊、眼睛等，装饰性很强，具有画龙点睛的效果。

译文：Daio (mode) stitch, one of the earliest stiches in embroidery, is also known as Jiezi stitch, Huanzi stitch and Dageda (making node). The method is to wind silk thread on needles to make nodes and form a dotted pattern for decorating stamen or eyes, and can produce an impressive effect.

此例子表述的少数民族的刺绣方法，即使是中国人，对此了解也不多，单纯把刺绣的方法翻译成拼音，信息量是不足的，因此，"making node"被加注在拼音之后，以帮助读者理解原文的意思。

例2：1968年建港，1993年建市，下辖港口区、防城区、上思县、东兴市，总面积6222平方公里，总人口约100万人，有汉、壮、瑶、京等21个民族，是京族的唯一聚居地、北部湾海洋文化的重要发祥地之一。

译文：The port was constructed in 1968, and the year 1993 witnessed the establishment of the Fangchenggang City. With Gangkou District, Fangcheng District, Shangsi County and Dongxing City under its jurisdiction, Fangchenggang has a total population of about 1 million, including 21 ethnic groups such as Han, Zhuang, Yao and Jing, covering an area of 6,222 square kilometers. It is the only settlement of the Jing people—the mainstay in Vietnam and accounting for 80% of Vietnam population—and one of the important birthplaces of the marine culture of Beibu Gulf.

在翻译这段话时，译者采取增译补充，对原文中一带而过的京族进行了补充说明，增加了关于京族的背景知识。考虑到目标语读者头脑中对京族可能没有任何概念，可能完全不了解，京族也称为越族，北部湾是京族在中国的唯一聚居地，增加了对京族的解释说明。京族是越南的主体民族，占到了越南总人口的80%。这样能使读者对北部湾民族人口构成有更好的了解，更深刻的认识，达到北部湾外宣文章有效传播的目的。

例3：它拥有世界唯一的国家级金花茶自然保护区，拥有多种国家重点保护动植物，森林面积近500万亩，森林覆盖率98%以上，生长着中国南方最好的热带雨林，有1890多种植物种类，空气负氧离子含量每立方厘米高达8.9万个，享有"华南第一天然氧吧""中国氧都"的美誉，是发展生态农业、生态旅游、健康养生的不可多得之地。

译文：It boasts the only National Nature Reserve for Golden Camellia in the world, various kinds of wildlife and plant under state protection, and the best-preserved tropical rain forest in south China with more than 1,890 plant species, an area of about 5 million mu（333 thousand hectares）and a forest coverage of over 98%. It enjoys the reputation of "The Best Natural Oxygen Bar in South China", and "Capital of Oxygen in China", since the content of negative oxygen ions in the air is as high as 89,000 per cubic centimeter here. All these make Fangchenggang city a rare place for developing eco-agriculture, eco-tourism, and health preservation.

在这段话的翻译中，译者增加了对"5 million mu"的注释。"亩"是中国市制土地面积单位，源于中国夏、商、周的井田制度所实施的井田模型，面积单位"亩"没有国际通用符号，英文读者无法从中获得相应的面积信息，因此，译者用国际通用的面积单位"公顷"进行了换算，方便读者了解金花茶自然保护区有多大。

二、删减法

"删减法"指的是从受众角度出发，对译文进行一些不必要信息的删减，减轻受众信息阅读负担的翻译方法。由于英汉两种语言在词汇、语法和文化修辞上的差异，一些在汉语中很自然的表达翻译成英文后，会显得内容重复、文字累赘，因此，译者需要在不破坏原文精神的前提下，省去不必要的信息及其成分，使译文更加简洁和通顺。

例4：每年的金秋，五洲四海的宾朋乘着歌声的翅膀款款而来，与中国南方美丽的城市——绿城南宁相约一年一度的世界民歌盛会，汇聚一起同台献技、倾心交流，民族的、现代的、世界的文化之流在这里汇集、交融，共同演绎出一首世界欢歌。

译文：Folk singers from outside Guangxi as well as from other countries are invited to the Folk Song Arts Festival. Singers show their own folk songs as well as get inspiration from others. They perform on the same stage, exchange views and skills, and share their merry songs that flow with ethnic, modern, and global cultures.

例4是关于南宁国际民歌节的介绍。在中文文本中使用了浓厚而华丽的修辞手段，"五洲四海的宾朋"在翻译的过程中被简化成"Folk singers from outside Guangxi"，来自外地的宾客，而"乘着歌声的翅膀款款而来，与中国南方美丽的城市——绿城南宁相约一年一度的世界民歌盛会"省去了所有的描绘性修辞，只留下了"来"的信息，翻译成"are invited to the Folk Song Arts Festival"。中文具有浓重的汉语修辞特征，文体重修辞，文字华丽而煽情，非常符合中国读者的审美习惯。但对于英语受众而言，过度的描述性修辞会使得文章过于花哨和浮夸，而且会让读者抓不到文章的主要信息。因此，在翻译的过程中需要进行"删减"。

例5：防城港市依山傍海，拥有靓丽的颜值和良好的空气，这里海湾多，半岛多，绿树多，三岛三湾环绕港城，海湾、江湖、岛屿、丘陵、田园、海上红树林等元素浑然天成，城市各项建筑布局有序，错落有致。

译文：Adjacent to mountain and sea, Fangchenggang city has many bays, peninsulas, and trees, which results in its remarkable scenery and good air quality. Buildings are set up in its well-planned layout, surrounded by three islands and three bays, and decorated with natural bays, rivers, lakes, islands, hills, bucolic sites, and mangroves.

在例5中，"城市各项建筑布局有序，错落有致"的信息有所重叠，而且

"错落有致"是中国独特的东方审美风格，这个信息即使翻译成英文，也无法让英文读者获得相应的美感。因此，在不影响整句话理解的基础上，作者把信息简化成了"well-planned layout"。

例6：八桂之南、边海之交、邕江之畔、绿城之中。广西大学坐落于风景如画的广西首府南宁，是广西办学历史最悠久、规模最大的综合性大学，是广西唯一的国家"211工程"建设学校，世界一流学科建设高校，教育部和广西壮族自治区人民政府"部区合建"高校。

译文：Guangxi University, established in 1928, is a regional comprehensive university with the longest history and largest scale. Being the only National 211-Project Key Construction University in Guangxi and the co-administrative university by both the national Ministry of Education and Guangxi Zhuang Autonomous Region, it has also been selected as a construction university within "First-class Discipline Project" and "National Plan to Promote the Comprehensive Strength of Midwest Colleges and Universities".

在例6中的第一句"八桂之南、边海之交、邕江之畔、绿城之中"点明了广西大学的地理位置，其中地域性的词汇"八桂""边海""邕江""绿城"可以为中文读者所理解，但对于缺乏广西地域文化背景的英文读者来说，这些信息毫无意义，广西大学的具体方位也不是读者关心的信息。因此，译者选择了将此句省略，不在英文译文中呈现，这就是外宣翻译中"删减法"使用的一个具体例子。

三、调整法

翻译中"调整法"指的是改变源语文本的内容和结构乃至风格，有效地转换话语形式，使得目的语文本更通顺、更清楚、更直接、更好地实现交际目的的翻译方法。外宣翻译本质上是一种跨文化交际活动，交际的成功与否取决于是否"方便目的语读者接受"（张健，2013：20）。简单地说，外宣译文要赢得读者，就得让英文读者喜欢读、愿意读、这样才能实现对信息的传播。如果译者不顾英汉两种语言行文习惯的不同，一味地机械翻译，就会译出不通顺流畅、翻译腔浓厚的文本。

例7：歌圩日，小伙子和姑娘们都穿节日盛装，男携礼物，女揣绣球，成群结队前往。<u>有的抬着刘三姐神像绕行歌圩一周，才开始对歌。有的则由姑娘们搭起五彩绣棚</u>，待小伙子到来，边对歌、边审度对方人品、才华。

译文：On the day of song fair, the young men and young women dress in festive costumes. Young men bring gifts while the females bring embroidery balls to come to the song fair in flocks. Then they will judge the young men from the side of character and talents while singing songs.

此句子描述了青年男女在歌圩中所做的事情，中文画线句子"有的抬着刘三姐神像绕行歌圩一周，才开始对歌。有的则由姑娘们搭起五彩绣棚"，在这个句子中并没有详细说明小伙子做什么而姑娘做了什么，但依据逻辑，应该是男子从事更重的体力活，因此，英文译文被调整为"Young men fetch the statue of Liu Sanjie to walk around for a time before they start to sing songs. Young women set up colorful embroidered sheds and wait for young men' comings."更清晰地展示信息的逻辑。

例8：总面积378平方公里，总人口近17万人。港口区三面环海，南濒北部湾，东邻粤港澳，西与越南隔海相望，是中国内地进出东盟各国最重要的中转基地和大西南最便捷的出海通道；是国家批准实施的《广西北部湾经济区发展规划》中重点建设的临海临港重要工业区；港口区拥有绵延300多公里的原生态海岸线，是旅游休闲的黄金地带。

译文：The Gangkou District is a prime area for tourism and entertainment, which has a total area of 378 square kilometers, a primary coastline of over 300 kilometers and a total population of 170,000. Surrounded by sea on three sides, with the Beibu Gulf in the south, Guangdong, Hong Kong and Macao in the East, and Uietnam across the sea to the west, playing as not only the most important gateway for China's inland area to enter ASEAN, but the most convenient sea passage in southwest China. It is an industrial zone adjacent to the sea and port and high on the agenda of Guangxi Beibu Gulf Economic Zone Development Scheme issued by the state.

中文的宣传文本往往"形散神不散",句子之间的连接不需要功能词,句子间靠共同的主题黏合在一起,最重要的信息往往出现在段落的尾部。英语语法比较严谨,重视句子之间形式上的配合,各个句子、段落通常用一些功能词和一些特定的短语进行连接,句子之间必须有严谨的逻辑关系,重要信息往往在段落开头就明确提出。在例7中,中文段落中最重要的信息为港口区是"旅游休闲的黄金地带"。因此,在把该段文字翻译成英文的时候,译者把最后一句的信息与第一句进行了合并,使得英文段落的信息重点更突出,逻辑更清楚。

另外,由于语言使用上的习惯,广西外宣材料的中文版本会大量使用一些中国特色词汇,例如在《广西防城港市投资指南》中就出现了"全国双拥模范城""中国白鹭之乡""中国金花茶之乡""中国长寿之乡""中国十大最关爱民生城市""中国科学发展城镇化质量示范城市"等具有中国特色的荣誉称号来形容防城港的发展状况。这些词汇在汉语语境下使用十分自然,也很容易为中文读者所理解,但如果在英文版本中不加变通地直译过去,很容易让英语受众难以理解,甚至造成误解,不利于达成良好的外宣效果。

第五节 提高广西外宣翻译质量的对策

一、从政府层面加强外宣翻译的管理

外宣翻译有其自身独特风格,较之其他类型的文本翻译,特点迥然不同,原因在于外宣翻译是政府对外宣传的工具,官方意志充斥其中,有塑造良好的国家形象、地方形象之重要作用,以达到促进对外经济文化交流的目的。但目前的翻译多为个体操作,整体外宣材料缺乏规划,缺少统一的翻译标准和质量评估体系。因此,政府应该在外宣翻译中发挥主导作用,主动牵

头，整合监管机构、人才支持和政策服务等各方面资源，提供地方性外宣翻译的服务平台和制度保障。一方面，制度保障极其重要，急需健全来保障外宣翻译的发展，更重要的是出台符合实际需求有科学依据的评判标准，以规范外宣翻译，使之业务流程标准化和规范化，推动和保障外宣翻译工作的良性发展。外宣翻译质量的管理亦可吸收国外有用的经验，洋为中用，助力广西外宣翻译走上新台阶。

欧盟便是很好的一个例子，加盟国众多，其官方语言多达20多种，重要的文件需进行多语种翻译，日常翻译工作量非常大。鉴于此，欧盟成立了欧盟翻译总部，细分为6大部分来处理繁杂的翻译工作，包括资源部、信息技术和开发部、翻译和多语言工具分析部、术语和语言支持服务部、自由职业译员部和培训部六大部门。这六大部门的设立可谓面面俱全，各司其职。资源部统筹译员的招聘和培训。人才为翻译的第一要务，根据翻译行业的特殊性，资源部需要招聘的翻译人员，既要有过硬的翻译技能，也要具备过硬的心理素质。信息技术和开发部负责翻译管理平台、翻译软件开发及计算机信息服务；翻译和多语言工具分析部主要负责翻译工具和软件；术语和语言支持服务部是站在最前沿的部门，当前不断涌现出新的学科和专业术语，将其进行准确翻译，使这些术语的表里统一，是术语和语言支持服务部的主要工作内容；自由职业译员部，顾名思义，总部翻译量太大，有时还需要借助市场上的职业翻译人员，因此该部负责招聘和校审场外译者，而培训部主管译员的培训，目的在于不断提升议员专业能力和翻译水平。欧盟翻译总部的6大部门，相辅相成，交相辉映，使语言问题不再成为欧盟的障碍。如此精妙的管理模式应当为广西政府所用，组织相应的翻译管理部门，促进本地外宣翻译工作的持续发展和不断进步。

除此之外，广西政府外宣主管部门还可以借助各个部门的力量，进行宏观资源整合，形成多方参与，分工协作的大外宣格局。例如，政府的文化部门可为广西的外宣翻译提供整体性指导，肩负外宣规划的职责；外宣文本的编写和翻译，考虑到内外有别和意识形态上的区别，应由广西翻译协会和各高校翻译研究所组织专业译员负责；而外宣文本的校对工作，可聘请外籍专业人员进行译文的校对和润色。通过多层质量监控，不但可以确保最终的外宣材料符合目标语读者的要求，还有助于形成广西外宣翻译的行业监管体系，从整体上提高广西壮族自治区对外宣传翻译的整体水平。

二、从教育层面加强外宣翻译人才的培养

　　新时代创新型外宣翻译，人才极为重要。合格的外宣翻译人才，要具备扎实的汉外语言能力，深厚的跨文化交际能力，同时良好的本国文化素养，牢靠的专业知识和专业相关技术缺一不可。这样的人才不是凭空出现的，而是需要大力培养的。十年树木，百年树人，广西各大高校应当肩负其对翻译人才培养的重任，在培养创新型翻译人才的过程中，以大力改革传统的外语教育模式为重点，科学规划课程，完善相关课程，提升课程教学质量，使课程配置与社会实际挂钩，必须保障课程设置与人才发展步调一致，根据实际情况，将广西少数民族文化和东盟十国文化的课程纳入教学体系，加强翻译实务课程的训练，完善学生知识、能力和综合素质结构。翻译课程内容应涉及与广西区域经济发展的各个领域，力求与市场需求接轨。

　　高校应对外承接外宣翻译项目，利用翻译实践开展翻译教学，鼓励学生从实践中来到实践中去，把外宣翻译技巧运用到实践，从而稳步提升外宣翻译的能力。广西各大高校不应与社会脱节，应该加强政府外宣部门和外企的合作，与社会中的相关部门和单位建立良好的合作关系，在地方政府的支持下，使学生有更多机会参加地方文化类外事活动或外宣工作中。例如，每年的中国—东盟博览会，广西大学外国语学院都派出大量的本科生和研究生志愿者，让学生参与到博览会的翻译、接待、联络等工作中。同时，通过加强与外企或者是专业翻译公司的合作，建立更多翻译实习实训基地，确保外宣翻译人才的培养符合市场的需求。

　　同时，高校还应搭建学生参与国际交流与学习的平台，积极采取措施鼓励学生参与国际交流与学习。广西大学外国语学院与泰国、越南等国家的高校建立了联系，让专业学生有更多途径出国交流学习，体验东盟国家和地区的风土人情，学习东盟国家的文化，拓宽国际视野。

三、从译者层面提高跨文化交际的意识

翻译是对源文化在跨文化交际时的二次解读。在中译英的过程中，译者要重视中英文化差异，不能忽视其所带来的各种冲突，既有显性冲突，又有隐性冲突。对于翻译文本，其内容要进行筛选，在读者能接受其内容的基础上，获得读者的喜爱。就语言而言，译者应该考虑英文读者所关心和感兴趣的内容，以信息的实用性来吸引读者。我们应知道，汉语写作风格与英语写作风格迥异，汉语宣传文本重修辞、喜工整；而英语宣传文本不重修辞，重简洁平实，不喜工整，而喜结构严谨，在翻译中，将两种语言风格进行巧妙转换，其重要性不言而喻；纵观汉英文章风格不难发现，汉语语篇常用归纳式结构，而英语语篇常用演绎式结构，因此在翻译中，译者需要将中式语篇结构调整为地地道道的英式行文结构，这样受众读起来才不会有违和感，这样的翻译才能有效传递我们想要传递的内核和价值，达到目标效果。

汉宣文本所蕴含的文化信息，译者需注重语言的有效传递。译者应从英文读者的文化背景出发，权衡译文的交际目的与文化传递间的关系，对文化背景信息进行适当增译或删减，增强其在跨文化交际中的效用。

四、加强广西外宣翻译平行语料库的建设

当前广西外宣文本的翻译存有大量问题，如过渡翻译、翻译水平不高和专业术语不统一等。要解决这些问题，就必须推进语料库相关研究。鉴于此，应在广西外宣翻译的实践中，下苦功夫建设和完善平行文本语料库，完美应用该语料库，使之辅助广西外宣翻译，提升广西外宣翻译的准确性。

相比传统的双语词典等翻译工具书，语料库检索便捷，材料能以最快的速度更新，语料鲜活，对于比较同一语言文本在不同语境中的译文有着天然优势，从而加快译者翻译速度，提升译者翻译质量，极大助力翻译活动。语料库把不同语言层面的相似点与差异显现出来，使译者能够洞悉这些特点，

翻译中把握规律，使外宣翻译达到规范化和质量化。广西外宣平行文本语料库的建设，对于提升广西壮族自治区的对外形象，推动区域经济发展，促进对外交流将发挥积极的助力作用。

五、加强外宣网站的建设

我们处在地球村的时代，全球各国的联系空前紧密，为了让对外宣传工作更加有效，建立带有中国特色的、高水平、高规格的对外宣传网站大有必要。目前，广西地方的对外宣传网站的主力是南宁市政府门户网站和中国—东盟博览会官网。南宁市政府门户网站外文版由政府主办，运营至今已有17个年头，有英、越、泰三大外文版本。获得过国内多项殊荣，如在2011年"第五届中国政府网站国际化程度测评结果发布暨智慧城市高峰论坛"，该网站获得69.4分，摘得国际化程度"领先奖"。

图5-1 南宁市政府门户网英文网站

中国—东盟博览会作为中国与东盟最盛大的经贸交流活动，以"促进中国自由贸易区的建设，分享，合作发展机遇"为主要目标，每年在南宁举办，是中国与东盟经贸交流的重要桥梁。在这样的大背景下，中国—东盟博览会官网由此建立，版面板块内容丰富，涵盖博览会简介、新闻、投资等各个方面，有英、越、印尼、泰四大外文版，有力地传播了国际区域性信息。

图5-2　中国—东盟博览会英文官网

但是，广西英文网站的建设绝非白璧无瑕，目前存在大量问题需要解决，如页面样式不够新颖、技术未能与当前最前沿的水平接轨、缺乏精密维护等，这显示出英文版网站未得到有关部门的高度重视，政府需认真解决存在的问题，做好网站外宣的规划。

参考文献

Crismore, A., & Farnsworth, R.（1989）. Mr. Darwin and his readers：Exploring interpersonal metadiscourse as a dimension of ethos[J]. *Rhetoric Review*, 8（1）, 91–112.

Crismore, A., Markkanen, R., & Steffensen, M. S.（1993）. Metadiscourse in persuasive writing：A study of texts written by American and Finnish university students[J]. *Written Communication*, 10（1）, 39–71.

Dafouz-Milne, E.（2003）. Metadiscourse revisited：A contrastive study of persuasive writing in professional discourse[J]. *Estudios Ingleses de la Universidad Complutense*, 11（1）, 29–57.

Dafouz-Milne, E.（2008）. The pragmatic role of textual and interpersonal metadiscourse markers in the construction and attainment of persuasion：A cross-linguistic study of newspaper discourse[J]. *Journal of Pragmatics*, 40（1）, 95–113.

Halliday, M. A.（1994）. *An Introduction to the Functional Grammar*[M]. London：Edward Arnold.

Hartmann, R. R. K.（1994）. *The Use of Parallel Text Corpora in the Generation of Translation Equivalents for Bilingual Lexicography*[M]. Martin, W. et al.（eds.）, 291–297.

Hickey, L.（2005）. Politeness in Spain：Thanks But No 'Thanks' In：Shickey, L., Stewart, M.（Eds.）, Politeness in Europe.

Hinds, J., Connor, U., & Kaplan, R. B.（1987）. Reader versus writer responsibility：A new typology [J]. *Landmark Essays on ESL Writing*, 63–74.

Holmes, J.（1982）. Expressing doubt and certainty in English [J]. *RELC Journal*, 13（2）, 9–28.

Holmes, J.（1988）. Doubt and certainty in ESL textbooks [J]. *Applied Linguistics*, 9（1）, 21–44.

House, J.（2007）. Covert translation, language contact and language change [J]. 中国翻译，28（03），17–25.

Hu, G., & Cao, F.（2011）. Hedging and boosting in abstracts of applied linguistics articles：A comparative study of English-and Chinese-medium journals [J]. *Journal of Pragmatics*, 43（11）, 2795–2809.

Hyland, K.（1998）. Persuasion and context：The pragmatics of academic metadiscourse [J]. *Journal of Pragmatics*, 30（4）, 437–455.

Hyland, K.（2004）. Disciplinary interactions：Metadiscourse in L2 postgraduate writing [J]. *Journal of Second Language Writing*, 13（2）, 133–151.

Kaplan, R. B.（1966). Cultural thought patterns in inter-cultural education [J]. *Language Learning*,16.

Kim, L. C., & Lim, J. M. H.（2013）. Metadiscourse in English and Chinese research article introductions [J]. *Discourse Studies*, 15（2）, 129–146.

Kong, K.（2006）. Linguistic resources as evaluators in english and chinese research articles [J]. *Multilingua-Journal of Cross-Cultural and Interlanguage Communication*, 25（1–2）, 183–216.

Kopple, W. J. V.（1985）. Some exploratory discourse on metadiscourse [J]. *College Composition and Communication*, 82–93.

Mauranen, A.（1993b）. Cultural Differences in Academic Rhetoric：A Textlinguistic Study. Peter Lang.

Mauranen, A.（1993a）. Contrastive esp rhetoric：metatext in Finnish-English economics texts [J]. *English for Specific Purposes*,12（1）, 3–22.

白蓝．（2010）.从功能翻译论视角谈张家界旅游资料英译 [J].中国科技翻译，23（03）：45–48.

蔡基刚．（2001）.英汉写作对比研究[M].上海：复旦大学出版社.

蔡基刚．（2003）.大学英语翻译教程[M].上海：上海外语教育出版社.

陈道德．（1996）.传播学教程[M].武汉：武汉测绘科技大学出版社.

陈宏薇．（1998）.汉英翻译基础[M].上海：上海外语教育出版社.

参考文献

陈小慰.（2011）.外宣翻译：从"新修辞"理论角度的思考[J].东方翻译，（05）：8-13.

陈小慰.（2012）.翻译教学中修辞意识的培养[J].外语教学理论与实践，3（03）：86-90.

陈小慰.（2014）.汉英商务画册语言的修辞对比与翻译[J].中国翻译，35（02）：97

陈小慰.（2014）.作为修辞话语的隐喻：汉英差异与翻译[J].福州大学学报（哲学社会科学版），28（02）：85-89.

仇贤根.（2010）.外宣翻译研究——从中国国家形象塑造与传播角度谈起[J].（Doctoral dissertation, 上海外国语大学）

邓志勇.（2001）.西方"新修辞学"及其主要特点[J].四川外语学院学报，17（01）：92-95.

董璐.（2008）.传播学核心理论与概念[M].北京：北京大学出版社.

方梦之.（2003）.我国的应用翻译：定位与学术研究——2003全国应用翻译研讨会侧记[J].中国翻译，（06）：47-49.

冯庆华.（2009）.英汉翻译基础教程[M].北京：高等教育出版社.

龚颖芬.（2015）.新修辞理论视域中的外宣翻译研究——以茂名市外宣翻译为例[J].广西师范学院学报：哲学社会科学版，（01）.

顾维勇.（2012）.实用文体翻译[M].北京：国防工业出版社.

衡孝军.（2011）.对外宣传翻译理论与实践：北京市外宣用语现状调查与规范[M].北京：世界知识出版社.

胡洁.建构视角下的外宣翻译研究[D].（Doctoral dissertation, 上海外国语大学）.

胡曙中.（1993）.英汉修辞比较研究[M].上海：上海外语教育出版社.

胡兴文，张健.（2013）.外宣翻译的名与实——张健教授访谈录[J].中国外语：中英文版，（03）：100-104.

黄建凤.（2010）.会展英语现场口译[M].武汉：武汉大学出版社.

黄友义.（2004）.坚持"外宣三贴近"原则，处理好外宣翻译中的难点问题[J].中国翻译，25（06）：27-28.

黄友义.（2005）.从翻译工作者的权利到外宣翻译——在首届全国公示

语翻译研讨会上的讲话[J]. 中国翻译, (06): 31-33.

贾文波.(2012). 应用翻译功能论[M]. 第2版. 北京: 中国对外翻译出版公司.

鞠玉梅.(2005). 肯尼斯·伯克新修辞学理论述评: 关于修辞的定义[J]. 四川外语学院学报, (01): 72-76.

鞠玉梅.(2011). 从伯克对修辞与人的定义看中西修辞学思想的差异[J]. 外语学刊, (05): 111-115.

李博.(2013). 基于语料文本的中英企业简介对比研究及英译启示[J]. 海外英语, (09): 129-130.

李定坤.(1994). 汉英辞格对比与翻译[M]. 武汉: 华中师范大学出版社.

李国南.(1992). 英、汉习用性比喻中的喻体比较与翻译[J]. 外国语, (05): 39-44.

李茜, 刘冰泉.(2011). 传播模式下的外宣翻译传播效果探析[J]. 黄河科技大学学报, (02): 83-86.

梁美清.(2018). 文化视域下民族特色旅游外宣文本翻译策略——以广西三江侗族为例[J]. 新西部, (03): 31-41.

林菲.(2015). 新修辞理论视域下的汉英旅游网站文本的修辞对比与翻译[J]. 西华大学学报(哲学社会科学版), 34(04): 81-86.

卢小军.(2012). 中美网站企业概况的文本对比与外宣英译[J]. 中国翻译, 33(01): 92-97.

卢小军.(2015). 国家形象与外宣翻译策略研究[M]. 北京: 外语教学与研究出版社.

吕俊, 侯向群.(2001). 研究生英汉翻译教程[M]. 上海: 上海外语教育出版社.

吕俊.(1997). 翻译学——传播学的一个特殊领域[J]. 外国语, (02): 40-45.

吕丽贤.(2016). 平行文本视域下的企业简介汉英翻译策略研究[J]. 常州工学院学报(社会科学版).

马慈祥.(2009). 民俗文化词语的可译性限度及其翻译策略[J]. 青海民

族研究，20（03）：109-111.

莫红利，金美兰.（2009）.目的论观照下的中文旅游宣传资料的翻译[J].安徽工业大学学报（社会科学版），（02）：66-69.

潘平亮.（2006）.翻译目的论及其文本意识的弱化倾向[J].上海翻译，（01）：13-17.

邵志洪.（2009）.汉英语言，修辞对比与翻译实践——TEM8（2009）汉译英试卷评析[J].外语教学理论与实践，（04）：65-70.

王丽丽.（2010）.目的论视角下的旅游网站翻译[J].齐齐哈尔大学学报：哲学社会科学版，（05）：118-120.

王银泉，钱叶萍，仇园园.（2007）.跨文化传播语境下的外宣电视新闻导语译写策略[J].中国翻译，28（02）：58-62.

王永泰.（2007）.旅游广告语及俗语外译的艺术美——从"桂林山水甲天下"英译文谈起[J].上海翻译，（01）：35-37.

王治奎.（2004）.大学英汉翻译教程[M].济南：山东大学出版社.

温科学.（2009）.中西比较修辞论：全球化视野下的思考[M].北京：中国社会科学出版社.

徐敏，胡艳红.（2008）.功能翻译理论视角下的企业外宣翻译[J].华中科技大学学报（社会科学版），22（03）：107-111.

杨惠莹.（2011）.外宣翻译的特点研究综述[J].赤峰学院学报（汉文哲学社会科学版），（02）：160-161.

杨琳，刘怀平.（2013）.广西边疆地区民俗文化翻译研究——民族身份认同与翻译策略互补[J].广西社会科学，（12）：46-50.

杨晓军.（2007）.基于语料库翻译研究和译者教育[J].外语与外语教学，（010）：51-55.

杨雪莲.（2010）.传播学视角下的外宣翻译[D].（Doctoral dissertation,上海外国语大学）.

余秋平.（2016）.国家形象视阈下外宣翻译策略刍议[J].西安外国语大学学报，24（01）：126-129.

张健.（2013）.全球化语境下的外宣翻译"变通"策略刍议[J].外国语言文学，30（01）：19-27，43.

张健.（2013）. 外宣翻译导论（应用翻译理论与教学文库）[M]. 北京：国防工业出版社.

朱丽田.（1993）. 英汉比喻修辞格的对比与翻译[J]. 沈阳师范大学学报（社会科学版），（04）：112-114.

附录1：英汉宣传语篇平行文本

大学简介的平行文本

广西大学简介

八桂之南、边海之交、邕江之畔、绿城之中。广西大学坐落于风景如画的广西首府南宁，是广西办学历史最悠久、规模最大的综合性大学，是广西唯一的国家"211工程"建设学校，世界一流学科建设高校，教育部和广西壮族自治区人民政府"部区合建"高校。

广西大学1928年成立于梧州，1939年成为国立广西大学。1950年与南宁师范学院合并，1951年与西江学院本科部合并。1952年，毛泽东主席亲笔题写广西大学校名。同年，广西大学农学院成为独立建制的广西农学院。1953年全国高校院系调整时，广西大学师生、学科专业以及设备和图书资料被调整到中南和华南地区的19所高校，为新中国高等教育的发展做出了重大贡献和牺牲。1958年，毛主席批准广西大学恢复重建。1961年，广西工学院和广西科技学院并入广西大学。1962年，广西林学院并入广西农学院。1970年，广西劳动大学并入广西农学院。1992年，广西农学院更名为广西农业大学。1997年，广西大学与广西农业大学合并，组建新的广西大学。

广西大学首开广西高等教育之先河，首任校长是被誉为教育界"北蔡南马"和"一代宗师"的我国著名教育家、科学家、民主革命家马君武博士。抗战时期，李四光、陈望道、陈寅恪、李达、王力、千家驹、梁漱溟、卢鹤绂、陈焕镛、施汝为、汪振儒、李运华、刘仙洲、纪育沣、熊得山、张映南、张志让、盛成、焦菊隐等一批名家曾在这里任教，其时人才荟萃，学科兴盛，是当时国内有较大影响的国立综合性大学之一。1997年两校合并以及进入"211工程"，使广西大学踏上了创建高水平大学的新征程。特别是十八大以来，学校改革发展取得一系列重大标志性成果：顺利完成中西部高校提升综合实力计划，创建国家重点实验室，获得多项国家级科技奖励，工程学、材料科学、农学、植物与动物学和化学5个学科进入ESI全球排名前1%，进入国家世界一流学科建设高校行列，成为"部区合建"高校，入选全国文明单位、全国高校就业工作50强、全国高校创新创业工作50强、全国首批深化创新创业教育改革示范高校等，学校进入内涵式发展新阶段。在九十多年的办学历程中，广西大学秉持"保卫中华，发达广西"的办学宗旨和"勤恳朴诚"的校训，积累和沉淀了鲜明的办学特色、深厚的人文底蕴和独特的西大精神。

学校占地面积2.13万余亩，其中广西亚热带农科新城（农林动科研教学实验基地）占地1.69万亩，校舍总建筑面积170多万平方米，教学科研设备总值25.32亿元，馆藏文献总量870万册（含学院资料室），其中电子图书465万册，电子期刊5.7万种，中外文数据库206个。学科门类齐全，哲、经、法、教、文、理、工、农、医、管、艺等11大门类，2020年招生本科专业67个，其中37个专业按15个大类招生。下设25个学院，在校全日制本科生27704人、全日制研究生11049人、留学生及港澳台生2267人，各类在读继续教育学生56165人。现有在职在编教职工3457人，其中具有正高级专业技术职务598人、副高级专业技术职务1015人，专任教师1955人。现有1个"世界一流"建设学科、2个"部区合建"一流学科群，2个国家重点学科，1个国家重点（培育）学科，8个广西一流学科，2个广西一流（培育）学科，13个广西特色优势重点学科，20个广西重点学科，19个国家一流本科建设专业；17个一级学科博士学位授权点，37个一级学科硕士学位授权点，25个硕士专业学位授权类别和11个博士后科研流动站。有1个国家重点实验室、1个省部共建国家重点实验室培育基地和1个国家级国际科技合作基地，2个省部共建协同创新中心，4个教育部重点实验室和工程研究中心，1个教育部战略研究基地，1个教育部区域与国别研究基地，1个国家林业局重点实验室和一批广西重大科技创新基地、重点实验室、工程技术研究中心、农业良种培育中心、高校人文社会科学重点研究基地、"2011协同创新中心"等。我校与全球48个国家和地区的270所高校及学术机构签署了学术合作交流协议，与东盟十国90所高校及学术机构合作交流密切。

学校坚持社会主义办学方向和立德树人根本任务，以提高人才培养质量为核心，教学发展和改革取得了一系列标志性成果。2007年至今共获得教育部"质量工程"建设项目、"本科教学工程"项目共81项，获得项目数居国家"211工程"高校前列。其中国家特色专业12个，国家精品课程3门，国家级双语教学示范课程2门，国家级精品开放课程7门，国家级一流本科课程6门，国家级教学团队3个，国家教学名师2人，国家级专业综合改革试点专业4个，国家级人才培养模式创新实验区1个，国家级大学生校外实践教育基地5个，实验教学中心24个，国家级实验教学示范中心5个，国家级虚拟仿真实验教学中心2个，国家虚拟仿真实验教学项目1个，自治区级实验教学示范中心17个，自治区级虚拟仿真实验教学中心（含培育项目）10个，自治区级虚拟仿真实验教学一流本科课程4门，15个专业入选教育部"卓越工程师教育培养计划""卓越法律人才教育培养计划"和"卓越农林人才教育培养计划"，国家一流本科专业建设点19个。赵艳林教授获2018年高等教育国家级教学成果奖二等奖。学校连续16年获得"广西普通高校毕业生就业工作先进单位""广西普通高校毕业生就业创业工作突出单位"称号。广西大学KAB创业俱乐部荣膺全国十佳。在第十六届"挑战杯"全国大学生课外学术科技作品竞赛获一等奖，并捧得"优胜杯"，在第六届中国"互联网+"大学生创新创业大赛全国总决赛获1银2铜，并在第二届全国农科学子大学生创新创业大赛、全国大学生电子设计竞赛、第十一届全国大学生广告艺术大赛、第十三届中国智能制造挑战赛全国总决赛等一系列竞赛中荣获一等奖。九十多年来，学校为国家和社会培养了50多万名各类人才，其中李林、党鸿辛、陈太一、沈善炯、卢鹤绂、文圣常、施汝为、韩斌等8位校友当选为两院院士，第十、十一届全国政协副主席李兆焯、民政部原部长李纪恒、全国人大财政经济委员会副主任委员陈武、广西壮族自治区主席蓝天立等一大批校友成长为各行各业的杰出人才。

学校着力提高教师水平和质量，加大高层次人才培养和引进力度，造就了一支品德高尚、业务精湛、结构合理、充满活力的高素质教职工队伍。现有院士1人、双聘院士4人、"万人计划"领军人才8人、长江学者特聘教授7人、长江学者讲座教授1人、青年长江学者1人、国家"杰出青年基金"获得者8人、国家"优秀青年基金"获得者2人、国家"百千万人才工程"人选14人、国家"杰出专业技术人才"3人、中国科学院百人计划人选13人、国家海外高层次人才引进计划人选10人、国家"有突出贡献中青年专家"8人、全国文化名家暨"四个一批"人才2人、科技部"中青年科技创新领军人才"5人、教育部"新世纪优秀人才支持计划"人选8人、鲁迅文学奖获得者1人，享受国务院政府特殊津贴专家39人。

学校注重科技创新，努力服务社会，产生了一批有重大影响的原创性成果。其中，王丕建教授在牛、猪杂交改良研究上成就显著，1978年获全国科学大会先进个人奖，1985年获首届世界水牛会议"科学先驱者"奖；张先程研究员主持的"籼型杂交水稻"项目获1981年国家特等发明奖；卢克焕教授（第二完成人）承担的"牛体外受精技术的研究与开发"项目获2000年国家科技进步二等奖；黄日波教授主持的"高活力α-乙酰乳酸脱羧酶的研制与应用"项目获2007年国家科技进步二等奖；王双飞教授主持的"造纸与发酵典型废水资源化和超低排放关键技术及应用"项目和"大型二氧化氯制备系统及纸浆无元素氯漂白关键技术及应用"项目，分别获2016年国家科技进步二等奖和2019年国家技术发明二等奖；郑皆连院士领衔的"大跨拱桥关键技术研究团队"荣获第二届全国创新争先团队奖牌，主持获得2018年度国家科技进步奖二等奖，获第16届中国土木工程詹天佑奖，获第36届国际桥梁大会（IBC）最高奖——乔治·理查德森奖。此外，2006年以来，学校还获得教育部等省部级科技奖励一等奖25项，获教育部高等学校科学研究优秀成果奖（人文社会科学）三等奖2项、三等奖4项，获广西社科优秀成果奖一等奖23项。学校服务国家和区域发展战略，履行社会服务职能，凸显服务亚热带特色资源保护利用与产业升级、服务面向东盟为重点的"一带一路"建设、服务南海及北部湾海洋资源开发与生态环境保护、服务边疆民族地区治理和团结进步的办学特色和科研优势，推进产学研结合和成果转化，大批成果转化取得巨大经济和社会效益。

近年来，广西大学的发展得到中央和广西壮族自治区党委政府的关怀和支持。1998年10月，时任中共中央总书记、国家主席江泽民为广西大学题词："百年大计 教育为本 团结奋斗 努力办好广西大学"；2018年12月，中共中央政治局常委、全国政协主席汪洋到广西大学视察慰问；贾庆林、宋平、尉健行、李岚清等多位党和国家领导人曾到广西大学视察，教育部和广西壮族自治区党委政府主要领导到校指导工作、解决问题。自治区党委政府先后批准印发《广西大学综合改革试点方案》《广西大学推进一流大学和一流学科建设方案》和《"部区合建"广西大学实施方案》，与教育部签署《教育部 广西壮族自治区人民政府关于"部区合建"广西大学的协议》，学校进入了以"双一流"建设和"部区合建"为主要目标的内涵式发展新阶段。

面向未来，学校将以习近平新时代中国特色社会主义思想为指引，深入贯彻党的十九大精神，坚持社会主义办学方向，落实立德树人根本任务，服务"建设壮美广西 共圆复兴梦想"的目标任务，按照建校"百年目标、三步实施、五个一流、六条方略"的规划思路，努力培养新时代有社会责任、有法治意识、有创新精神、有实践能力、有国际视野的"五有"领军型人才，加快推进"双一流"建设和内涵式发展，为实现中华民族的伟大复兴做出新的更大贡献！

马来西亚博特拉大学简介

ABOUT US

UPM, a leading research university in Malaysia is located in Serdang, next to Malaysia's administrative capital city；Putrajaya. As a world renowned centre of learning and research, UPM has attracted students and staff from all around the world making it a well-respected global entity.

Corporate Information

UPM is recognised by the independent government assessments as one of Malaysia's leading research Universities. Founded in 1931 as the School of Agriculture, the University today combines impressive modern facilities and a dynamic approach to teaching and research with its proud heritage of quality services and achievements.

The Mace
Our Vision/Mission/Value/Goals
University Policy
Logo
The UPM Anthem
Client Charter
UPM's Tagline

The Mace

The Universiti Putra Malaysia (UPM) mace, a symbol of the University's authority, was bestowed by His Royal Highness the Yang Dipertuan Agong on 30 July 1977 in conjunction with the installation of UPM's first Chancellor, His Royal Highness Sultan Salahuddin Abdul Aziz Shah Ibni Al-Marhum Sultan Hishamuddin Alam Shah Al-Haj, D.K., D.M.N., S.P.M.S., D.K. (Brunei), D.K. (Terengganu), D.K. (Kelantan), D.K. (Perlis), D.K. (Johor), S.P.D.K (Sabah), D.P. (Sarawak), D.U.N.M. (Melaka), P.J.K.

The mace, made of gold and silver, measures 1.4 metres in length and weighs 8 kilogrammes. It comprises:

– the Torch;

– the Bowl; and

– the Shaft.

The torch represents the role of the university as a source of knowledge, while its base is surrounded by the verse, "Bismillahhirrahmanirrahim", which illustrates that all activities in gaining knowledge are only possible and achievable with the consent of ALLAH. Below the verse is an inscribed carving of UPM's former name, "Universiti Pertanian Malaysia", in Roman alphabets.

The bowl represents knowledge. The topside is carved with emblems of all the states in the country, while Malaysia's official national emblem, the Hibiscus flower, is carved alongside the UPM logo around the bowl to represent knowledge. The bowl base is carved with paddy flowers. These petals are placed on five open books, which represent the quest for knowledge. The books also embody the five pillars upon which the development and extension of the university are based. The book covers are carved with the images of the National Mosque, the Royal Headdress, the Keris, the Federal emblem, the Parliament, a judge in session, a justice scale, a law book, the Malaysian flag and the four major races of Malaysia.

The shaft consists of three parts which symbolise the university's main functions. Carved motifs on each part reflect the three functions, which are:

– Teaching;
– Research; and
– Services.

The pointed curves on the shaft are carved with five symbols that depict the nation's cultural aspects:

– Islam;
– Lifestyle;
– Education;
– Traditional instruments; and
– Traditional Games.

The base, carved with thin lines, represents electronic circuits which signify the qualities of a 21st century university that is progressive in ICT and multimedia.

Our Vision/Mission/Value/Goals

As a premier institution of learning, widely recognised for leadership in research and innovation, UPM continues to strive for excellence. In order to motivate the entire university community towards achieving excellence, it ensures that all the members, both students and members of staff, share the responsibility of strictly adhering to the demands of the University's vision, mission and goals.

VISION》To become a university of international repute.

MISSION》To make meaningful contributions towards wealth creation, nation building and universal human advancement through the exploration and dissemination of knowledge.

GOALS

》Goal 1

Enhancing the Quality and Competitiveness of Graduates

》Goal 2

Creating Value through a Strong and Sustainable RDCE

》Goal 3

Boosting Industry and Community Networking Services

》Goal 4

Strengthening UPM as a Centre of Excellence in Agriculture

》Goal 5

Enhancing the Quality of Governance

UPM'S POLICY

Policy is one of the important elements in the administration system. Policies guarantee the sustainability of the university and also serves as a basic framework for planning and implementation action to achieve mission, vision and goals of the university. UPM practice these policies:

UNIVERSITI PUTRA MALAYSIA POLICY (QUALITY MANAGEMENT SYSTEM) 2017

UNIVERSITI PUTRA MALAYSIA (ENVIRONMENTAL MANAGEMENT SYSTEMS) POLICY 2013

UNIVERSITI PUTRA MALAYSIA (INFORMATION SECURITY MANAGEMENT SYSTEM) POLICY 2014

UNIVERSITI PUTRA MALAYSIA (OCCUPATIONAL SAFETY AND HEALTH) POLICY 2013

UNIVERSITI PUTRA MALAYSIA (BUSINESS CONTINUITY MANAGEMENT) 2017
UNIVERSITI PUTRA MALAYSIA (GREEN POLICY) 2011

History

The journey from 1931 to 2012 has seen UPM being transformed from what was once a small agricultural school into what is today a leading learning and Research University which is well respected both nationally and internationally.

The Story Behind UPM

Universiti Putra Malaysia was first established as the School of Agriculture in 1931. The school was located on a 22-acre piece of land in Serdang and offered two programmes—a three-year diploma programme and a one-year certificate course in Agriculture. In 1947, the school was declared the College of Agriculture Malaya by Sir Edward Gent, the then Governor of the Malayan Union. The establishment of Universiti Pertanian Malaysia came about when the College of Agriculture in Serdang merged with the Faculty of Agriculture, University of Malaya. Dr. Mohd. Rashdan bin Haji Baba, the then principal of the College of Agriculture Malaya, was appointed as the first Vice-Chancellor by virtue of the provisions of Section 18 of the Universities and University Colleges Act, 1971. With the first intake of 1,559 students, Universiti Pertanian Malaysia had its first academic session in July 1973 in the three central faculties and one basic division: the Faculty of Veterinary Medicine and Animal Sciences, Faculty of Forestry, Faculty of Agriculture, and a Division of Foundation Studies. In the early 80s, UPM extended its area of studies to include the field of Science and Technology (S&T). In 1997, the name Universiti Pertanian Malaysia was changed to Universiti Putra Malaysia by former Prime Minister, Tun Dr. Mahathir Mohammad, as a strategic gesture to portray the status of UPM as a centre of higher education capable of providing various fields of studies, especially in science and information technology, which facilitate national development in the new millennium.

Our Previous Chancellors

马来西亚马来亚大学简介

About UM

OUR HISTORY

Universiti Malaya, or UM, Malaysia's oldest university, is situated on a 922 acre (373.12 hectare) campus in the southwest of Kuala Lumpur, the capital of Malaysia.

It was founded on 28 September 1905 in Singapore as the King Edward VII College of Medicine and on 8th October 1949, it became the University of Malaya with the merger of the King Edward VII College of Medicine and Raffles College (founded in 1928).

The University of Malaya derives its name from the term "Malaya" as the country was then known. The Carr-Saunders Commission on University Education in Malaya, which recommended the setting up of the university, noted in its Report in 1948: "The University of Malaya would provide for the first time a common centre where varieties of race, religion and economic interest could mingle in joint endeavour ... For a University of Malaya must inevitably realise that it is a university for Malaya."

The growth of the University was very rapid during the first decade of its establishment and this resulted in the setting up of two autonomous Divisions on 15 January 1959, one located in Singapore and the other in Kuala Lumpur. In 1960, the government of the two territories indicated their desire to change the status of the Divisions into that of a national university. Legislation was passed in 1961 and the University of Malaya was established on 1st January 1962.

On June 16th 1962, University of Malaya celebrated the installation of its first Chancellor, Tunku Abdul Rahman Putra Al-Haj, who was also the country's first prime minister. The first Vice-Chancellor was Professor Oppenheim, a world-renowned Mathematician.

Currently, His Royal Highness The Sultan of Perak Darul Ridzuan, Sultan Nazrin Muizzuddin Shah is the Chancellor of UM.

YBhg. Dato' Prof. Ir. Dr. Mohd Hamdi Abd Shukor was appointed as the 13th Vice-Chancellor of UM on 1 November 2020

UM FACTS

University of Malaya has its roots in Singapore with the establishment of King Edward VII College of Medicine in 1905. In 1949 University of Malaya was formed with the amalgamation of King Edward VII College of Medicine and Raffles College in Singapore. University of Malaya Kuala Lumpur was established in 1962.

UMIQUE

Universiti Malaya offers some unique places for students and visitors.

Museum of Asian Art

The Museum of Asian Art (Muzium Seni Asia) is located within University of Malaya, Malaysia's first and oldest university. The outstanding education-oriented museum is a treasure trove of local and Asia art objects.

Botanical Gardens

Rimba Ilmu is an 80-hectare botanic garden located within the University of Malaya, campus. The words Rimba and Ilmu are of the Malaysian language that literally means Forest of Knowledge.

Symphony Orchestra

In March 2003, His Royal Highness Sultan Azlan Muhibuddin Shah, the Chancellor of the University of Malaya inaugurated the University of Malaya Symphony Orchestra (UMSO), breathing life into an artistic first for higher learning institutions in Malaysia.

Experimental Farm

The seven hectares that make up UM's Experimental Farm offer facilities for research by staff, post-graduate and undergraduate students in various branches of animal and plant science and a range of other biological science disciplines.

Museum of Zoology

The Museum of Zoology is home to a precious collection of insects (50,000 insects), 150 mammals (144 species), 600 birds (261 species), 445 reptile specimens (186 species), and 2,000 specimens (mostly freshwater species)

Field Studies Centre

The University of Malaya Field Studies Centre of the Ulu Gombak Biodiversity Centre, sited on 120–hectares of secondary and primary forest is a veritable fount of biological & ecological knowledge, with the area's fauna and flora extensively studied and documented throughout the site's 40-year history.

Community Engagement

As a top ranking university in Malaysia, UM has made great strides in institutionalising not only excellent academic programmes but also university-community engagement projects. These community projects must address local community needs and societal problems leveraging on technology developed through research and expertise within the campus community for possible solutions.

UM Living Lab

The starting point for research conducted at the Living Lab is the natural environment. The Living Lab engages in joint research with national and international scientists within a range of sustainability-related areas. We view sustainability in a holistic fashion, considering environment, humanity and economy as the three primary variables to be taken into account as we work toward a more sustainable future for Malaysia and the world.

List of Awards

CAREER

The UM Strategic Plan of 2016– 2020 forms the last phase of the transformation plan that has a fifteenyear horizon (2006–2020), with a guiding objective that is founded on seven Thrusts, that is, to be "A Globally Influential and Preferred University". This Plan incorporates specific Goals and leading

Strategies and Action Plans, which are aimed at achieving greater collaboration with world-renowned institutions of higher learning, higher impact on research and outputs, and achieving financial sustainability. The Action Plans are driven by our Key Performance Indicators（KPIs）.

新加坡南洋理工大学简介

About NTU Singapore

A research–intensive public university, Nanyang Technological University, Singapore（NTU Singapore）has 33,000 undergraduate and postgraduate students in the Engineering, Business, Science, Humanities, Arts, & Social Sciences, and Graduate colleges. It also has a medical school, the Lee Kong Chian School of Medicine, set up jointly with Imperial College London.

NTU is also home to world-class autonomous institutes—the National Institute of Education, S Rajaratnam School of International Studies, Earth Observatory of Singapore, and Singapore Centre for Environmental Life Sciences Engineering—and various leading research centres such as the Nanyang Environment & Water Research Institute（NEWRI）and Energy Research Institute @ NTU（ERI@N）.

Ranked amongst the world's top universities by QS, NTU has been placed the world's top young university for the past seven years. The University's main campus is frequently listed among the Top 15 most beautiful university campuses in the world and it has 57 Green Mark-certified（equivalent to LEED-certified）building projects, of which 95% are certified Green Mark Platinum. Apart from its main campus, NTU also has a campus in Novena, Singapore's healthcare district.

Under the NTU Smart Campus vision, the University harnesses the power of digital technology and tech-enabled solutions to support better learning and living experiences, the discovery of new knowledge, and the sustainability of resources.

Vision & Mission

A great global university founded on science and technology, nurturing leaders and creating societal impact through interdisciplinary education and research.

美国斯坦福大学简介

About Stanford

A place for learning, discovery, innovation, expression and discourse

Facts

Welcome to Stanford

Located in the San Francisco Bay Area, Stanford University is a place of learning, discovery, expression and innovation. Founded in 1885, Stanford's areas of excellence span seven schools along with research institutes, the arts and athletics. Stanford's faculty, staff and students work to improve the health and wellbeing of people around the world through the discovery and application of knowledge.

History

A History of Stanford Stanford University was founded in 1885 by California senator Leland Stanford and his wife, Jane, "to promote the public welfare by exercising an influence in behalf of humanity and civilization."

When railroad magnate and former California Gov. Leland Stanford and his wife, Jane Lathrop Stanford, lost their only child, Leland, Jr., to typhoid in 1884, they decided to build a university as the most fitting memorial, and deeded to it a large fortune that included the 8,180-acre Palo Alto stock farm that became the campus. The campus is located within the traditional territory of the Muwekma Ohlone Tribe. The Stanfords made their plans just as the modern research university was taking form.

Leland Stanford Junior University—still its legal name—opened Oct. 1, 1891.

The Stanfords and founding President David Starr Jordan aimed for their new university to be nonsectarian, co-educational and affordable, to produce cultured and useful graduates, and to teach both the traditional liberal arts and the technology and engineering that were already changing America.

Their vision took shape on the oak-dotted fields of the San Francisco Peninsula as a matrix of arcades and quadrangles designed for expansion and the dissolving of barriers between people, disciplines and ideas.

From the start, stewardship of the founders' extraordinary land gift has helped support university endeavors, and has made room for a multiplicity of institutes, schools and laboratories that cross-fertilize each other with innovations that have changed the world. Computer time-sharing, the first isolation of highly purified stem cells and the first synthesis of biologically active DNA, among many other breakthroughs, all originated at Stanford.

The early years were difficult, however, as even the Stanfords' wealth proved inadequate to their vision. After her husband's death, Jane Stanford kept the fledgling university open through her leadership. The 1906 earthquake dealt a further blow, killing two people and destroying several campus buildings, some so new they had never been occupied.

University benefactor and trustee Herbert Hoover, future U.S. president and member of Stanford's Pioneer Class of 1895, professionalized university operations in the 1920s and helped to put Stanford on a sound financial footing. He founded an institute to collect global political material—today's Hoover Institution Library and Archives—and led the creation of the Graduate School of Business, both now world leaders in their respective fields.

Engineering Professor Frederick Terman, dubbed the "Father of Silicon Valley," left his stamp by encouraging Stanford students not only to develop but also to commercialize their ideas. In 1937, physicists Russell Varian, Sigurd Varian and William Hansen developed the klystron ultra-high-frequency vacuum tube, paving the way for commercial air navigation, satellite communication and high-energy particle accelerators. In 1939, graduate students William Hewlett and

David Packard developed the precision audio oscillator, first low-cost method of measuring audio frequencies, and spun it into the company now known as HP. In 1951, the university developed its Stanford Research Park to house firms led by such innovators. Varian Associates became the first tenants.

The post-World War II era saw many research advances. In 1959, Stanford Medical School moved from San Francisco to the main Palo Alto campus. The 1950s also saw planning of today's SLAC National Accelerator Laboratory, managed under license from the U.S. Department of Energy and opened in 1962. The first website in North America went online at SLAC 29 years later. Advances in particle physics developed at SLAC led to the Linac Coherent Light Source, whose ability to capture ultra-fast images of chemical changes at atomic scale has made it a global destination for pharmaceutical research. The Cold War also gave rise to "the Dish," the radio telescope that is a familiar landmark in the foothills behind campus. The hill housing the Dish is a conservation area open to the public, and more than 2,000 people run or hike "Dish Hill" each day.

Deep in the foothills beyond the Dish, a much smaller structure yielded epochal discoveries when it became home to the Stanford Artificial Intelligence Laboratory (SAIL), founded by John McCarthy and Les Earnest in 1965. SAIL researchers devised the first interactive system for computer design, as well as pioneering work on computer vision, robotics, laser printing and automated assembly. The world's first office desktop computer displays appeared at SAIL in 1971.

In the 1970s, Stanford sought new ways to transform society and preserve the environment. It severed its links to classified defense research and forged new paths for service and stewardship. Stanford reduced its dependence on the automobile by adding campus housing and the free Marguerite shuttle, named after a 19th-century horse that pulled a jitney between campus and Palo Alto. The Jasper Ridge Biological Preserve was designated in 1973 to help preserve the green "lungs" of the Peninsula and access to the biological data compiled there that helped establish the field of population genetics.

The multidisciplinary Stanford Humanities Center, first of its kind in the nation and still the largest, opened in 1980 to advance research into the historical, philosophical, literary, artistic and cultural dimensions of the human experience. At this and 30 other humanities-related centers on campus, scholars ranging from distinguished undergraduates to mid-career fellows create new understandings of the world and humanity's place in it.

From the start, Stanford has valued experiential education. Generous funding helps its undergraduates of diverse economic backgrounds to enjoy parity of experience and opportunity. In 2015, 85 percent of students received some form of financial assistance and 78 percent of Stanford undergraduates graduated debt-free. More than 1,000 undergraduates conduct faculty-directed research and honors projects each year, while 1,000 take part in public-service projects and 1,000 study overseas, all without regard for ability to pay. Since 1992, all undergraduates are guaranteed four years of on-campus housing, in keeping with Stanford's emphasis on residential education and the experience of a small liberal arts college within the matrix of a large research university.

A significant physical transformation followed the 1989 Loma Prieta earthquake, which again challenged the university's resilience and vision. Stanford's main Green Library renovated its heavily damaged west wing as the Bing Wing, while the similarly damaged Stanford Art Museum reopened in 1999 as the Iris & B. Gerald Cantor Center for Visual Arts.

In 1985, the B. Gerald Cantor Rodin Sculpture Garden opened as the largest collection of Rodin bronzes outside Paris. It became the nexus for a world-class collection of 20th- and 21st-century sculpture, nearly all of it freely accessible to the public. Today, the museum and sculpture garden are part of a Stanford arts district that includes the Bing Concert Hall, the McMurtry Building for experiential arts learning and the acclaimed Anderson Collection of 20th-century American painting.

The James H. Clark Center for Biomedical Engineering and Sciences opened in 2003 as the geographic and intellectual nexus between the schools of

Engineering and Medicine and the home of Bio-X, a pioneering interdisciplinary biosciences institute led by Professor Carla Shatz. Its collaboration-friendly architecture set the tone for future building, furthering the interdisciplinarity that became a hallmark of university President John Hennessy's tenure. The environmentally sensitive construction seen in the Clark Center, the Science and Engineering Quad, the School of Medicine and elsewhere fulfills the university's deep commitment to sustainability in research, teaching and institutional practice. In 2015, Stanford Energy System Innovations' electric heat recovery system joined the university's solar and geothermal power procurement initiatives to reduce campus emissions by roughly 68 percent.

The Hasso Plattner Institute of Design at Stanford opened in the School of Engineering in 2005, bringing students and faculty from radically different backgrounds together to develop innovative, human-centered solutions to real-world challenges. Using techniques from design and engineering, the institute, known on campus as the d.school, instills creative confidence and draws students beyond the boundaries of traditional academic disciplines.

Development campaigns of unprecedented scope carry forward the Stanford family's vision. The 2000 Campaign for Undergraduate Education raised $1 billion, while the Stanford Challenge concluded in 2012 after raising $6.2 billion, then the largest fundraising campaign undertaken by a university, to fund bold new initiatives. Meanwhile, the $1 billion Campaign for Stanford Medicine is rebuilding Stanford's two hospitals for adults and children to advance the mission of precision health.

During 2016, Stanford celebrated its 125th year of transformational impact. A revamped Roble Gym opened with a dedicated "arts gym" to help make art an integral part of the student experience. "Old Chem," one of Stanford's first buildings, received new life as the Sapp Center for Science Teaching and Learning. The School of Humanities and Sciences launched the Humanities Core, a new certificate and minor program providing undergraduates a structured pathway to explore fundamental questions of human existence. That year, Stanford also expanded its Bing Overseas Studies Program, enhanced undergraduate research opportunities and played a pioneering role in exploring how best to use online technologies to expand access to high-quality education.

Stanford University today comprises seven schools and 18 interdisciplinary institutes with more than 16,000 students, 2,100 faculty and 1,800 postdoctoral scholars. Stanford is an international institution, enrolling students from all 50 U.S. states and 91 other countries. It is also an athletics powerhouse, with 900 current student-athletes and a history of 128 national titles and 22 consecutive Learfield Sports Directors' Cups, awarded to the top intercollegiate athletics program in the nation.

At the 2016 Global Entrepreneurship Summit, hosted by Stanford, President Barack Obama praised the university as "a place that celebrates our ability as human beings to discover and learn and to build, to question, to reimagine, to create new ways to connect and work with each other."

景点介绍的平行文本

桂林独秀峰王城景区介绍

王城景区由明靖江王城和独秀峰组成。王城为全国重点文物保护单位。位于桂林市中心，著名的独秀峰就屹立在王城的正中位置。元顺帝妥懽帖睦尔继位前曾在独秀峰前的大圆寺修行。朱元璋称帝封藩时，将其侄孙朱守谦封藩于桂林，称靖江王。王城就是靖江王的王府。

千年一述（风水王城）

自古以来，王城景区被奉为桂林的风水宝地，更是整个桂林城市的发祥地。这里曾经走出了2位皇帝、11代14位靖江王；清代，这里是广西贡院，屡出状元；民国时期，孙中山曾驻跸于此，为北伐大本营，筹划北伐大计；李宗仁、白崇禧、黄旭初都曾在此办公。世间传颂"北有北京故宫，南有桂林王城"。靖江王府的选址与建筑布局,堪称是明代风水学说的理想之作,王府北面有三峰屏列、彩翠相间的叠彩山作为靠山,南面有形神俱肖的象鼻山作为案山,府中有高标独秀的独秀峰作为镇山,且三山自南向北一线排列,周围群山环拱,大有唯我独尊的气势。如此紧切传统风水的理想格局宅址,在桂林仅此一处。历代靖江王都为此而自豪,按庄简王之说是其地位"广西甲甚"。

明代藩王王城

靖江王府位于桂林市中心的独秀峰下,是明朝开国皇帝朱元璋分封给其侄孙的府邸,距今有600多年的历史,是目前中国保存最完整的一座明代藩王府,被评为"国家重点文物保护单位"。朱守谦在明洪武五年(公元1372年)开始建府,历时20年才完工。整个王府占地面积为18.7公顷,约合283亩地。它有承运门、承运殿、寝宫,左建宗庙,右筑社坛,亭台阁轩,堂室楼榭,无所不备,红墙黄瓦,云阶玉壁,辉煌壮观。王城周围是3里长的城垣,内外以方形青石修砌,十分坚固。城开东南西北四门,分别命名为"体仁"(东华门)、"端礼"(正阳门)、"遵义"(西华门)、"广智"(后贡门)。坚城深门,气势森严。靖江王府共有11代14位靖江王在此居住过,历时280年之久,系明代藩王中历史最长及目前全中国保存最完整的明代藩王府。后来被清朝定南王孔有德所占而成为定南王府。农民军李定国攻克桂林后,孔有德纵火自焚,使有250多年历史的王城化为焦土。现在王城尚完好。

Tower of London

From the modern London Eye to the historic Tower of London, the top 10 tourist attractions in London are a must–see on any London sightseeing trip. Even better, many London landmarks are free to visit. Use the London attractions map to find them all.

There are also plenty of kid-friendly places to visit in London. Get up close and personal with underwater creatures at SEALIFE London Aquarium or explore the Science Museum, London's interactive hub of science and technology. Both are perfect for fun family days out in London.

You could also soak up some culture at London museums, visit the Queen at Buckingham Palace, or take the perfect picture with Big Ben, just some of the many iconic places to go in London.

The top 10 free London attractions list is based on visitor numbers: start your sightseeing in London now with these popular spots. Book tickets with visitlondon.com for the top 10 bookable London attractions.

Coronavirus information: Many outdoor attractions have reopened, while indoor attractions are due to reopen from 17 May at the earliest, following the proposed easing of coronavirus restrictions. Check back nearer the time for confirmation and be aware that some venues listed may still be closed after those dates. You may also need to book tickets in advance, even if entrance is free.

If you're not yet able to visit London, check out attractions, online exhibitions and more activities to enjoy from home with the Virtually London guide.

Royal Botanic Gardens, Kew

Discover beautiful glasshouses including the iconic Palm House and its exotic rainforest; the Princess of Wales Conservatory which invites you to explore 10 of the world's climatic zones; and the Waterlily House with its amazing, giant lily pads.

Visitors of all ages love the 59ft (18m) high Treetop Walkway, which soars into the tree canopy offering a bird's-eye view of the gardens. Enjoy a stroll along the Great Broad Walk Borders, home to more than 60,000 plants, and step into history at Kew Palace, the former summer residence of King George Ⅲ.

Plus, relax with refreshments in one of our inviting cafes. Kew Gardens is less than 30 minutes from central London, and easily reached by road, rail, and London Underground.

Warner Bros. Studio Tour London

Step on to authentic sets, discover the magic behind spellbinding special effects and explore the behind-the-scenes secrets of the Harry Potter film series.

Discover the iconic Hogwarts Great Hall and explore the Forbidden Forest, all before boarding the original Hogwarts Express at Platform 9 ¾ and wandering down Diagon Alley.

Located at the Studios where all eight films were produced, the Studio Tour showcases the British talent, imagination and artistry that went into making the impossible a reality on screen. Visitors will relive the magic through the eyes of the filmmakers who brought the Harry Potter film series to life.

London Mithraeum

The Temple of Mithras, originally constructed around AD 240, was discovered in 1954 during the excavation of a Second World War bomb site. This discovery captured the imagination of the public, with more than 400,000 people visiting the uncovered remains over two weeks.

London Mithraeum Bloomberg SPACE returns the temple to the location of its discovery in the City of London, beneath Bloomberg's new European headquarters.

Descend seven metres below modern street level to explore the ancient temple through an immersive experience. See the bustling world of Roman Londinium brought to life, as the stories of the City's first Londoners are unlocked. Plus, discover a remarkable selection of Roman artefacts found during the excavations, alongside a series of contemporary art commissions responding to one of the UK's most significant archaeological sites.

附录2：英汉翻译语篇平行文本

中国企业中英文简介

广西北部湾银行

广西北部湾银行是顺应国家实施北部湾经济区开放开发战略，在原南宁市商业银行基础上改制设立的省级城市商业银行，于2008年10月挂牌成立。目前已在南宁、桂林、柳州、北海、贵港、钦州、防城港、崇左、玉林、百色、梧州、河池等12个设区市和桂平、横县、凭祥等42个重点县域设立了分支机构，在田东、宾阳、岑溪发起设立了3家村镇银行。全行共有一级分支机构21家，营业网点超220家，职工人数超3400人。逐渐成长为总资产超3000亿元，存款余额超2200亿元，贷款余额超1600亿元，具有良好公司治理和风险管理机制的现代商业银行。2020年主体长期信用等级提升至AAA，成为广西区内第一家主体长期信用等级获评AAA的城商行。

广西北部湾银行努力打造"支持地方经济发展的省级主力金融平台、金融创新平台、地方金融人才培养平台"，作为"广西自己的银行"，北部湾银行牢记使命担当，累计提供省内外融资逾1.4万亿元服务广西经济社会发展，其中从区外引进资金4000亿元以上，累计实现营业收入超400亿元、经营利润超250亿元、上缴税金超90亿元，朝着"地方金融的领头羊、国内一流的精品银行、加快上市步伐"三大目标稳步迈进，努力建设让地方党委政府、监管部门、股东、客户、合作伙伴和员工六方"高兴"和满意的银行。

十二载砥砺奋进，广西北部湾银行书写了"广西自己的银行"的靓丽答卷，全行整体呈现解放思想、担当实干新气象。在2020年英国《银行家》杂志全球银行1000强排名中升至第423位，中国服务企业500强中升至第384位。先后荣获"金融机构支持地方经济发展突出贡献奖""全国银行业金融机构小微企业金融服务先进单位""全国十佳城商行""全国七五普法中期先进集体""广西优秀企业"和"广西企业100强""广西服务业50强""广西地方税纳税百强""服务八桂综合贡献奖"等荣誉。

Profile of Guangxi Beibu Gulf Bank Co., Ltd.

Guangxi Beibu Gulf Bank Co., Ltd. is located in the center junction of multi-region cooperation, such as China-ASEAN Free Trade Zone, Pan-Beibu Gulf Economic Cooperation Zone, the Greater Mekong Subregion, Pan-Pearl River Delta Economic Cooperation Zone, Southwest Six Provinces, Southcenter Five Provinces, having advantages of coastal opening up, riverside opening up and board opening up. At the same time, it is located in the heartland of China-ASEAN Free Trade Zone, connecting China and ASEAN, having the regional advantage of connecting China and ASEAN by two-way communications, and being recognized as an important base and "bridgehead" of promoting all-round cooperation between China and ASEAN. To serve Guangxi economy and the opening up and development of Guangxi Beibu Gulf Economic Zone and the construction of China-ASEAN Free Trade Zone, "Guangxi Beibu Gulf Bank Co., Ltd., as one of the ten major opening up and development projects in Guangxi Beibu Gulf Economic Zone, came into being.Guangxi Beibu Gulf Bank Co., Ltd.—Regional, International and Joint-stock High-quality and Featured Bank

Development Purpose：Adhering to the concept of serving Guangxi economy, the opening up and development of Beibu Gulf and China-ASEAN Free Trade Zone, Guangxi Beibu Gulf Bank Co., Ltd. further improves the organizational form of property rights and operating mechanism, innovates on the management system, integrates financial resources, intensifies risk control, and improves asset quality to become a modern commercial bank with good company governance and risk management mechanism, providing powerful financial support to the economic development of Guangxi, the opening up and development of Beibu Gulf Economic Zone, and the construction of China-ASEAN Free Trade Zone.

Function Positioning: Important pillar of regional finance, powerful support of local economy, partner of enterprises, and high-quality and featured bank serving the public.

Strategic Focus: Adhering to different development strategies, Guangxi Beibu Gulf Bank Co., Ltd. creates core competence to contribute to the economic development of Guangxi, the opening up and development of Beibu Gulf Economic Zone, the construction of China-ASEAN Free Trade Zone, the development of enterprises and the development of individual customers.

Business Concept: Complying with the requirements of being a "Excellent Bank", Guangxi Beibu Gulf Bank Co., Ltd. sets up the business objective of "First-class Business Performance, Sound Corporate Governance Structure, Good Internal Control Mechanism and Management Level, Satisfying Services" and the business concept of "Customer-centered, Benefit-oriented, Risk Control-focused".

Business Innovation: Guangxi Beibu Gulf Bank Co., Ltd. will vigorously develop international business, intensify cooperation with financial institutes at home and abroad, and build a modern financial system serving China-ASEAN Free Trade Zone.

漳州片仔癀药业股份有限公司

漳州片仔癀药业股份有限公司是以医药制造、研发为主业的国家技术创新示范企业、中华老字号企业，现市值超1500亿。拥有1家研究院、35家控股子公司、7家参股公司。经营6大品类、470多个产品系列。在全国7个省、直辖市建立23个科研、生产和药材基地。

Zhangzhou Pien Tze Huang Pharmaceutical Co., Ltd. is a time-honored national high–tech enterprise. In December 1999, the Zhangzhou Pharmaceutical Factory established in 1956 was restructured into Pien Tze Huang Pharmaceutical. In June 2003, the company was listed on the Shanghai Stock Exchange. After two additional issues and one allotment, the company has now issued 603 million shares. Currently, the company has 34 holding subsidiaries, 8 joint-stock companies and 4 industry funds with more than 2,100 employees.

核心产品

国宝名药片仔癀，为国家中药一级保护品种，处方和工艺受国家保护，传统制作技艺列入国家非遗名录，单品种出口连续多年位居中国中成药外贸单品种出口前列，成"海丝"路上"中国符号"。

Core Products:

Originating from an imperial secret recipe of the Ming Dynasty. Pien Tze Huang was listed as one of the national protected varieties of traditional Chinese medicine and it has unique curative effect on liver diseases and cancer and health care; the relevant traditional production techniques were also included in the national intangible cultural heritage list. Our products have been exported to all parts of the world and become a "Chinese Symbol" on the Maritime Silk Road. For more than 20 years, our export volume ranks No.1 among the country's foreign trade single variety of Chinese patent medicine.

片仔癀荣誉

公司荣获中国主板上市公司价值百强、全国文明单位、全国质量标杆、国家级"绿色工厂"、全国慈善会爱心企业、福建省工业企业质量标杆、福建省劳动关系和谐企业、福建省节水型企等20多项称号，被授予（第六届）

福建省政府质量奖。企业技术中心通过国家评定，研发实力居中国中药研发实力前10强（列第7位），片仔癀连续多年居"中药大品种科技竞争力"排行榜清热解毒领域第一名。品牌连续六年获评"健康中国"肝胆用药第一品牌，以566.96亿列"2020年中国最具价值品牌100强"第55位，居2020年胡润品牌榜医疗健康行业第1位。

The Glories of Pien Tze Huang:

The Pien Tze Huang brand has remained in the Hurun brand list for many years; it has been rated as the No.1 brand of "Healthy China" hepatobiliary drugs for three consecutive years and won the top Chinese brand award "China Spectrum Award". With a brand value of RMB 24.903 billion, it ranked second on the "Brand Value Ranking List of China Time-honored Brands for 2018". In December 2017, with a brand value of RMB 35.048 billion, it was listed as one of the "2017 World's 500 Most Influential Innovation Brands". Chairman Liu Jianshun was awarded as the "Model Worker of Fujian Province for 2018" and the "2017-2018 National Outstanding Entrepreneur"

经营业绩

2020年，公司实现营收65.07亿元，比增13.72%；利润总额19.82亿元，比增20.53%；净利润16.94亿元，比增22.12%；上缴税收8.7亿元，比增29.33%，再创同期历史新高。全球投行Torreya发布2020年《全球1000强药企报告》，公司排名从2019年的第80位上升至第49位，位居中国前10强。

Business Performance:

The annual compound growth rate of Pien Tze Huang's main economic indicators exceeds 20%, which is more than twice of the growth rate of the National Strategic Plan for TCM Development, ranking at the top of the industry. The company was included in the list of China's top 100 pharmaceutical companies, and won the titles of Demonstration Enterprise of China's Intellectual Property Protection, Pilot Demonstration Enterprise of National and Provincial Brand Cultivation, and Quality Benchmark Enterprise in Fujian. It was rated as the most respected listed company by investors in the country and listed as one of the Top 100 Main Board Listed Companies in China.

In 2017, Pien Tze Huang achieved operating revenue of RMB 3.714 billion, up 60.85% year-on-year; its total profits reached RMB 942 million, up 54.55 percent; the net profit was RMB 780 million, up 53.99%; the tax revenue was RMB 452 million, up 16.83% year-on-year. In the first quarter of 2018, the company realized an operating income of RMB 1.222 billion, up 42.06% year-on-year; its total profits reached RMB 384 million, up 47.31%; the net profit was RMB 326 million, up 48.34%; the tax revenue was RMB 145 million, up 91.16% from a year earlier.

马来西亚征阳集团

1989年起，征阳集团陆续开发轻型工厂、商业单位以及住宅等多个项目。如今，已成为马来西亚一个多向发展、高效管理、不断推出高产值和高素质开发项目的房地产上市公司。

征阳集团目前集中力量在马来西亚中部区域积极拓展大型发展项目，打造商业型发展项目、永久地契的豪华服务式公寓以及高级住宅等。自2013年起，征阳集团制定长期发展大蓝图，在布城南端、沙叻丁宜兴建一座占地525英亩的征阳城，城内心脏地带设有中国第一所海外大学分校——厦门大学马来西亚分校，周边国际名牌商城林立，潜力无限。

Sunsuria Berhad

Since 1989, Sunsuria Group has been developing light factory, commercial unit and residence. Today, Sunsuria Group has become a multi-oriented development, efficient management, constantly launched high production value and high-quality development projects of the property listed companies in Malaysia.

At present, Sunsuria Group is focusing its efforts on developing large-scale development projects in Malaysia's central area. Such as creating commercial development projects, luxury serviced apartments of permanent land deeds and high-end residential buildings. Since 2013, Sunsuria Group has formulated the grand blueprint of long-term development, and built a 525-acre city at the southern end of Putrajaya and in Yixing of Sarat. In the heart of the Sunsuria City, there has China's first overseas university branch—Xiamen University Malaysia branch. Surrounded by a number of famous international shopping malls, the university has huge potential of development.

缅甸金山集团

缅甸金山集团是缅甸的领先企业之一，拥有多元化的商业利益组合，专注于六个核心领域，包括建筑材料、分销、工程和建筑、基础设施投资、生活方式和房地产。

除此之外，缅甸金山集团是缅甸最大的雇主之一，至今为止拥有超过7000名员工。

Shwe Taung Group

Shwe Taung Group is one of the leading corporations in Myanmar. It has a diversified portfolio of business interests in six core sectors—building materials, distribution, engineering and construction, infrastructure investment, lifestyle, and real estate.

It is one of Myanmar's largest employers with a workforce of over 7000 employees.

东盟博览会产品介绍

果味伏特加

1. VISS

VISS, a premium Vodka liqueur with the taste of refreshing fruity flavor combined with shimmery colors to create a glorious spiral galaxy effect through party bash! VISS Introduced six (6) flavors and colors to full your taste buds：

Vintage Claret/ Yellow Passion/ Lime Sorbet/ Ballet Blue/ Blush Blossom /

Forest Berries.

威斯天然花香与水果的美味组合呈现出缤纷闪烁的色彩结合了星系旋转效果。

威斯利口酒推出6种不同花香与水果的口味：石榴红/百香情/青柠冰/深海莓/樱花粉/野莓紫。

2. KHRRRSO VODKK（Original）

Kharaso Vodka Original is made from premium selected sugarcane and refined it into molasses spirits, following by fermentation and distillery process more than 3 times with special charcoal filtering process for the crystal clear and brilliant liquid with a smooth and balanced taste. Kharaso Vodka has been marketed in Malaysia for more than 22 years and with its strong reputation, the brand has been awarded GOLD MEDAL in China Wine and Spirits 2016（CWSA）competition, SILVER MEDAL in International Wine and Spirit Completion 2017 and BRONZE MEDAL in San Francisco World Spirits Competition.

卡拉索原味伏特加选用精选顶级甘蔗压出来的糖汁，经过发酵，以纯手工艺加工酿制而成。在经过蒸馏器多次蒸馏与活性炭过滤后使其酒质更加晶莹澄澈，无色且清淡爽口。其口味极其顺滑，口感淡香凛冽，带有独特的焦糖风味。卡拉索原味伏特加在马来西亚过去22年已建立其口碑和品牌并荣获2016年中国环球葡萄酒伏特加大赛金奖，2017年 国际葡萄酒和烈酒大赛银奖和2017年旧金山国际烈酒大赛铜奖。

3. Kharaso Apple

Kharaso @ apple vodka offering a pleasing aroma and a long fruity aftertaste.

It is perfectly garnish with cinnamon sticks and star anise to makes this sweet concoction a perfectfall drink for the ultimate treat.

卡拉索@苹果伏特加附带浓郁的香气，口感清脆。

此伏特加独特香醇，混合肉桂与八角可使其精华完全萃出香味甘甜的口感，让人为之心旷神怡，饮用时更可享受其辛辣的香料，温暖而浑厚的味道，令人难忘。

4. Kharaso Lemon

Kharaso @ lemon vodka strikes a delicate balance between the sweet and tart flavors of its unique fruits, also renowned for its fragrant aroma and richly flavored juice. This vodka creates a perfect choices for many cocktails.

卡拉索@柠檬伏特加有着浓郁强烈的柠檬口味，口感顺滑芳醇，带有柠檬和酸橙的清爽甘味，亦能感受到清爽适宜的酸度，使其成为有特点的伏特加酒。此酒本身的素质结合也适合调配其他的鸡尾酒。

5. Lime Sorbet青柠冰

A Vodka liqueur with its vibrantly green colour consisting of lemon and lime infusion creates a perfect combination of sweet and sour twist, this drink is surprisingly refreshing.

青柠味利口酒口感清凉，特别是青柠清爽的感觉直击味蕾，让人有种透心凉的感觉。其味道很清新，有股淡淡的清香，有一点青涩、有一点甜蜜，如单纯青柠般的初恋。

6. Ballet Blue深海莓

A Vodka liqueur with tangy sweet taste of fresh blueberry aroma bursts into flavours, it gets the deep ocean blue sparkle from the fusion to make a crowd pleaser.

在这片深山丛林中，生长着一种神秘的野果，它有着夜空一样神秘深邃的宝石蓝色，有着"蓝色妖姬"般的蓝紫色，隐隐透出一股深山老林的悠然寂静。蓝莓利口酒就是一位神秘的情人，甜配以酒精的浓醉，调出了一种独有的神秘的美味使其酒香与蓝莓果香层次分明，余韵悠长。品鉴时，感受酒液在口中每秒的千变万化，微微闭上双眼，你的心已在那神秘、深邃的蓝莓酒的指引下拥入大自然的怀抱。

7.Blush Blossom樱花粉

A Vodka liqueur with a soft scent and flavour of beautiful cherry blossoms, this refreshing drink embodies your sense of spring in a blossoming garden.

樱花总是给人带来浪漫的气息，如同一场唯美的恋爱，淡淡粉色，道着不可言说的故事。在盛开的樱花树下，感受花瓣温柔落下所带来的柔美香味。多用于庆祝的时候。不但可以闻到樱花的香味治愈心灵，还可以在品尝的时候闭上双眼想象眼前樱花盛开的景象。

8. Forest Berries 野莓紫

A Vodka liqueur bursting with fully mature wild berries, having a file fruit favour and lovely purplish in colour, it would be the perfect sip and sparkle your night.

紫色是一种神秘的色彩，它充满了浪漫，让人遐想、回味。而喜欢紫色的人，优雅高贵，细腻敏感，宛若翩翩仙子般美好却又难以接近，威斯利酒散发出令人愉悦的野山莓香气。香气迷人，充满浪漫和梦幻。在浓郁的果香中，透出丝丝来自太平洋的海洋浪漫气息，独特而令人回味无穷。

广西民俗中英翻译语篇

壮族与铜鼓

Zhuang Ethnic Group & Bronze Drum

壮族铜鼓文化源远流长。从公元前5世纪的战国时期算起，到公元19世纪的清代末叶，壮族铸造和使用铜鼓的历史长达两千多年。至今，桂西、桂西北地区的壮族群众仍珍藏着许多明清时期的铜鼓，这些祖传的宝物，在壮族村寨中扮演着重要的角色，它是壮族历史的见证，同时也是节日喜庆活动中不可或缺的珍贵器物。

The bronze drum culture of the Zhuang minority is of long standing and well established, From the Warring States period in the 5th century B.C. to the late Qing dynasty in the 19th century. Zhuang people cast and used bronze drums for over two millenniums. To this day, in west and northwest Guangxi, many bronze drums made in the Ming and Qing dynasties have teen garnered by the Zhuang people. These precious heirlooms play an important role in villages. They are the witnesses of the Zhuang's history and the indispensable rarities in festivals.

说书讲古——广西传统曲艺
STORYTELLING WITH THE MUSIC
The Traditional Folk Art Form within Guangxi

广西曲艺综合了诗歌、音乐、表演三种艺术形式，表演时连说带唱，以唱为主，兼具抒情和叙事功能，有曲目丰富、篇幅短小、唱词押韵的特点。其唱腔曲调与各地方言相结合，风格因地而异，常以管弦乐器伴奏。

The folk art from within Guangxi synthesizcs three artistic forms, poems, the music and performances. In performance there are talking and singing, with singing as the major from. It is lyric and narrative. The song is rich in content, short in size and rhymed. With a combination of local dialect and generally accompanied with wind instrument, its singing tone differs due to different regions.

广西文场表演
Guangxi Wenchang Performance

广西文场又称"文玩子"，是流行于桂林柳州一带的民间曲艺，以坐立清唱为主，扬琴伴奏为辅。曲体为板腔体、曲牌体混合结构，基本的唱腔曲牌和器乐曲牌近百个。

Again named "Wenwanzi", Guangxi Wenchang is a Chinese folk art form popular among the people in Guilin and Liuzhou. It is dominated by the form of singing in seat and supplemented by the accompaniment of dulcimer. The song is constructed with combinations of plate cavity and joint music based on nearly one hundred pieces of singing and instrument tunes.

桂林渔鼓表演
Guilin Fishing Drum Performance

桂林渔鼓以渔鼓为主奏乐器，音乐为四句一组的单曲体徵调式，外加大小过门，是源于道情流行于桂柳方言区的代表性民间说唱艺术形式。

With the fishing drum as the main instruments, Guilin Fishing Drum is the Dangunti (single tune torn) and Zhi mode (sol) with additional ritornellos, its music is groups containing four sentences. Being a representative folk vocal art which is popular in the Guilin dialect region, its lyric contents are originated from

Taoism story.

侗族琵琶歌演奏

Song of Chinese Lute by Dong

琵琶歌流行于广西三江侗族地区,以侗族琵琶伴奏。琵琶歌以小型琵琶伴奏时,是单纯的抒情歌;以大型琵琶伴奏时带有叙事说唱性质,属民间曲艺,主要内容多为侗族神话传说、民间爱情故事。

Accompanied by the Dong lute, the Song of Chinese Lute is popular among the Sanjiang Dong areas within Guangxi. When the song is accompanied with small lute, it is the pure lyric song. And when it's accompanied with big lute, it has singing and talking. Being the folk art form, its major themes are Dong myths and legends and folk love stories.

壮族末伦表演

Witch-telling Song of Zhuang

壮族末伦源于桂西壮族巫婆在非正式场合所唱的散板巫调,内容多为叹苦情、思离别和诉衷肠,经历了从单口清唱到多口说唱的表演形式转变。句式一般为"五二分"的七言句,押腰脚韵。

Witch-telling Song of Zhuang is originated from Sanban (Ad libitum) witch tune sung by the Zhuang witch in western Guangxi in informal occasions. Its contents are sigh of affliction sentiment of parting and venting grievances. Its forms have changed from solo singing without accompaniment to multiple singing and talking. The lyrics are five-two divided seven-word sentences with rhymes in the middle and end.

婚恋礼俗

Etiquette and Custom of Marriage

婚姻是人生大事,包括婚制、择偶、婚仪等内容。自古至今,广西各民族有自由恋爱的传统,婚恋保留了各自的民族特点。从情窦初开的青年男女发展为喜结良缘的恩爱夫妇,其间的故事仪礼浪漫有趣,反映出各民族深厚的历史文化积淀。

Marriage is an important event in one's life and it covers the marriage system, mate selection and wedding ceremony etc. From the past to the present, Guangxi's ethnic groups have kept the tradition of free love with their own ethnic features. For boys and girls to have their first awakening of love and for a married couple with conjugal love, their stories and wedding rituals are romantic and interesting, showing deep historical and cultural deposits of different ethnic groups.

闻乐起舞——广西传统舞蹈

Dancing with the Music—The Traditional Dances of Guangxi

广西传统舞蹈题材广泛、形态多样、内涵丰富。每逢岁时节庆，舞者们常闻乐起舞，内容既有拟生产劳动舞蹈与拟鸟兽动物舞蹈，也有民俗风情类舞蹈宗教祭祀类舞蹈，不同程度地反映本民族的民族心理、审美情趣和风俗习惯等。

The traditional dances of Guangxi have wide themes, various forms and rich connotations. At festivals or celebrations, the dancers will dance with the music. The contents are imitations of birds and beasts moves as well as folklore, religious and sacrificing dances, which, to a different degree, reflects the ethnic psychology, aesthetic sentiment and habitual custom.

追古述艺

Ancient Technologies

服饰既是民族的标志，也是性别、年龄和婚姻状况的象征。各民族因生活环境、历史传统、风俗习惯、审美意识的不同，服饰的材质、款式、纹样和风格等也各不相同。人们把美的感受、自然崇拜和生活的热爱统统集中在服饰中体现出来。服饰的发展与演进，始终与社会文化的变迁紧密相连。服饰是民族"活"的历史、文化的表征，具有很高的艺术、研究和欣赏价值。

Clothing is not only the sign of nation, but also the symbol of gender, age and marital status. Because of the differences in living environment, historical tradition, customs and aesthetic consciousness, each nation has shown its characteristics in costumes' materials, design, pattern and style. People express their sense of beauty, natural worship and love of life with costumes whose development and evolution has always been closely connected with the change of social culture. Clothing possessing high art, research, and appreciation value is the representation of nations' history and culture.

纺织是服饰工艺的基础，满足着人们的物质和精神需求，并延伸到生活的方方面面，通过服饰影响社会。在长期的社会实践中，广西各民族发展了纺织材料和织造技术，经历了草叶毛羽裹身到葛麻丝棉制衣的历史过程。从甑皮岩的骨针、石脚山的纺轮到独具特色的竹笼机，从罗泊湾汉墓的麻织物、唐代郁林等地的贡布到闻名天下的壮锦，广西的纺织工艺呈现出独特面貌。

Textile, the basis of garment industry. caters for the people's material and spiritual demands, covers all aspects of life and influences the society through garments. Through long term social practice the ethnic groups in Guangxi developed textile materials and technologies, and experienced the process from grass-or feather-made clothes to hemp-, silk- and cotton-made ones. From the bone needles of Zengpiyan Site and the spinning wheel of Shijiao Mountain to the unique bamboo-cage boom from the hemp products unearthed in the Luobowan Tomb and the Tang Dynasty's tribute cloth from Yulin, to the world famous Zhuang brocade. Guangxi shows its special outlook in textile technologies.

纺织生产技术是世界各族人民长期创造性劳动经验积累的产物，世界三大文明发祥地对于发展纺织技术都有突出的贡献，大约公元前5000年，世界各文明发祥地区都已就地取材开始了纺织生产。进入18世纪，纺织生产机械化，世界各地的家庭手工业生产逐步被集中性大规模工厂生产所代替。特别是21世纪以来，原始的手工纺织技艺正在逐渐失传，古老的文化也在还渐消失。只有少数地区仍然保留着古老的手工纺织技艺。

Textile production technology is a kind of product made by people of all ethnic groups in the world by way of accumulating creative labor experience for a long time. The world's three largest birthplaces of civilization offered outstanding contributions for the development of textile technology. Around 5000BC, the world's civilized origins stared to use local materials for textile production mechanized, cottage industry production around the world was gradually replaced by centralized large-scale factory production. Especially since the 21st century, original manual textile art along with ancient culture is gradually lost and disappears with the old manual textile craft only remaining in a few areas.

挑花

The Cross Stitch

挑花主要分为"十字挑花"和"数纱挑花",是各民族绣法中最常用的一种。技艺手法是在脉络清晰的面料上根据经纬线走向挑出十字或者线段,并通过每个细小单元组合成各种图案。

The cross stitch is mainly divided into "cross-stitch" and "shusha" cross stitch, a most commonly used stitch of various ethnic groups. This technique is to stitch crosses or line segments on the fabric with legible warp and weft and form various patterns by combining small cells.

马尾绣

The Horse Tail Embroidery

马尾绣是利用棉纱或丝线将马尾毛裹缠后再钉缝于布料上的一种技艺。马尾绣主要是应用于制作背带、服饰、鞋、帽等。其中马尾绣背带图案精美、内容丰富、色彩绚丽,制作工艺复杂,在刺绣艺术中独具特色。2006年,"水族马尾绣"被列入国家第一批非物质文化遗产名录。

The horse tail embroidery is a handicraft wrapping the horse tail hair with yam or silk and then stitching on the fabric. The horse tail embroidery is mainly used in making straps, costumes, shoes, hats etc. It is unique with exquisite patterns, rich contents, gorgeous colors and complicated techniques. In 2006, the Horse Tail Embroidery of the Shui people was inscribed to the intangible cultural heritage list of China.

锁绣

Chain Stitch

锁绣是古代最早采用的针法之一。锁绣的特点是曲展自如、流畅圆润,用来表现线条或图案的轮廓,可以形成严整清晰的边线。锁绣的针迹呈链状结构,图案如锁链圈圈相套。

Chain stich, one of the earliest stitches, features free and smooth contours for lines or patterns, with dear and complete borders, and traces linked chain.

辫绣

Braid Stitch

辫绣是将绣线分三股编成辫状丝带后再将其依纹样轮廓弯曲，钉缝固定于底布上的一种制绣技艺。辫绣的绣迹走向明里，不打皱褶，如行云流水，有浅浮雕感。

Braid stitch is to split silk threads into three strands, braid the strands according to the pattern and then fix it on the backdrop cloth. The traces of braid stitch feature obvious directions. It is smooth and has no wrinkles. It feels like bass-relief.

打籽绣

Daio（mode）Stitch

打籽绣是古老的制绣基本针法之一。俗称"结子绣""环籽绣"，民间叫"打疙瘩"。打籽绣的方法是用丝线缠针缠绕圈形成颗粒状，绣一针成一籽，构成点状纹样，多用于表现花蕊、眼睛等，装饰性很强，具有画龙点睛的效果。

Daio（mode）stitch, one of the earliest stitches in embroidery, is also known as" Jiezi stitch, Huanzi stitch and Dageda（making node）. The method is to wind silk thread on needles to make nodes and form a dotted pattern for decorating stamen or eyes, and can produce an impressive effect.

京族服饰

Garments and Ornamentation of the Jing People

京族服饰清新雅致，独具风格。过去，京族男子剪短发，穿窄袖对襟长衣，束腰带，着长裤；女子留中分长发结辫，两侧流"落水"，扎"砧板蟹"，耳挂银环，上穿无领对襟短衣，内挂菱形遮胸布，下着宽筒长裤。现在的京族女子上穿对襟或斜襟紧身高衩长衣，下着阔腿长裤，外出时戴竹笠，轻盈飘逸；男子衣着大多与汉族相同。

The garments and ornamentation of the Jing people are fresh and elegant and have the unique style. In the past, the males of Jing people grew short hair, and wore narrow-sleeve coats and gowns with buttons down the front, girdles and trousers. The females of the Jing people wore long queues with flat buns, sliver earrings, collarless short coats with buttons down the front and diamond-shoes corsets inside and flares pants. Today, the Jing females wore gowns with buttons down the front or slanting front, flares pants and bamboo hats. The Jing males wear similar clothes with the Han people.

回族服饰

Garments and Ornamentations of the Hui People

广西回族与其他地区的回族一样，服饰尚白，如白衬衫、白帽子、白色盖头等。男子常戴"礼拜帽"。妇女有戴红、白、绿盖头和披搭式巾帕的习惯。20世纪七八十年代以后，回族除红白喜事和礼拜节庆时仍着传统服饰外，日常衣着大多与汉族相同。

The Hui people in Guangxi are the same with those in other regions. They favor the white clothes, such white shirts, white hats and white scarves. The men often wear Muslim hats, and the women wear red, white or green veils and scarves. After the 1970s and 80s, the Hui people wear the same with the Han people in daily life, and their traditional costumes on the occasion of weddings, funerals, celebrations or festivals.

剪贴绣

The Cutting and Applique Embroidery

剪贴绣是先用剪刀在纸上剪出各种图案，把剪纸图案贴于底布上，再用各色丝线在针的引导下裹缠覆盖而成，具有一定的凹凸立体感。多在壮族、侗族、苗族等少数民族中使用。

The cutting and applique embroidery is to cut patterns with paper, then paste the patterns on the backing fabric and then cover the patterns with threads to make the patterns to have the effect of relief. This technique is mostly used among Zhuang, Dong, Miao and other ethnic groups.

雕塑

Sculpture

雕塑是利用各种材质通过雕凿或捏塑形成的造型艺术。广西境内主要有石雕、木雕、竹雕、贝雕、角雕和泥塑等，多采用浮雕、平雕、镂雕和堆塑等技法。各族雕塑，因其文化传统和艺术风尚的不同而各具特色，形象栩栩如生，或神形兼备，大凡生灵万物，尤其是吉祥物体或人物造型，均有所涉及。

Sculpture is a three-dimensional artwork created by shaping or combining all kinds of materials. In Guangxi, there are stone carving, wood carving, shell carving, ivory carving and clay sculpture etc. Most of which adopt basso-relievo, line carving, openwork and molding, etc. The sculpture covers widely and makes mascots and figures as the first choice. These sculptures have different features thanks to various cultural traditional and artistic fashions.

生产生活是人类生存文化的主体，人类依赖食物得以生存。由此衍生出的采集、狩猎、游牧、渔业和农耕等生活在不同民族中得以创造、传承。生产生活用具最能从细微处展示一个民族、一个地区的文化特征以及人们的生活状态，有利于我们理解他们的生计方式、饮食习惯和审美情趣。

Production and living is the main part of culture of human existence. Human rely on food to survive in different ways of living which have been creating and inheriting in different nations, such as gathering, hunting, nomadic, fishing and farming. Production and living appliances is the best representation of a nation and a region's cultural characteristics and status of people's lives. They help us to understand people's mode of living, eating habits and aesthetic taste.

山地生活

Mountain life

广西山地聚居着壮、汉、瑶、苗、侗、毛南、彝、水、仫佬等民族，他们在长期的生产实践中逐步创造出极具特色的山地生产生活方式。干栏式房屋是这些山地民族村寨最主要的传统民居建筑。他们因地制宜，垦山垒田，垦荒造地，勤劳耕种；他们护林造林，广种经济作物；历史上，采集狩猎也曾是山地民族食物来源的重要补充，他们的生产工具、生活用具、捕猎工具，形式多样，各具特色，充分展示了各个山地民族出神入化、巧夺天工的智慧。

The people of ethnic groups such as Zhuang, Han, Yao, Miao, Dong, Maonan, Yi, Shui and Gelao live in compact communities in Guangxi's mountainous regions. During the long practice, they have created mountainous production and living styles with striking features. The wooden railing house is the most important traditional bulling in villages. The people adjusted measures to local conditions, reclaimed mountains and wasteland and farmed industriously. They planted and protected trees and sowed economic crops widely. In history, farming and hunting served as important supplement for mountainous groups to search food. Their production implement, living utensils, hunting tools were various and full of special features, which reveal fully their superb wisdom.

绘画是审美的过程，是人类表达情感和对生活理解的最直接的方式，也是沟通心灵，传递信息的桥梁。世界各民族就地取材，在各种材料上创造出令人叹服的经典艺术。在艺术作品中感受艺术家抒发感情，自由生活的历程也可以激发出我们对于生活的热爱。

As a process of beauty-appreciation, painting is the most direct way to express emotion and understanding of life. It's also the bridge of mind communication and trans information. Ethnic groups all over the world use various local materials to create admirable classical art works which enable us to feel the artist's emotions and their free life. Simultaneously, painting inspires our love for life.

岩画

Cliff Painting

广西岩画是我国乃至世界岩画艺术宝库中的重要组成部分，多绘制于山洞或沿江崖壁上，图案粗犷，画风古朴，色彩鲜红，画面大多以群体性祭祀活动为主。其中左江流域的岩画主要出现在战国至东汉时期，是左江流域骆越文化的艺术结晶，是广西岩画艺术的代表。唐宋以后，扶绥、金秀和靖西等地出现的岩画，画风与左江岩画迥异，人物造型逼真，内容多与民俗信仰有关。

The cliff painting in Guangxi serves as an important part in the art treasury in China and even in the world. Most cliff paintings were painted on walls of caves or cliffs along rivers, unrestrained in patterns, simple in styles and bright in colors. Most scenes show the sacrificial activity in groups. The cliff paintings along the Zuo River emerged in the Warring States period and the Eastern Han dynasty.

They are the artistic crystal of Luo Yue Culture in the reaches of Zuo River and the representative of cliff paintings in Guangxi. After Tang and Song dynasties, new paintings showed up in Fusul, Jinxiu and Jingxi etc. However, their styles are totally different from counterparts in the Zuo River. They have vivid figures and most contents are related to folk customs and belief.

乡村大世界导游词

导游路线：
乡村大世界—门卫—沿主干道—球馆门口停车场—兄弟连野战营—球馆—沿主干道—二门卫—经餐厅前的小叶榄仁林荫小道（100米）—回主干道—鱼塘—途经马术俱乐部—会议室—碧雅轩（客房）—餐厅—游客服务中心（结束）
各位游客：
　　早上好！欢迎大家来到乡村大世界。我是×××，在接下来的时间里，由我带领大家游览乡村大世界。
　　（全景导览图前）乡村大世界位于南宁市兴宁区三塘镇，距市中心约15公里，距南宁市快速环道约6公里。乡村大世界占地1000多亩，建筑面积约10000多平方米，是威宁公司独自投资规划建设，由南宁威宁生态园有限责任公司经营管理的大型全生态休闲度假村，是一个集运动、休闲、观光度假、会议培训、农业示范及推广等多种功能、极具乡土风情，倡导健康休闲理念的特色生态园。
　　（葡萄园）从大门右手这条小路进去，是我们的葡萄园，占地约200亩，是迄今为止桂南地区最早种植日本红提葡萄面积最大的种植基地。我们种植葡萄是采用绿色的生产技术，使用制作有机肥取代化肥，套袋生长。因此我们的葡萄是非常绿色环保的。品种主要以无核红提、美人指等欧亚品种为主，近两年来新增了红珍珠、巨峰、温克等优良品种。每年6—10月是我们的葡萄采摘节，从2005年至今已经是第九届了。由于有了一定的知名度，许多南宁市及周边的游客都慕名而来，体验葡萄采摘的乐趣。因此我们的葡萄园应该说是南宁周边重要的集观光、采摘、品尝于一体的葡萄生产基地。

（汽车旅游营地）我们的右手边是我们的汽车旅游营地，占地20亩，是广西首批南宁唯一的汽车旅游营地，2007年9月开营，可同时容纳200人安营扎寨。2007年10月的东盟博览会期间，成功接待了越南政府组织的近百辆自驾车队；2010年五一期间南宁、昆明两地旅游局共同开展了南宁与昆明自驾车互游活动，我们的露营地成功地接待了来自昆明的自驾车队。2010年10月在成都举办的首届中国国际汽车自驾游博览会上荣获"优秀露营地"称号。

（简单介绍豆腐坊）我们的左手边是乡村大世界豆腐坊，豆腐坊于2006年开始自产腐竹，有着多年的传统手工制作经验。"乡邕"腐竹品牌正式创立于2010年，是目前南宁市唯一一家获得QS认证的腐竹生产企业。我们的腐竹以精选上等黄豆为原料，采用传统木材烧制工艺，产品不含任何添加剂，纯天然无公害。很多客人吃了我们餐厅用腐竹做的菜后都会带一些回去，而且也经常有客人回来再次购买。

乡村大世界整体分两个区域，目前我们所在的是娱乐活动区域，主要项目有野战营、烧烤场、球馆等娱乐项目。

（兄弟连野战营）从我们左手这座桥过去是兄弟连野战营，是华南地区规模最大的户外野战拓展基地，占地60亩。基地根据战争年代设计的地道战区、游击战区、CS反恐战区、桥梁争夺战区、丛林战区等，游客可根据自己的喜好，选择镭战或是彩弹，选择喜欢的战区进行体验。

（球馆）在我们前方是我们的球馆，同时拥有气排球、乒乓球、桌球等，适合各单位举办大型的运动会和比赛。像现在这个季节就是运动会的旺季，这个月以来我们已经接待了好几个单位的运动会了。右手边是我们的室外烧烤场，可以同时容纳400人左右进行烧烤。

（二门卫）从这里开始我们所在的这个区域以静为主，客房、餐饮、会议室、垂钓等项目在这个区域。

（水岸别墅）我们的水岸别墅区环境优美，鸟语花香，6栋别墅错落有致地坐落在白鹭湖畔，睡莲、椰树林、小溪、湖水、白鹭以及满湖的鱼儿让这里充满了生机。每年十月，飞来过冬的白鹭聚集在这里安营扎寨，自然环境条件优越，是广西第二大白鹭栖息地。每天清晨，您总能见到白鹭在湖边散步，鱼儿在水中悠游，白鹭在湖边嬉戏，时而振翅直窜云霄，白鹭欢声与竹涛呼应伴奏，组成一幅绝美的田园画卷。别墅分别以中式、欧式、乡村风格进行装修，除住宿外还有卡拉OK房及棋牌等设施，是小型聚会的最佳选择地。

（垂钓基地）从我左手这条小路下去是我们的垂钓基地，乡村大世界共有20张鱼塘，总面积约200多亩水面，目前已开发主要的开钓池是综合池，鲫鱼池和罗非池，从2006年开始就成为广西区钓鱼协会的比赛基地，每年在此举办几十场大型钓赛活动，场面十分壮观，吸引无数游客前来观赛。

（马术俱乐部）您可能已经发现在如此优美的鱼塘边有几个蒙古包，那是我们的群英会马术俱乐部。群英会马术俱乐部拥有正规的马场训练场地、调教圈、盛装舞步场地等；专业教练的马匹：澳洲进口纯血马、蒙古马和广西特有的德保矮马，可以全面满足不同层次的游客和马术爱好者的需求；还拥有技术过硬的教练队伍，可提供一对一的专业马术教学。

骑马是所有运动项目中对身体最有益处的、最健康的有氧运动；群英会马术俱乐部可以使你从零开始，从认识马、亲近马、到学会控制马、在马背上慢步、跑步，甚至学会跨越障碍等，使你感受到马术的无穷乐趣。

（返回山月居，途中可简单介绍一下百果园）马术俱乐部的左边，是我们占地百亩的百果园，百果园荟萃着台湾大青枣（11月—2月成熟）、美国甜杨桃（12月—2月成熟）、台湾火龙果（8月—9月成熟）、木瓜、香水柠檬、黄皮果等。每到百果丰收时，硕果累累，果香醉人，游客可入园体验采摘的乐趣，感受丰收的喜悦，这份浓郁的乡村风情让来这里的游人无不流连忘返。

（会议室）左手下面这个区域是会议区，景区内共有大小会议室7个，能满足不同规模的会议接待。在这个区还有两间棋牌室，棋牌室内配有电动麻将及扑克桌，节假日我们的棋牌接待非常满，几乎处于供不应求的状态。

（客房）景区共有绿雅苑、碧雅轩、山月居、观鹭小院四个住宿区，拥有121间客房，同时可接待近300人左右。住宿客房均是按乡村田园风格建设的四合院，环境十分优美，非常适合同学聚会和单位训培。特别是早晨起来时，空气清新，鸟儿争鸣，非常惬意。

（餐厅）由二个大厅和5个包厢组成；大厅可同时容纳40台，再加上5个包厢，整个餐厅可同时容纳600人用餐。餐厅主要是以经营农家菜为主，特色菜：自养鸡、自养鸭、清蒸鱼、上汤野菜以及山庄豆腐坊自作的豆浆、豆腐、腐竹等豆制品系列；同时还可以品尝到乡村独有的自酿葡萄酒和百香果汁等。

（游客服务中心）前面右手边就是我们的游客服务中心，也就是我们山庄的总台，这里提供所有项目的预订、接待、咨询等相关综合服务，同时，在游客服务中还可以购买到我们乡村大世界全生态的农特产品——腐竹、葡萄酒、不同季节的水果、土鸡蛋等，大家可带上一些特产跟家人和朋友一起分享。

各位游客，今天对乡村大世界的介绍就到这里结束了，接下来希望你们能来好好体验一下我们乡村的各个项目，也衷心地希望大家可以抛开城市的喧嚣与压抑，给自己的身心放个假，感受乡村的休闲与自在，实现您回归田园生活的梦想。

谢谢！

The Tour Guide Speech of the Nanning Country World

Ladies and Gentlemen：

Good morning! Welcome to the Nanning Country World. I am XXX. I will be your guide on the tour of the Country World in the following hours.

（Before the Panoramic Map）The Nanning Country World is located in Santang Town, Xingning District of Nanning. It is about 15 kilometers from the city center and 6 kilometers from the express ring road. The resort covers an area of over 66 hectares, with a building area of over 10000 square meters. It is a large total ecological resort, invested and constructed by Nanning Weining Asset Management Co., Ltd., and operated and managed by Nanning Weining Ecosystem Park Co., Ltd.. This characteristic ecological park combines sports, relaxation, sightseeing, vacation, meeting, training, agricultural demonstration, popularization and other functions together, embodying the local customs and proposing health and leisure concept.

（Vineyard）Go through the entrance, take the right road and we will reach the vineyard, which covers an area of about 13 hectares. It is so far the earliest and largest planting base for Japanese red grapes in southern Guangxi. Environmentally-friendly technologies are used for planting the grapes, such as bagging the grapes and substituting the chemical fertilizer with the organic one. Thus the grapes are especially healthy to body. The most widely planted grapes here belong to the Eurasian grape variety, such as Red Seedless and Manicure Finger. Flame Seedless, Kyoho, Vink and other improved varieties have also been brought in over the past two years.

The Grape-Picking Festival is held from June to October every year and it has been held for nine years since 2005. Attracted by its reputation, many tourists come here to enjoy the experience of picking grapes from Nanning City and other nearby regions. Therefore, the vineyard can be regarded as an important grape planting base near Nanning City which combines the functions of sightseeing, picking and tasting together.

(Motor Camp) On the right is the motor camp, which covers an area of about 1.3 hectares. It is one of the earliest developed motor camps in Guangxi and the only one in Nanning. The camp was put to use in September, 2007 and it can receive 200 people at a time. During the China-ASEAN Expo in October, 2007, the camp accommodated a self-driving car team organized by Vietnam government, which included nearly a hundred cars. In 2010 May Day holiday, the tourism administrations of Nanning and Kunming held jointly a self-driving activity and this camp accommodated the self-driving car team from Kunming. In October, 2010, the motor camp won the title of "Excellent Camp" in the first China International Self-driving Car Tour Expo in Chengdu.

(A Concise Introduction of the Tofu Workshop) On our left is the tofu workshop of the Nanning Country World. It started producing fuzhu (rolls of dried soybean milk cream) in 2006 with traditional handicraft experience of many years. Created formally in 2010, "Xiang Yong" brand is so far the only fuzhu brand whose manufactory has obtained quality safety certification in Nanning City. The workshop uses the well-chosen first-rate soy beans as the raw material, and adopts the traditional wood burning technique. The products are natural and harmless without any additive. Many tourists will take some fuzhu back home after tasting the fuzhu dish, and some of the tourists will come back and buy more.

The Nanning Country World is divided into two areas. Now we stand in the recreation area which mainly includes the field battle camp, the barbecue site and the arena for the ball games.

(Brothers' Camp for Field Battle) Go across the bridge on our left and we will see the Camp for Field Battle. It is the largest outdoor base for the field battle in Southern China, covering an area of 4 hectares. Based on the wartime situation, the camp is divided into tunnel warfare zone, guerrilla zone, Counter-Strike zone, bridge fighting zone, bushwhacking zone and other zones. The tourists can choose laser strike or paintballs and the war zone as they like.

(The Arena for Ball Games) In front of us is the arena for ball games, where you can play soft volleyball, ping-pong and billiards. It provides a good place for the organizations to hold large-scale sport meets and games. Now it is the busy season for sport meets. Several organizations have already held sport meets here this month. On the right is the outdoor area for barbecue which can receive about 400 people.

(The Second Gate Sentry) Now the area where we stand is mainly for relaxation without too much exercise. You can find room service, restaurant, meeting room, and fishing site in this area.

(Waterside Villas) The waterside villas are surrounded by fine scenery. Birds sing around and flowers smell sweet. Six villas are located in proportion by the Egret Lake that is stirring with new life with water lilies, coconut palms, brook, lake water, egrets and fish swimming hither and thither. Egrets fly and camp here to spend the winter in October every year. It is the second largest egret habitat in Guangxi with the favorable natural environment. Each morning you can always see egrets strolling by the lake and fish swimming in the water. The egrets may flutter and soar high into the sky every now and then. The joyful cry of the egrets chimes in with the waves of bamboo leaves. All these picturesque views form a fascinating pastoral scroll. The villas are separately decorated in

Chinese, European, or pastoral style. Besides the accommodation, the villas are also equipped with Karaoke rooms, Chess & Poker rooms and other facilities. The place is the best choice to have small social gatherings.

(Fishing Base) Go straight along the road on the left and we will see the fishing base. The Nanning Country World has altogether 20 fishponds which cover a water area of over 13 hectares. In the present, crucian pond, tilapia pond, and pond with mixed fish have been opened to the public and the fishing base has been a contesting site of Guangxi Fishing Association since 2006. Every year, dozens of large-scale fishing contests are held here. The fine spectacle attracts numerous tourists to come and watch.

(The Saddle Club) You may have found there are several Mongolian yurts stands beside such a beautiful fishpond, it is our "Heroes Equestrian Club". The club owns normal horse training site, tuning loop and dressage site. Also, the club provides different kinds of professional coach horses, such as Imports of Australian thoroughbred, Mongolian Horse, DeBao Pony of Guangxi unique, can fully meet the needs of different levels of tourists and equestrian enthusiasts demand. And, the club has a skilled coach team, may provide one to one professional equestrian teaching.

Horse-riding is the most beneficial and healthy aerobic exercise among all the sports. Our club may let you learn from scratch, from know about horse, close to the horse, to learn how to control the horse, walk on horseback, real riding, even learn to overcome obstacles, etc. The learning may make you feel the joy of equestrian.

(Return to Moon Compound and Egret-watching Yard, and introduce the Fruits Orchard briefly on the way) On the left of the saddle club, is our Fruits Orchard which covers an area of Mu about 100. The Orchard provides different kinds of fruit, such as Taiwan jujube (ripe from November to February) Taiwan Pitaya (ripe from August to September), pawpaw, the perfume of lemon, Clausena lansium, etc. When the harvest season comes, the Orchard is always fruitful with the thick fruit fragrance. At this time, visitors can park to experience the fun of picking, and feel the joy of harvest. A strong country style let visitors indulge in pleasures without stopping here.

(Meeting Room) Ahead on our left is the meeting area, including seven meeting rooms of different sizes, which can hold meetings of different scales. In this area, there are two Chess & Poker rooms equipped with electric mahjong tables and poker tables. In the holidays, the rooms are always too busy to meet the demand.

(Guest Rooms) The scenic spot has four residences: Green House, Jade Block, Moon Compound and Egret-watching Yard. There are 121 guest rooms that can accommodate about 300 people. The guest rooms are constructed in the form of quadrangles with pastoral characteristic, where guests can enjoy delightful environment. The place is best suited for the gathering of classmates and the training program for different working units. Imagine when you get up in the morning, you can feel the fresh air and hear the birds' whistles. How pleasant it is!

(Dining Room) The dining room consists of two halls and five boxes. The halls contain 40 tables, and plus the five boxes, the whole dining room can hold 600 people. It mainly provides farmhouse cooked food. Special dishes are self-raised chicken, duck, steamed fish, potherb soup, and self-made soy-bean milk, tofu, fuzhu and other soya products of the tofu workshop. Particular self-made vines and passion fruit juice are also provided here.

(Tourist Service Center) Ahead on our right is the tourist service center, which is also the reception desk of our resort. It provides reservation, reception, consultation and relevant services. Special ecological agricultural products can be bought in the service center, such as Fuzhu (dried bean—curd stick), vines, fruits of four seasons and country chicken eggs. Take some local specialties home and share them with your family and friends.

Ladies and gentlemen, that's all for today's introduction and guidance. We hope you could enjoy all activities in our resort. We hope you can break from the urban noise and pressure, take some time to relax your mind and body, and enjoy the leisurely and free atmosphere in the countryside, realizing your dream of returning to the pastoral live.

　　Thank you!

广西防城港市投资指南

Investment Guide of fangchenggang city in 2019

城市名片
Visiting cards of city
"东兴国家重点开发开放试验区"
"Dongxing National Key Experimental Zone for Development and Opening-up"
"中国东兴—越南芒街跨境经济合作区"
"China-Vietnam（Dongxing-Mong Cai）Cross Border Economic Cooperation Zone"
"开放型经济新体制综合试点试验地区"
"Pilot Area for New Open Economic System"
"沿边金融综合改革试验区"
"Border Financial Comprehensive Reform Pilot Area"
"中国首批边境旅游试验区"
"First Pilot Site for Border Tourism in China"
"全国双拥模范城"
"National Double Support Model City"
"中国科学发展城镇化质量示范城市"
"Model City for Scientific Approach to Urbanization in China"
"中国转变经济发展方式示范城市"
"Model City for Transforming Economic Mode in China"
"中国十大最关爱民生城市"

"China's Top 10 Cities for Improving People's Livelihood"

"全国投资成本最低十佳城市"

"China's Top 10 Cities with Lowest Investment Cost"

"中国优惠政策密度最大的城市"

"The City with Most Preferential Policies in China"

"中国唯一的'上山下海出国'旅游天堂"

"The Only Tourist Paradise Offering Tours to Mountains and Seas as well as Cross-Border Odyssey in China"

"中国唯一的红树林国际示范区"

"The Only International Demonstration Area for Mangrove in China"

"城市环境空气质量全年优良率100%"

"The City with a 100% Excellent Rate of Air Quality"

"'互联网+'指数全国第二"

"The City Ranking Second in China in 'Internet Plus' Index"

"全国地级城市小康经济指数100强"

"Top 100 of Economic Index of Prefectural-Level Cities in China"

"广西人均GDP最高的城市"

"The City with the Highest GDP Per Capita in Guangxi"

"中国白鹭之乡"

"Home to Egrets in China"

"中国金花茶之乡"

"Home to Golden Camellia in China"

"中国长寿之乡"

"Home of Longevity in China"

"中国肉桂八角之乡"

"Home to Cinnamomum and Illicium Verum in China"

"中国氧都"

"City of Oxygen in China"

县市区简介
Brief Introduction of Counties and Districts

上思县
Shangsi County

总面积2816平方公里，总人口约25万人。上思县自然资源禀赋突出，旅游发展条件得天独厚，被授予"中国氧都""中国老年人宜居宜游县""全国十佳生态休闲旅游名县"等称号。上思是广西林业大县，全县森林覆盖率60%左右，被纳入广西重点生态主体功能区范围。上思还是产糖大县，甘蔗种植面积45万亩左右。

Shangsi County has a total population of about 250,000 people, covering an area of 2,816 square kilometers. With rich natural resources and favorable natural conditions for tourism, the county has been awarded the titles of "Capital of Oxygen in China", "Livable and Tourist County for the Elderly in China", and "China's Top 10 County for Ecotourism and Leisure Tourism". Shangsi is a large forestry county, with a forest coverage rate of about 60%, which has been included in the key ecological major function-oriented zone in Guangxi. It is also an important sugar producer, with a sugarcane planting area of about 450,000 mu (3.01 hectares).

重点发展产业：制糖、水泥建材、木材加工、黏土加工、制药、能源开发、生态休闲旅游等。

Key Industries: sugar refinery, cement industry, timber processing, clay processing, pharmacy, energy development, ecotourism and leisure tourism, etc.

东兴市
Dongxing City

总面积590平方公里，常住人口30万人。东兴是我国唯一与越南海陆相连的国家一类口岸城市，先后获得"中国最佳生态旅游城市""中国长寿之乡""中国十大养老胜地""中国最具海外影响力城市""中国最具竞争力百强县""全国电子商务百佳县""中国红木文化城""全国双拥模范城""中国十佳特色文化旅游名县"等荣誉称号。

Covering a total area of 590 square kilometers, Dongxing, a city with a resident population of 300,000, is the only first-class national port city that shares both sea and land border with Vietnam. It has been awarded many honorary titles, including "The Best Ecotourism City in China", "Longevity Town in China", "China's Top 10 Destination for the Old", "China's Most Influential City Overseas", "China's Top 100 Counties for Competitive Strength", "China's Top 100 Counties for E-Commerce", "China's Rosewood Town", "National Support Model City", and "China's Top 10 Tourist Counties".

重点发展产业：商贸、加工、旅游、金融、电商、物流等跨境产业。

Key Industries: business and trade, manufacturing, tourism, finance, e-commerce, logistics and other cross-border industries.

港口区

Gangkou District

总面积378平方公里，总人口近17万人。港口区三面环海，南濒北部湾，东邻粤港澳，西与越南隔海相望，是中国内地进出东盟各国最重要的中转基地和大西南最便捷的出海通道；是国家批准实施的《广西北部湾经济区发展规划》中重点建设的临海临港重要工业区；港口区拥有绵延300多公里的原生态海岸线，是旅游休闲的黄金地带。

The Gangkou District has a total population of 170,000, covering an area of 378 square kilometers. Surrounded by the sea on three sides, it plays the role of the China's most important transfer base to ASEAN countries as well as the most convenient sea passage in southwest areas, with Beibu Gulf on the south, Guangdong, Hong Kong and Macao to the east, and Vietnam across the sea to the west. It is an industrial zone adjacent to the sea and port, which is highlighted on *Guangxi Beibu Gulf Economic Zone Development Scheme* issued by the state. Besides, it is a prime area for tourism and entertainment owning a pristine coastline of over 300 kilometers

重点发展产业：高端钢铁生产加工、有色金属加工、新能源开发、装备制造、粮油食品加工、化工及高新技术等。

Key Industries: high-end iron & steel, non-ferrous metal, new energy development, equipment manufacturing, oil and foodstuff processing, chemical engineering, and high and new technology.

防城区
Fangcheng District

总面积2426平方公里，总人口43.85万人。防城区地处十万大山南麓山支脉附近地区，全区森林面积240.7万亩，森林覆盖率高达65.99%，素有"植物界大熊猫"和"茶族皇后"之称的金花茶主要分布在防城区，防城区被授予首个"国家级金花茶生态原产地产品保护示范区"称号。防城区拥有峒中口岸、里火口岸、江山边地贸口岸、滩散互市贸易点和茅岭海关监管卸货点5个对外开放窗口，是西南地区开展"一带一路"发展战略的重要出边通道。

Located near the south foot of Shiwan Mount, Fangcheng District, with a total population of 438,500, covers a total area of 2,426 square kilometers, among which 2.47 million mu (165.5 hectares) are forests, reaching a forest coverage rate of 65.99%. The precious golden camellia, known as "the panda in the plant world" and "queen of camellia" are growing in Fangcheng District, which makes it the first "National Nature Reserve for the Origin Area of Golden Camellia". With five ports connecting the outside world, including Dongzhong Port, Lihuo Port, Jiangshan Port, Santan Port and Maoling Port, Fangcheng District is an important passage for the strategic implementation of the Belt and Road Initiative in southwest China,

重点发展产业：香料加工、制糖、冶金、造纸、化工、制药、能源等。

Key Industries: spice processing, sugar refinery, metallurgy, paper industry, chemical engineering, pharmacy, and energy production etc.

防城港国际航线通商通航图
The Chart for International Routes of Fangchenggang City

防城港 Fangchenggang City，列宁格勒Leningrad，莫斯科 Moscow，都柏林 Dublin，

伦敦 London，柏林 Berlin，巴黎 Paris，罗马 Rome，雅典 Athens，伊斯坦布尔Istanbul，

耶路撒冷Jerusalem，阿尔及尔 Algiers，开罗 Cairo，德黑兰 Teheran，巴格达 Baghdad，

卡拉奇 Karachi，卡萨布兰卡Casablanca，雅温德Yaoundé，摩加迪沙 Mogadishu，

金沙萨Kinshasa，卢萨卡Lusaka，哈拉雷 Harare，约翰内斯堡 Johannesburg，

开普敦Cape Town，塔那那里弗Tananarive，伊斯兰堡Islamabad，喀布尔Kabul，

加德满都Kathmandu，新德里New Delhi，科伦坡Colombo，达卡Dhaka，曼谷 Bangkok，

新加坡 Singapore，雅加达 Jakarta，胡志明市Ho Chi Minh City，马尼拉 Manila，

香港 Hong Kong，台北 Taipei，北京 Beijing，乌鲁木齐Urumqi，平壤 Pyongyang，

西雅图 Seattle，旧金山San Francisco，芝加哥 Chicago，波士顿 Boston，纽约New York City，

华盛顿Washington D.C.，盐湖城Salt Lake City，洛杉矶Los Angeles，亚特兰大Atlanta，

休斯顿 Houston，奥兰多 Orlando，迈阿密Miami，墨西哥城Mexico City，利马 Lima，

里约热内卢 Rio De Janeiro，圣地亚哥 San Diego，布宜诺斯艾利斯

Buenos Aires

生态环境优美
Beautiful Environment

防城港市依山傍海，拥有靓丽的颜值和良好的空气，这里海湾多，半岛多，绿树多，三岛三湾环绕港城，海湾、江湖、岛屿、丘陵、田园、海上红树林等元素浑然天成，城市各项建筑布局有序，错落有致，是一座"海在城中，城在海中，人在景中"的全生态海湾城市，可以恣意享受"推开门窗观碧海，歇坐阳台闻涛声"的优美意境。防城港市主要河流水质，饮用水源和近岸海域水环境质量优良，滩涂生物资源，浅海海底生物种类，沿海鱼类、虾类、贝类、藻类种类繁多。著名的十万大山自东向西横贯防城港的腹地74.4公里，既是一座天然的防台风屏障，更是一座能造福人民的宝山。它拥有世界唯一的国家级金花茶自然保护区，拥有多种国家重点保护动植物，森林面积近500万亩，森林覆盖率98%以上，生长着中国南方最好的热带雨林，有1890多种植物种类，空气负氧离子含量每立方厘米高达8.9万个，享有"华南第一天然氧吧""中国氧都"的美誉，是发展生态农业、生态旅游、健康养生的不可多得之地。

Adjacent to mountain and sea, Fangchenggang city has many bays, peninsulas, and trees, which results in its remarkable scenery and good air quality. Buildings are set up in its well–planned layout, surrounded by three islands and three bays, and decorated with natural bays, rivers, lakes, islands, hills, bucolic sites, and mangroves. In this natural bay city surrounded by sea, one may find embraced by the intoxicated scenery depicted in the line, "Windows and doors open on an emerald expanse of seas； verandas send in the sound of waves". The water quality is good due to its clear rivers, drinking water sources and marine environment. Many kinds of neritic benthos, costal fish, shrimp, shellfish, and algae, as well as many plants and animals live on the tidal flat.

The famous Mt. Shiwandashan runs 74.4 kilometers through this city from east to west, which provides a natural barrier against typhoon as well as numerous resources to local people.

The famous Mt. Shiwandashan runs 74.4 kilometers through this city from east to west, which is not only a natural barrier against typhoon, but a mountain that can benefit people.

It boasts the only National Nature Reserve for Golden Camellia in the world, various kinds of wildlife and plant under state protection, and the best-preserved tropical rain forest in south China with more than 1,890 plant species, an area of about 5 million mu (333 thousand hectares) and a forest coverage of over 98%. It enjoys the reputation of "The Best Natural Oxygen Bar in South China" and "Capital of Oxygen in China", since the content of negative oxygen ions in the air is as high as 89,000 per cubic centimeter here. All these make Fangchenggang city a rare place for developing eco-agriculture, eco-tourism, and health preservation.

产业配套完善
Complete Industrial System

防城港市交通网络发达便捷，高速公路和高速铁路直达港口，距离南宁、北海两大机场均一个多小时车程，动车可直达南宁、桂林、广州等地。防城港作为广西沿海重要工业基地，已初步形成了以钢铁、有色金属、能源、粮油食品、石化、装备制造为六大支柱的一批产业，建有自治区级高新区，建成广西最大临港工业基地防城港经开区，以及中国第一大植物油籽加工基地和磷酸出口加工基地。防城港市是全国能源基地，全市装机容量超500万千瓦。位于防城港的我国西部首座核电站已实现商运，柳钢防城港基地，中铝生态铝项目已开工建设。海洋渔业发展迅猛，据统计，防城港1万平方公里左右的海域内，有海洋鱼类500多种、虾类200多种、头足类40多种，中华白海豚、海猪、海马等珍稀海洋生物在此生息繁衍。海产品远销北京、上海、成都等大城市。

Fangchenggang city owns a developed and convenient traffic network, with direct access to the port by expressway and high-speed railway as well as more than an hour's drive from Nanning Airport and Beihai Airport, and is directly linked with Nanning, Guilin, and Guangzhou by bullet trains. As an important industrial base in the coastal area of Guangxi, it has initially formed an industrial layout, with iron and steel, non-ferrous metals, energy, oil and foodstuffs, and equipment manufacturing as six pillar industries, and put in place the high-tech zone of autonomous region level, the Fangchenggang Economic and Technological Development Zone—the largest harbor industrial zone in Guangxi, and China's largest vegetable oilseed processing base and phosphoric acid export processing base. Besides, it is a national energy base. The city's installed capacity is over 5 million kilowatts. The first nuclear power plant in western China has been put into commercial use, and the Fangchenggang base of Liuzhou Iron and Steel Group Company Limited as well as the green ecological aluminum project of the Aluminum Corporation of China have been under construction. Fangchenggang city's marine fishery develops rapidly, and marine products are sold to Beijing, Shanghai, Chengdu and other big cities. According to statistics, there are more than 500 kinds of marine fishes, 200 kinds of shrimps and 40 kinds of cephalopods in Fangchenggang's seas of about 10,000 square kilometers, with rare marine creatures, marine organisms such as Chinese white dolphins, finless porpoise, and seahorse living here.

市场空间广阔
Board Market Prospect

防城港市前有东盟6亿人口大市场，背靠中南西南6亿人口经济腹地，人流、物流、资金流密集，2018年，其边境贸易占全广西的1/5，互市贸易占全广西的1/3。外贸进出口位居广西前列。企业入驻后可借助跨境经济合作等平台，开拓东盟市场乃至全球市场。目前，防城港市已经站在了改革发展新的起点上，正全面掀起新一轮大开发大建设热潮，积极寻求与广大客商合作，是防城港在新时期深化对外开放，提升发展水平的战略选择。

The labor-abundant Fangchenggang city sees thriving logistic industry and strong capital flow, since it has access to two huge markets: the ASEAN market as well as the market in central south and southwest China with a population of 600 million respectively. In 2018, its total volume of foreign trade import and export ranked in the forefront of Guangxi, of which the volume of frontier trade and that of border trade account for 1/5 and 1/3 respectively. After settling in, enterprises can take advantage of the platform for cross-border economic cooperation and other platforms to explore the ASEAN market and even the global market. Fangchenggang city, where a new round of development and construction is surging, is now standing at a new starting point for reform and development and seeking cooperation with potential clients, which are strategic choices for Fangchenggang to deepen its opening-up and develop better in the new era.

优惠政策叠加
Multiple Preferential Policies

防城港市拥有东兴试验区，跨境经济合作区，沿边金融综合改革试验区，构建开放型经济新体制综合试点试验，边境旅游试验区等多个国家级平台，享有沿海、沿边、少数民族、西部大开发等多重叠加优惠政策，先后获批人民币与越南盾特许兑换业务试点，个人跨境贸易人民币结算试点，进境粮食指定口岸，进境种苗（景观树）指定口岸，海港进境水果指定口岸等，创新形成了34证合一商事改革制度，"六个一"市场监管新模式，企业登记全程电子化等，一枚公章管审批等先行先试成果，支持政策富集，营商环境宽松，有力保障企业持续健康发展。

Fangchenggang city owns many platforms at the national level, including Dongxing Experimental Zone, Cross Border Economic Cooperation Zone, Border Financial Comprehensive Reform Pilot Area, Comprehensive Pilot Area for New System of Open Economy, and Border Tourism Experimental Zone. It benefits from multiple preferential policies for coastal areas, border areas, minority nationality, and western areas. It has been approved as the trial for the exchange between RMB and VND, the trial of settling cross-border trade accounts in RMB, designated port for imported grain, designated port for imported seedlings (landscape trees), and designated port for imported fruits. It is at the forefront of the commercial system reform that merges 34 forms of certification of businesses into one certificate, the new market regulation system— "Six Ones", and provides electronic service for enterprise registration and one-step service. These supportive policies make them easier to do business and ensure a sound and sustained development of enterprises.

▶ 到2020年12月31日前，新办的享受国家西部大开发减按15%税率征收企业所得税的企业，在东兴试验区范围内经批准免征地方分享部分后，企业最低可按9%缴纳企业所得税。

By December 31, 2020, newly established enterprises that enjoy a preferential corporate income tax rate of reduced 15% for the Development of China's Western Region shall pay the enterprise income tax at a minimum rate of 9%, upon approval of exemption from the tax share of enterprise income tax going to by local tax authorities in Dongxing Experimental Zone.

▶ 对新设立的加工贸易企业在形成生产能力并开展加工贸易业务后，符合有关条件的，按实际到位资金给予（0.5%以内）一次性补助。

Processing trade enterprises that meet relevant conditions Manufacturers shall be given a one-time subsidy (less than 0.5%) according to funds actually being put in place, after forming production capacity, doing business, and meeting relevant conditions.

▶ 对新设立或新迁入的金融机构，根据机构类型、组织形式和注册资本情况，财政给予最高1000万元人民币的一次性补助。

Newly established or newly moved move-in financial institutions shall be given a one-time subsidy of up to 10 million yuan by the government according to the type of institution, organization form and registered capital.

▶ 对于优先发展产业且用地集约的工业项目，以及以农、林、牧、渔业产品初加工为主的工业项目，可按不低于所在地土地等级相对应《全国工业用地出让最低价标准》的70%确定土地出让底价。

For the industrial projects encouraged by the state with intensive land use

use of land and industrial projects focusing on initial processing of agricultural, forestry, animal husbandry and fishery products, the base price for land assignment may be determined as not lower than 70% of the minimum price set out in the National Standards for *the Minimum Prices for Assignment of Land for Industrial Purposes*, corresponding to the land grade of the place the project is located.

▶ 对于自治区出台的《关于进一步降低实体经济企业成本的意见》的"新28条"措施,以及《关于切实做好招商引资工作的意见》《广西招商引资激励暂行办法》等配套文件,对符合条件的重大招商引资项目,按项目当年实际到位资金的0.5%给予项目业主一次性奖励。

Owners of projects to attract investment that meet relevant conditions shall be given a one-time reward of equal to 0.5% commission of the project's funds actually put in place that year, according to 28 new measures of Opinions on Further Reducing the Costs of Real Economy Enterprises and supporting documents such as Opinions on Working Effectively to Attract Investment issued by Guangxi Zhuang Autonomous Region.

▶ 广西第一个境外边民入境务工试点,在东兴试验区投资置业,可按相关规定招收越南边民入境务工。

The pilot program of allowing border residents enter Guangxi for jobs has been launched, which means enterprises making investments in the Dongxing Experimental Zone may recruit Vietnamese border residents as workers in accordance with relevant provisions.

▶ 边民互市进口商品收购企业按月将收购业绩及纳税情况报当地边贸行政主管部门,互市贸易区(点)所在地政府财政部门,按收购企业所缴纳增值税和企业所得总额的10%定期扶持收购企业的发展。

Enterprises purchasing import commodities in the border trade area (post) shall report monthly the purchasing performance and tax payments to the local border trade administrative departments. The local financial department of local government in the location where the border trade area (post) situates shall support the development of these enterprises by regularly providing them subsidies with 10% of the VAT or corporate income taxes they paid

▶ 每个边民每天不低于8000元人民币免税互市商品入境，可充分利用好越南等东盟国家的资源，大力发展资源落地加工。

Each border resident may import duty-free goods with a value not less than RMB 8,000. It is encouraged to develop processing industry based on resources from Vietnam and other ASEAN countries.

后　记

　　我最初的翻译经历可追溯到20世纪90年代。大学时代毛遂自荐到当地杂志社实习，翻译了几篇英文文章，得以印成铅字正式出版，便不知天高地厚地认为入了翻译的门。多年之后，我成了大学老师，担任了翻译课程的教学，也承担了一些翻译任务，才深感翻译的不易与艰辛。语言易学，文化难悟。翻译之难，不仅难在语言本身，更难在文化和思维，难在对不同文化中语篇修辞风格的掌握。为更好地研究翻译，帮助学生提高翻译质量，我申请了广西社科课题《中英会展平行文本的修辞对比与广西外宣翻译研究》，并在此研究的基础上完成了本部书稿的写作。

　　这部书稿完成于2021年，整本书的成稿时间恰逢广西大学改革之际。我处于读博、工作和家庭琐事的重重压力之中，同时经历着失眠症和颈椎病的折磨。每当夜幕降临，在床上辗转反侧难以入眠之际，内心就开始激烈交战。一个声音在说：放弃吧，你还读什么博，搞什么学术研究，人到中年，苟且过日便可。而另一个声音却在说：人总要进步，总要成长，不求完美，但求尽力呀。于是，在无数次想放弃的念头中，我还是坚持着完成了书稿。修辞学是一门具有严密体系与悠久历史的传统学科，翻译学则是具有庞大内容分支与实践导向的应用学科。在写作的过程中，我深深感到"心余力绌"的压力。没有身边各位朋友、家人、同事和领导的帮助和鼓励，本书不可能付梓。

　　一路走来，需要感谢的人太多太多。首先要感谢关熔珍教授和温科学教授。温教授以严谨务实的学术精神和几十年如一日的专注态度致力于修辞学的研究，启发了我的写作思路。关熔珍教授在翻译领域的研究上见解独到，诲人不倦，对本书稿给予了很多建设性修改意见。感谢李晓滢和吴虹老师在我思路枯竭之际给予的巨大帮助与启发。

感谢广西大学外国语学院给予我担任翻译课程教学和提供翻译实践的机会，促进了我对翻译的兴趣和研究。感谢学院管理制度给予我时间上的灵活性，使我在教学之余仍有时间写作和修改此书。感谢广西大学外国语学院英语专业2017级和2018级的本科同学和2018级MTI研究生同学，教学相长，同学们所提出的问题是本研究的动力，而同学们收集的广西翻译语料，为本研究提供了珍贵的素材。

最后，感谢一直在身后给予默默支持的家人。每逢看到我在电脑前码字，儿子就自觉地放低声音，甚至贴心地帮点外卖或到学校饭堂打饭。在赶书稿的过程中，往往需要牺牲家务和休息时间，感谢家人的耐心和一如既往的支持，正是这一切才让这本书得以问世。

因本人水平有限，书稿中难免存在错误及不足之处，欢迎广大读者批评指正。